Uncommon Solutions to Common Everyday Problems

Household How-Tos, Fix-Its, and Money-Savers

Publisher's Note

This book is intended for general information only. It does not constitute medical, legal, or financial advice or practice. The editors of FC&A have taken careful measures to ensure the accuracy and usefulness of the information in this book. While every attempt has been made to assure accuracy, errors may occur. Some websites, addresses, and telephone numbers may have changed since printing. We cannot guarantee the safety or effectiveness of any advice or treatments mentioned. Readers are urged to consult with their professional financial advisors, lawyers, and health care professionals before making any changes.

Any health information in this book is for information only and is not intended to be a medical guide for self-treatment. It does not constitute medical advice and should not be construed as such or used in place of your doctor's medical advice. Readers are urged to consult with their health care professionals before undertaking therapies suggested by the information in this book, keeping in mind that errors in the text may occur as in all publications and that new findings may supersede older information.

The publisher and editors disclaim all liability (including any injuries, damages, or losses) resulting from the use of the information in this book.

Therefore, there is now no condemnation for those who are in Christ Jesus, because through Christ Jesus the law of the Spirit who gives life has set you free from the law of sin and death.

Romans 8:1-2 (NIV)

FC&A Publishing®
103 Clover Green
Peachtree City, GA 30269

Produced by the staff of FC&A

ISBN 978-1-935574-60-6

Table of Contents

Appliance know-how

7 steps to lengthen your refrigerator's life. With just a little tender loving care, you can keep your refrigerator running smoothly and looking new.

- Wash the rubber gaskets that seal the doors with warm water and mild detergent, never bleach. Rinse and let dry. You can use a toothbrush to get down in the grooves of the gasket.
- Clean the compressor coils about once a month. You'll find the coils on the bottom of most newer models, while older models may have them on the back.
- Remove and wash the defrost pan once a month. Look for it behind the toe plate or on the back of the refrigerator.
- Clean behind and beneath the refrigerator regularly, and check to make sure it's level after you roll it back in place.
- Wash the outside with a sponge and warm, soapy water, then rinse and dry.
- Wash shelves and drawers by hand in warm, soapy water. Never use petroleum-based cleaners on any plastic parts.
- Wax the outside of the refrigerator once a year with a good appliance wax or paste auto wax to guard against rust.

Banish bad refrigerator odors fast. Put a handful of charcoal briquets in a bowl in the refrigerator, and throw them away once the odors disappear. Just don't use briquets that have been treated with lighter fluid.

4 refrigerator problems you can fix in a jiffy. Some problems you don't have to live with, like these common refrigerator complaints.

- If the temperature in your refrigerator is too warm, clean the condenser coil and make sure air can circulate around it freely.
- A noisy refrigerator could point to loose parts, but a simpler solution is to check that it's level and the floor beneath structurally sound.
- Does your refrigerator sweat on the inside? See if the doors are aligned and if the gaskets seal properly when you close the doors.
- If your refrigerator sweats on the outside, see if the energy-saver switch is turned "on."

Snap a lid on refrigerated liquids. Cover that open can of soda before you stick it in the refrigerator. Otherwise, you'll overwork your refrigerator. Refrigerators remove humidity to help keep food cold. An open container of liquid keeps your refrigerator busy constantly.

Secrets to keeping stainless steel looking new. You don't need to use expensive cleaners every day on your stainless steel appliances. Try these thrifty super heroes instead.

- Glass cleaner. To remove fingerprints, whip out your glass cleaner spray and a clean cloth.

- White vinegar. If your stainless steel develops water stains, wipe them away with white vinegar.

- Baking soda. For bits of food that have stubbornly glued themselves to the stainless steel, apply a mixture of warm water and baking soda, and rub gently with a sponge.

- Baby oil. You may even be able to make scratches fade almost instantly by buffing them with baby oil or mineral oil and drying with a clean cloth.

Organize your deep-freeze. Do you have a large freezer that's become a mixed-up jumble of frozen foods? Organize it with plastic milk crates. They're easy to stack and lift. And you can even sort your foods by color — perhaps green for vegetables, red for meats, and a yellow crate for your frozen fruits.

Fill er up! Your freezer can be a wonderful time and money saver, but to really work efficiently, it needs to be at least two-thirds full. If you don't have enough food to keep it this full, fill plastic milk jugs or plastic food storage containers with water and place them in the freezer. Once the water turns to ice, you can count on a peak performance from your freezer.

Communicate with your freezer

To avoid food poisoning, don't eat food that has been thawed and refrozen. But how can you know if your freezer ran continuously while you were on vacation?

Easy. Place a plastic bag containing a few ice cubes in the freezer before you leave. If the power goes off for any length of time, the ice cubes will melt and refreeze into a block. If you come back to ice cubes, all is well. But if you return to a frozen block of water, throw out your frozen food.

Say goodbye to baked-on spills. Want to hear an amazingly simple way to remove grime from a blackened oven? Sprinkle a thick layer of salt on spills while they're still hot and soft — and keep cooking. The food will burn to a crisp you can easily scrape off once the oven cools.

Clean a glass cook top with baking soda. Combine the scratch-free scrubbing power of baking soda with lemon slices or hot water, and you may be surprised at how easy cleaning your glass cook top can be. Just try one of these clever techniques:

- Lemon method. Scatter baking soda across your cook top, and use a slice of lemon to rub it across the entire surface. With a damp cloth, wipe down the cook top to remove any leftover baking soda and lemon juice. Buff with a dry cloth.

- Hot water method. Fill a bowl with hot water and a squeeze of dish soap. Drop a large cleaning rag into the water, and let it get thoroughly wet. Wring it out slightly so it stops dripping, but it's still very wet. Open up the rag, and rest it flat on the cook top for about 20 minutes. For really stubborn messes, leave the rag on a few minutes longer. When time is up, use the rag to scrub the entire surface of your cook top with baking soda. Wipe off the baking soda with a clean, damp cloth. Dry the surface and enjoy the scratch-free shine.

Release grease from oven fans. That disgusting, greasy buildup on the fan filter above your oven isn't hard to clean. All you need to do is take the filter out, put it on the top rack of your dishwasher, and run it through a full wash cycle.

Encourage finicky oven racks. Grease and grit can build up on your oven racks, and this causes trouble sliding the racks in and out. Clean the racks by rubbing their edges and guides with a soap-filled steel wool pad. For extra slide, grease the edges with vegetable oil after they've dried.

Say no to a hot dish. Want to know if a glass container can be used in the microwave oven? Do a quick test by putting the empty dish in the microwave on high for one minute. If it's still cool, you can safely use it for cooking. If it's lukewarm, it's OK for short periods of reheating. If it's warm, don't use it in the microwave oven.

Protect yourself from microwave mishaps

Liquids heated in microwaves can "superheat" and erupt. That's because your microwave can heat inner layers of liquid to a boiling point while the surface remains calm. When you move the container, the inner layer can explode and cause serious burns.

To make sure this doesn't happen to you, use a conventional stove for heating liquids whenever possible. When microwaving, always use a container at least one-third larger than the liquid being heated.

Before heating a liquid in the microwave, stir it well, and place something in the container to spread out the heat energy. You can use a tea bag or stirring stick. Break up heating time and stir liquid at least twice while microwaving, and again when it's done. Never exceed the recommended heating time.

Let your microwave clean itself. Why use elbow grease to clean the inside of your microwave oven? Try this clever trick instead. Wet a sturdy paper towel thoroughly. If your paper towels aren't sturdy, tear off several, pile them together, and then wet them. Toss your paper towel in the microwave, and heat for four minutes. After it's done, don't open your microwave right away. Let the steam work its magic while you put on rubber gloves. After a couple of minutes, open the microwave door, and use the paper towel to wipe down the inside of your microwave. You'll be amazed at how easily the grime just wipes away.

If you'd like to deodorize your microwave as well as clean it, switch to this method. Combine one-third cup of lemon juice with two-thirds cup of water in a microwave-safe bowl. Bring the liquid to a boil in your microwave, and let boil for about three minutes. Carefully remove the bowl and immediately wipe down the interior with a wet cloth.

6 secrets to spotless dishes. Tired of wasting time and money rewashing dishes? Make your dishwasher do it right the first time with these can't-miss tips.

- Prerinse dishes only if your dishwasher is more than five years old. Newer machines can handle the grime.
- Lean glasses against the tines in the rack. Placing them over the tines can leave water marks.
- Load some silverware handle up and others handle down to keep the pieces from nesting.
- Resist the temptation to load plates and bowls facing in the same direction. Reverse direction when you reach the middle of the rack. Plates and bowls should face the center.
- Buy only as much detergent as you can use in two months, and throw it out if it gets old. The older the detergent, the worse it cleans. Store it in a cool, dry pantry — not under your kitchen sink.

- Load flat cookie sheets, pans, and platters along the sides, but not along the front. They could block the detergent tray from opening. Move your silverware basket to the middle of the rack if you need more side space.

Smart way to stop losing small lids. Small plastic items — like cup lids, corncob holders, and storage container lids — need to go in your dishwasher's top rack, but the dishwasher isn't usually set up so you can keep them in one place. Buy a mesh lingerie bag for dishwasher use. Fill it with your small plastic items and hook it onto the tines of the top rack. When your dishwasher's cycle is finished, your items will still be in the same place, but they'll be clean.

Wash half your dishes at half the cost. Save money on your water and energy bills and use the forgotten cycle on your dishwasher — the rinse-and-hold cycle. If your dishwasher isn't full, this is perfect. The rinse-and-hold cycle will wash food off your dishes before it gets caked on, but it won't waste the hot water and the electricity of a full cycle.

Enhance your dishwasher's performance. A safety pin can help you get maximum performance from your dishwasher. That's because it's great for de-clogging the spray holes in your dishwasher's arms. Usually the bottom arm has the most clogs since it sits in the water, but make sure to clean the top arm's holes, too. For a complete cleaning, give the arms a bath under a sink faucet. Take the arms out of the dishwasher by removing the racks and then undoing the hubcap that holds them in place.

Exterminate dangerous fungus lurking in your dishwasher

After checking nearly 200 dishwashers on six continents, scientists found that 62 percent of them contained fungus, especially in the rubber seal around the dishwasher's edge. The fungus survived in spite of the detergents and high water temperatures in the dishwashers, but they won't survive this.

Scrub down your dishwasher's rubber seal with a mixture of vinegar and baking soda, making sure to completely remove any black moldy deposits if you find them. When you are done, fill a bowl with two cups of vinegar, place it on the top rack, and run the dishwasher on its hot setting. For the final blow against the fungus, pour one cup of baking soda on the floor of your dishwasher, and run it again.

3 garbage disposal fixes you can do yourself. Don't panic when your garbage disposal stops working. It might be easier to fix than you think.

- Check the power. Make sure the garbage disposal really is the problem. If your unit plugs into the wall, check that the plug hasn't been dislodged. If it doesn't plug into the wall, make a quick trip to your fuse box to see if the circuit breaker for the disposal has tripped and turned off the power.

- Try the reset button. If electricity is not the problem, check the user's manual for your garbage disposal to see if it has a reset button. Most have a red or black button on the part of the unit underneath your kitchen sink. Push the button, and your garbage disposal may work just fine.

- Dislodge a jam. If something is caught in your disposal, don't put your hand down there to fish it out. Not only is that incredibly dangerous, but better tools are available. First, turn off the garbage disposal or cut power to it. Grab long-handled tongs, extra-long needle-nose pliers, chopsticks, or even a bent coat hanger. With help from a flashlight, find the caught object, and use your tool to coax it out. If you don't need to fish out the item, some experts recommend inserting a broom handle carefully into the disposal and using it to gently turn the disposal blade. That may be enough to release the item.

Declare war on stubborn disposal odors. When throwing lemon or orange peels in your garbage disposal isn't enough to get rid of an awful smell, call in more powerful reinforcements. Pour some baking soda down the drain, but don't rinse. Instead, let it sit there and hammer away at the odor for several hours before you turn on the water and disposal. To get rid of odors even faster, measure 4 tablespoons of Borax into the drain, and let it sit for an hour or longer. Then turn on the water, run the disposal, and declare victory.

Secret to a problem-free garbage disposal. Clogged garbage disposals are one reason why the day after Thanksgiving is Roto-Rooter's busiest day of the year. Garbage disposals can handle many foods, but some items are a clog waiting to happen. Unfortunately, those foods may be more likely to find their way into disposals at Thanksgiving and Christmas. To keep your disposal problem-free every day, make sure these notorious cloggers never go into your disposal.

- Stringy or tough foods. This includes food with clingy fibers and fruits or vegetables with tough parts or peels like potato skins, corn husks, asparagus ends, artichokes, celery, string beans, chard, carrot peels, banana peels, onion skins — and, strangely enough, eggshells.

- Expandable foods. Rice, pasta, and other starchy foods expand in your pipes and disposal just as they do on your stove.

- Oils, fats, or grease. These can create a clog by accumulating into a solid mass or by building up over time.

- Hot water. If grease is in your disposal, hot water helps it accumulate into a clog.

Whip blender into tip-top shape. Cleaning your blender has never been easier. Add a few drops of dish soap and warm water, then blend on high speed for 15 to 30 seconds. Next, dump the water and take apart the blender. Buff stainless steel blades with glass cleaner. Gently clean plastic parts with baking soda and warm water. Rinse everything and let air dry. To keep your blender blades cutting-edge sharp, don't wash them in your dishwasher.

Boost your dehumidifier's efficiency

Make your dehumidifier work more efficiently with two changes. If the dehumidifier is in a cold room, turn on a space heater. This helps dry the air faster because dehumidifiers work better in warmer air. Placing your dehumidifier in the center of the room may dry the room faster, too.

Keep in mind that your dehumidifier works fastest when it only has to dehumidify one room or one closed-off space. If you have two rooms separated by an open door, putting a smaller dehumidifier in each room will dry the rooms faster than one large dehumidifier in one of the rooms.

Scrub away melted plastic. If plastic wrap has melted on your toaster or toaster oven, you can get rid of the mess with a damp cloth and some baking soda.

No waffling with your waffle iron. Use a clean, soft toothbrush to oil and clean your waffle iron.

Unstick your waffle iron. Has your waffle iron lost its nonstick ability? You can restore it by inserting two sheets of wax paper into the waffle iron and letting it heat. When the paper gets dark brown, remove it. Now your waffles should come out easily again.

Silence a vibrating washer. Your brand new washer is so loud it could wake the dead, and it vibrates so hard it actually moves a few inches by the time each load finishes. You could try putting carpet scraps under the feet to dull the noise, but check this first.

When the washer is empty and not running, check the tags and stickers until you find one with instructions for removing the bolts that hold the washer drum in place during shipping. These bolts should be removed during installation, but installers often forget. If you don't find any information on the back of the washer, check your washer's manual or the manufacturer's website for information on removing shipping bolts.

If the shipping bolts have already been removed, you may need to balance the washer legs. To check the balance, place a carpenter's level on the surface of the washer, and make sure the machine is not tilted in any direction. If the washer is tilted, play it safe, and ask someone to help you level it.

Before you begin, get your adjustable wrench and a block of wood or 2x4. Ask your assistant to tilt the washer so the front legs come off the floor. While the washer is tilted, shove the wood under the washer. Now your assistant can lower the washer, but the wood will keep the washer legs from touching the floor. Each washer leg has a locking nut that holds it in place. Loosen each one with the wrench so you can adjust the legs. When the legs are adjusted, tighten the locking nuts. Ask your helper to tilt the washer up again so you can remove the wood.

To level the rear legs, tilt the washer forward so you raise them about 4 inches off the floor. Unlike the front legs, the rear legs are self-leveling, so they should adjust to the proper height when you set them back on the floor. Use your carpenter's level to make sure the legs are balanced from left to right and from front to back.

Banish mold and mildew from your washer. Whether you own a conventional washing machine or HE washer, experts say you can help prevent mold, mildew, and bad odors by simply leaving the door open between washes. It gives everything a chance to dry out.

Say goodbye to washing machine odors. You might be surprised to learn that washing machines can develop mold, mildew, gunky buildup, and even smelly germs, in spite of regular washing with hot water. But that doesn't mean you have to break out nasty-smelling cleaners. Just use vinegar and baking soda.

For a front-loading washer, pour one cup of vinegar and one-fourth cup of baking soda into your machine. If you have a top loader, pour in four cups of vinegar and three-fourths cup of baking soda. Choose a hot water wash, allow the washer to agitate for a minute or two, and then let sit for 45 minutes. When you restart your washer, let it run through the rest of the wash and rinse cycles. After it empties, wipe down the tub with vinegar to remove any leftover residue.

This washing process works well with conventional washers, but cleaning a high efficiency (HE) washer works differently.

Some HE washers have a maintenance cycle you should run on a regular basis, but you can also run your own version of the cycle using a hot water or stain setting, along with an extra rinse cycle. Check your HE washer manual to find out the right way to run a maintenance cycle for your machine. Plan to run this cycle without any laundry in the washer. In general, you should run the maintenance cycle every month with one-fourth cup of bleach, a cup of white vinegar, or the cleaner specified by your user's manual.

After the HE cleaning cycle finishes, wipe down the inside of the washer with white vinegar to remove any lingering residue. In addition, scrub the rubber seal around the washer door with bleach or vinegar before wiping it dry with a fresh cloth.

No. 1 strategy to maintain your washer

Have you ever given your washing machine a birthday party? With this one ingenious, life-extending tip, you'll want to buy it candles and a cake. Periodically check the rubber fill hoses that carry water to your washer. Look for bulges, cracks, blisters, and bare spots, and consider replacing them every five years — their average life span.

Super solutions for hard water problems. Hard water clogs appliances with mineral deposits and makes soaps and detergents less effective. Take these steps to protect your appliances.

- Pour vinegar instead of water into the reservoir when your coffee maker is empty, and run the coffee maker as usual. If this doesn't remove all the mineral deposits in your coffee maker's carafe, repeat the process until the deposits are gone.

- Turn your water heater down to 130 degrees to reduce the mineral deposits you see on your dishes. Also, pour vinegar into the rinse agent slot, or spoon some vinegar into a cup or bowl on the dishwasher rack before running each load of dishes.

- Add one-third cup of washing soda to your rinse cycle for cleaner clothes if you use powdered detergent. If you are not completely satisfied with the result and your water is very hard, try this with the next load. Add one-half cup of washing soda. That should give you a better result.

Dry clothes in half the time. People who switch from fabric softener to wool dryer balls say their clothes dry up to 50 percent faster — and that means a lower electric bill. These balls separate clothes, increase the air flow between them, and absorb moisture. Wool dryer balls also get rid of wrinkles, soften your clothes, and reduce static in every load. Best of all, they last for years, so you can stop spending money on fabric softener sheets and liquids. Depending on how much fabric softener you use, you could save $15 to $100 every year.

Here's another reason to switch to wool — fabric softeners can coat your dryer's lint trap with waxy buildup so your clothes take even longer to dry. For best results, clean your lint trap to remove this buildup before using dryer balls for the first time.

Shop around to discover the best deal on wool dryer balls. You'll find them at fabric stores, Target, and Etsy.com, as well as other internet sources.

Vacuum your carpet like a pro. Back-and-forth vacuuming isn't the best way to clean your carpet. Instead, treat your vacuum cleaner as if it were a lawn mower for your carpet. Before you vacuum a room, quickly examine the carpet for any clutter or small items that could jam up your vacuum. After all, you would remove your hose and other items from the grass if you were mowing, so take a similar approach for inside.

When you're ready, turn on your vacuum and start cleaning in one direction in long strips. Let your strips overlap just slightly to be sure you never miss a spot. Also, remember to go slowly to give the vacuum more time to suction up the dirt. When you need to save time, you can vacuum a little faster in low traffic areas that may be less dirty. Change your vacuuming direction every few weeks or months to help suction up dirt that may have escaped the vacuum on previous passes.

The most important do-it-yourself dryer maintenance. Lint traps only catch some lint. The rest gets blown out through the tube that vents your dryer to the outside. Replace your white plastic vent tube with a rigid metal tube. Building codes no longer allow vinyl, or plastic, tubing because it can easily catch fire. Flexible foil or plastic vent tubes and those with ridges are much more likely to trap lint, creating another fire hazard. Rigid metal tubing is least likely to trap lint and can help contain a fire should one start.

No matter what type of vent tube you use, be sure to clean it regularly. Clean the entire length of the pipe, and make sure you remove the lint completely. Long, flexible brushes designed just for this chore make it a snap. Vacuum up lint behind and underneath the dryer, too, and clean the lint screen every time you use your dryer.

Stop wasting energy in the laundry room

Your dryer must work harder and longer to dry your clothes when the lint trap is clogged. That means wasted utility dollars. You know you need to keep both the filter and the exhaust tube clean or you risk burning your whole house down.

Professionals could charge you $100 or more to clean this tube, but why not take five minutes and take care of the problem yourself? Try this fix that's even easier than a brush. Take your outdoor leaf blower and insert the nozzle into the exhaust opening in your dryer. A couple of short blasts of air should blow out any lint caught in the tube.

Clean your hair dryer with a toothbrush. If your hair dryer smells like burning hair, it usually means hair and lint is trapped in the air intake. Rubbing an old toothbrush over the holes of the intake will get rid of the problem.

Unclog your steam iron. Return your clogged iron back to its old, steamy self with a half-and-half mixture of vinegar and water. Pour the combo into the water chamber, sit the iron upright, and select the "steam" setting. After five minutes, unplug your iron and let it cool. Empty out the water chamber, and your iron should be clog free.

Super smart way to fill your iron. Keep water handy for your steam iron by storing it in a recycled sports water bottle or mineral water bottle with pop-up top. The small spout is the right size for pouring water into the iron's water tank.

Foil a dirty iron. Don't you just hate it when the face of your iron gets coated with burnt starch or residue from polyester fabric? Fortunately, you can remove it easily. Rub it with aluminum foil, or apply a baking soda paste with a soft cloth. Even an iron with a nonstick coating can get a buildup of starch. To get rid of it, scrape it away gently with a scrubber made for cleaning nonstick cookware when your iron is cool.

Automotive answers to keep you on the road

Find the perfect time to buy a car. When you buy a car may affect how much you pay for it. One rule of thumb is the later the better. Do your car shopping at the end of the month, and you may get a deal because the dealership wants to boost its sales figures for that month. The same logic applies to the end of the year. Shop for your car right before the next year's model is due to come out, and the dealership may be eager to clear the lot — and make a deal.

You may even save just by shopping near the end of the day. The salesperson may want to hammer out one more sale before heading home for the night. If you don't mind rain or snow, you can snag a sunny deal. That's because new car sales usually drop when the weather is lousy. Brave the elements, and you just might find a desperate dealer willing to negotiate.

Watch out for dealer tricks. Going to a car dealership is like entering a lion's den. If you're not careful, you could end up in big trouble. Follow these tips to avoid being ripped off.

- Do not hand over your driver's license. Some dealers will hold your license hostage as a way to keep you at the dealership longer. Make photocopies instead.

- Say no to unnecessary add-ons. You have better things to spend your money on than gimmicks like rust proofing, fabric protectant, lifetime wax protection, or VIN etching.

- Refuse to be bullied into an extended warranty. Even if you think you may want one, you can always buy it later — even if the salesman is pressuring you to say "yes" right away.

- Look at the big picture. When it comes to financing, look at the total cost, not just the monthly payment. Longer loans mean more interest charges.

- Divide and conquer. Don't let dealers group your trade-in and financing in with the price of the car. Negotiate a fair price for each separately.

Get financing before buying. Your car loan doesn't have to come from your car dealer. Often, you can find a better rate before setting foot on the lot. First, check your credit report to make sure everything is accurate — then try to improve your credit score. Next, shop around for the best rate through online lenders, banks, and credit unions. You can even pay for your car with a home equity loan or line of credit. After settling on a fair price for the car, let the dealer know you have your financing. Then see if he will beat your lender's best rate.

Crash safety test results at your fingertips. The internet does more than help you find good deals on new or used cars. You can also find out which cars are the safest. Two websites provide helpful crash safety test information for a variety of vehicles.

At the Insurance Institute for Highway Safety's website, *www.iihs.org*, you can find ratings based on front, side, and rear impact. See if the car you're considering ranks as Good, Acceptable, Marginal, or Poor in these situations. You can also find a list of the safest cars by year and class.

Go to *www.safercar.gov* to view the National Highway Traffic Safety Administration's crash safety ratings. Using a five-star system, it measures how cars stack up in front and side crashes, as well as the car's risk of rolling over during an accident. Although not every car has been tested, these sites can help narrow your search for a safer vehicle.

Sweet way to sidestep lemons

A simple background check on a used vehicle can save you from buying a lemon. Go to CarFax at *www.carfax.com* to trace a car's history. Discover if the car has been in a major accident, flooded, or damaged by fire.

You can also check for odometer fraud. You'll need the vehicle identification number, or VIN. Your trusty mechanic can also give the car a once-over — and may not even charge you. Despite your precautions, if you do end up with a lemon, you can find a lawyer to handle your case at *www.lemonlawamerica.com.*

Go online to save time and money. Want to save big bucks on a new car? Then spend some time on your computer before heading to the dealership. Thanks to the internet, you can save hundreds — even thousands — on a new car. It's the secret weapon car salesmen don't want you to know.

Spending more time online can save you time — and money — at the dealership. A recent study found that people who researched their car online spent an average of 80 minutes less at the dealership and 25 minutes less taking test drives and negotiating prices. Another study found that people who studied price-related information online paid about $400 less than other buyers.

That's because when you come to the dealership armed with information, you're in a better position to make a deal. And you can find a wealth of automobile information online. You can compare prices and features of different models, read reviews, and discover the true value of a vehicle by looking at the dealer cost or invoice price.

Some helpful automobile websites include:

- Edmunds Car Buying Guide at *www.edmunds.com*
- Kelley Blue Book at *www.kbb.com*
- Autobytel Network at *www.autobytel.com* or *www.myride.com*
- Cars.com at *www.cars.com*
- AutoTrader.com at *www.autotrader.com*

Explore these sites to find out all the information you need before buying a new or used car. It may take some searching, but it's better and, ultimately, cheaper than getting all your information from a fast-talking salesman.

Protect yourself from flood-damaged cars. Whenever superstorms, hurricanes, or flash floods recede, they leave behind a deluge of water-damaged vehicles — hundreds of thousands of cars corroded from salt water, ruined by silt, and overrun with mold. Unfortunately, many of these will be spiffed up on the outside by swindlers and sold to unsuspecting buyers. Don't let that be you.

The most incriminating evidence will be deep inside the car's engine, transmission, brakes, electrical system, and other innermost parts, and may not even impact the car's functionality for months or even years. But there are ways you can spot a storm-damaged car if you know how.

- Sniff. Mold and mildew have a distinctive odor which is a dead giveaway, but even the overpowering aroma of air freshener or disinfectants should raise a red flag.

- Look inside the trunk and pop the hood. Hunt for silt, lines, or water stains, especially around the spare.

- Check under the carpet, on the seats and seatbelts, around metal screws and hinges, and along the door panels. You're looking for silt, discolorations, rust, and warping. Make sure the headlights and taillights aren't fogged or have water lines.

- Take it for a test spin and note if the engine is rough or lurches.

Of course, the best precaution is to have the vehicle inspected by a qualified mechanic before you buy.

Use VIN to check title

If you want to be sure a car's title is "clean," get the vehicle identification number (VIN) from the seller and dig a little deeper. Go online to the Department of Justice's National Motor Vehicle Title Information System (NMVTIS) at *www.vehiclehistory.gov* or the National Insurance Crime Bureau database at *www.nicb.org*, and request a report on the vehicle's damage history.

The NICB report is free, but there's a small fee for reports via NMVTIS. You can also pay a few extra dollars for a more in-depth report from AutoCheck at *www.autocheck.com*. If the seller will not give you the VIN, walk away from the deal — they have something to hide.

Beware of title scams. Never purchase a used car without giving its title a thorough inspection — front and back. Those extra minutes could save you from an expensive, and potentially life-threatening, mistake. What you're looking for are danger words, part of a branding strategy to warn unsuspecting buyers that a vehicle has suffered severe damage from a collision, theft, or disaster. Branding terms include flood, salvage, rebuilt, fire, junk, and irreparable.

But be aware that a "clean" title is sometimes misleading. Criminals can take a branded title to a state that does not require branding, register the vehicle there, and get a new, clean title. This is called "title washing." If you suspect someone is trying to sell a damaged car with a washed title, contact your auto insurance company, local police, or the National Insurance Crime Bureau (NICB) at *www.nicb.org*.

Smart features help seniors drive safer and longer. Arthritic knees, diminished hand strength, hip pain, and failing eyesight all make driving more of a challenge than it was years ago. But these common symptoms of aging don't necessarily mean you must throw in the car keys. The University of Florida National Older Driver Research and Training Center in conjunction with AAA have recommendations that address the challenges senior drivers face. Take advantage of existing features in your car or look for these specific elements if you're thinking of buying another vehicle.

- Safety features — front and rear warning systems, antilock brakes, adjustable head restraints with extra padding, dynamic stability control, backup cameras, parallel parking assistance, and dual-stage air bags.

- Ergonomics — adjustable seats, low door thresholds, adjustable accelerator and brake pedals, and tilting and telescoping steering wheels.

- Comfort — thick steering wheels, automatic door openers and closers, power mirrors and seats, heated mirrors and seats, large dashboard buttons, pushbutton ignition, and keyless entry.

In addition, you can add inexpensive assistive devices to your car — like pedal extenders, swivel seats, leg lift straps, lumbar supports, and hand controls — either through your car's manufacturer or a third party. Just make sure any add-ons don't compromise the existing safety features in your car. Find out by contacting an occupational therapy-driver rehabilitation specialist (OT-DRS) online at *www.aota.org/olderdriver* or by calling 301-652-6611. If you want help selecting a vehicle that fits your needs, visit the interactive website *SeniorDriving.AAA.com/SmartFeatures*.

Super strategies for selling your car. It may take more time and effort, but you can get a better price selling your car yourself rather than trading it in at a dealership. Here's a quick guide to selling your vehicle.

- Get a feel for the market. Research the value of your make and model with tools like Kelley Blue Book. Look at local classifieds for similar cars to see what the going rate may be.

- Set your price accordingly. You'll also want to take into account mileage, condition, location, gas mileage, and any special features or improvements. Boost your price by a few hundred dollars to leave room for negotiation.

- Advertise your car. You can do this simply by putting a "For Sale" sign in your window. You can also place classified ads in local papers, tack up signs on neighborhood bulletin boards, or list your vehicle online. Make sure your ad includes important information like the year, make, model, color, mileage, condition, color, and price. If you're open to negotiations, include "OBO," for "or best offer." If you're set on your price, include the word "firm."

- Show off the car. Park your car, with its "For Sale" sign, in places where it may generate the most interest. Remember that your appearance counts, too. If potential buyers want to test drive your car, ride with them so you can answer any questions. Feel free to bring a friend along if you're uncomfortable.

- Once you agree on a price and decide on a method of payment, close the deal. Make sure you know your state's laws regarding title transfers and any other paperwork you'll need to complete. You can usually find the necessary information on your state's department of motor vehicles website.

Top tips for trade-ins. When you buy a new car, it's easier to trade in your old one than sell it yourself. But it's also easier to get shortchanged on the deal. Here's how to make the most of your trade-in.

- Know your car's value. Use the internet to research trade-in values for your make, model, and year. That way, you'll know if you're getting a fair offer.

- Make sure your car is in good shape and looks good. Bring maintenance records as proof of your tender loving care. If you don't value your car, why should the dealer?

- Shop around. You may get a better offer at another dealership. But don't insist on an unrealistic price for your car.

- Don't be fooled. Dealers may act disinterested in your car, but they can earn big profits from reselling trade-ins.

- Keep negotiations for your trade-in and your new vehicle separate so you get a good deal on both. As a bonus, most states only tax you on the difference between the new car's sale price and what you received for your trade-in.

Bust a gas-saving myth. Changing your car's air filter will certainly improve acceleration, but it won't get you more miles to the gallon. Today's cars have fuel-injected, computer-controlled engines, and the air filter simply doesn't affect fuel economy. This myth is a holdover from the days when cars had carburetors — those built prior to the 1980s.

So change your air filter when it's dirty because it's good for your car, but don't expect to save any money at the pump. What will make your car more fuel-efficient? Drive with an empty trunk, keep your tires inflated properly, use cruise control when possible, eliminate jackrabbit starts and sudden stops, don't drive with a loose or missing gas cap, and fix serious problems like a faulty oxygen sensor.

Surprising ways to keep your windshield clear. A fogged windshield can cost you your life. Think about it. Here's the item to carry in your glove box to remove the haze instantly. It's unusual, but inexpensive — and it works. Just rub the windshield with a chalkboard eraser to fix the problem. You can also repel rain from your windshield. Simply dampen a cloth, dip it in baking soda, and wipe it on the windshield inside and out. To keep frost away from the inside of your windows, rub them with a solution made of two teaspoons of salt in a gallon of hot water. Then wipe them dry.

10 ways to find the best repair shop. Car problems are bad enough. Don't make things worse by taking your car to a shifty repair shop. Instead, follow these tips from the National Institute for Automotive Service Excellence (ASE).

- Shop for a repair shop before you actually need one, so desperation doesn't enter into your decision.
- Ask friends and coworkers for recommendations.

- Check out a shop's reputation through a local consumer organization, like AAA.
- Do not choose a shop just for its convenient location.
- Look for a tidy, well-organized shop with modern equipment.
- Make sure the shop handles your make and model.
- Look for ASE certifications and other signs of mechanics' competence, like trade school diplomas and certificates of advanced coursework.
- Ask questions of the staff. They should be courteous and helpful. You can even ask for names of some customers as references.
- Look for clearly posted labor rates, diagnostic fees, and guarantees.
- Start small. Take your car to an unfamiliar shop for a minor job first.

Beware of shady mechanics' dirty tricks. Not all auto mechanics are honest. Some just want your money. Watch out for these warning signs that your mechanic may be ripping you off.

- Recommending extra and expensive services, like engine or transmission flushes. Check your owner's manual for recommended scheduled maintenance items.
- Passing off old parts as new. A mechanic may just clean up your old part, put it back, and charge you for a new one. Always ask to see the old, broken part or receipts for new parts.

- Swapping multiple parts. Your mechanic may replace one part, only to find that the real problem is something else that also requires replacing. While a misdiagnosis can be an honest mistake, you should get a refund for the first repair or a discount for the second.

Clean critters from your windshield

Anyone driving in the state of Florida, or other "buggy" locales, knows too many dead critters on the windshield can be a safety hazard. Get rid of them with this homemade windshield cleaner.

Make a paste using about 70 percent baking soda and 30 percent liquid dish detergent. Dip a wet sponge into the paste, scrub the windshield, and rinse thoroughly. Don't use the mixture on other parts of the car.

Drive your car longer for bigger savings. According to a *Consumer Reports* survey, driving your car past 200,000 miles is cheaper than buying a new car every five years. In fact, it can save you more than $30,000.

Of course, the key is to buy a safe, reliable vehicle and take good care of it. That means strictly following the maintenance schedule and using only recommended parts and fluids. It also involves keeping an eye out for problems by regularly looking under the hood. You should also keep the car clean to prevent rusting.

Yet, it doesn't always pay to hold onto an old vehicle. If it needs repairs that cost more than its value, spends more time in the shop than on the road, or has been in a flood or serious accident, give up on it.

Wash greasy hands with olive oil. Olive oil is great for your heart. It's also great for greasy hands. After working on your car, drizzle some olive oil or vegetable oil on your dirty hands and rub it in. Wash your hands in hot soapy water, and the grease will come off much easier.

10 great gas-saving tips. With gas prices so high, it's more important than ever to find ways to get more mileage for your money. Here are 10 easy ways to improve your mileage — and your finances.

- Use cruise control. Maintaining a constant speed improves mileage.
- Tighten a loose gas cap. An unsealed cap allows gasoline to vaporize and can reduce your mileage by up to two miles a gallon.
- Clean out your trunk and back seat. Extra weight takes its toll on fuel economy.
- Consolidate trips. Instead of making several short trips around town, do all your errands at once. You'll cut down on cold starts and help your engine run better.
- Avoid rush hour. Idling just wastes gas.
- Open your windows when driving in town, but use your air conditioner on the highway. Open windows create drag at speeds above 40 mph.

- Ditch the rooftop carrier. Your car burns gas trying to overcome wind resistance.
- Skip the warm-up. Start driving immediately. Your engine warms up faster that way.
- Ease into stops and starts. Don't slam on the brakes or floor the accelerator at green lights. Smooth driving not only saves fuel, it also extends the life of your brakes, transmission, and tires.
- Keep tires properly inflated. If a tire is underinflated by just 2 pounds per square inch (psi), it increases fuel consumption by 1 percent.

Running on empty can empty your wallet. Refill your gas tank when the needle hits a quarter of a tank. Otherwise, you can stir up sediment that collects at the bottom of your tank. This dirt can clog or damage parts, including your fuel injector and filter. It may even require an entire fuel-system flush and cleaning, which can cost $1,000. It's cheaper just to keep an eye on the fuel gauge.

Lay trunk clutter to rest with old pillowcases

Stick an old pillowcase in your trunk to use as a handy storage bag. It can hold a change of clothes, shoes, tools, or other supplies. You can also keep your trunk clean and dry by slipping muddy shoes or a wet umbrella in the pillowcase.

Terrific tips for top-notch tires. You may not give your tires too much thought, but you should. As the only part of your car that touches the road, tires are key to your safety. Follow these guidelines to keep your tires on a roll.

- Check the tire pressure. Do this once a month with a tire gauge. For an accurate reading, check tire pressure on cold tires, or those that haven't been driven on for at least three hours. Both overinflated and underinflated tires pose dangers. Make sure you stick to the recommended tire pressure, measured in pounds per square inch (psi), listed in the owner's manual. You may also find the information on the vehicle door edge, door post, glove box door, or trunk lid.

- Check the tread depth. It should not fall below 1/16 of an inch. You probably know the old penny trick. Stick a penny in the tread, and if you can see the top of Lincoln's head, it's time for new tires. Recently, Consumer Reports recommended using a quarter — and 1/8 inch — as your benchmark instead.

- Rotate the tires. Periodically switching tires from front to back and from side to side prevents uneven wear.

- Buy wisely. When you need to replace your tires, shop around for the best price. You also want to get the proper size and pay attention to a variety of rankings, including speed, treadwear, traction, and temperature. Fresh tires are best. The last four digits following the "DOT" indicate the week and year of manufacture.

Put the squeeze on dirt and grime. Fill an empty, clean, squeeze dish detergent bottle with water and store it in your car. Use it to wash your hands after changing a flat tire or checking under the hood. You can also use it to clean off your windshield if you're out of wiper fluid.

Mayo jar fights road tar. Mayonnaise does more than perk up your sandwich. You can also take road tar off your car with this simple kitchen condiment. Just slather some mayonnaise over the tar. Let it sit a few minutes, then wipe it with a clean rag.

4 hot tips for cold car care. You and your car can survive the fury of Old Man Winter with these clever tips that will make frosty outings less troublesome.

- Apply a coat of wax to your car's alloy wheels. This protects them from the corroding effects of road salt.

- Slip a pair of long socks over your wiper blades whenever your car sits outside during a freeze. Then when you're ready to go, pull off the socks without fighting any ice.

- Drain and refill your radiator with fresh antifreeze just before winter hits. Since antifreeze needs to be fairly pure to protect your engine properly from cold temperatures, experts recommend you do this every other year.

- Keep a stash of plastic grocery bags in your car, and tie one around each side-view mirror before a frost. Remove in the morning, and you're on your way with no scraping.

Limit risk of lockouts. A few simple tricks can help you avoid the hassle of getting locked out of your car. Instead of using the inside door locks, always lock the door with your key. Keep an extra key in your wallet or somewhere else where you can always get to it. If you do get locked out, your best bet is to call a locksmith. If you have an older car, you may be able to unlock the door with a bent coat hanger, but you can damage newer vehicles — and possibly injure yourself by triggering the air bag. If it's a true emergency, like a baby locked in the car, call the police.

Don't leave home without these 10 items — and 6 you should always leave at home

Keep in your car

- blanket
- flashlight
- shovel
- tire gauge
- emergency phone numbers
- first-aid kit
- ice scraper
- jumper cables
- spare tire with jack
- flares

Never leave in car

- Electronics — they contain information that could be used for identity theft.
- Important ID — a Social Security card or passport contains your confidential data.
- Your mail — it can give crooks critical personal information.
- A GPS unit — thieves not only have the GPS, but now they know where you live.
- Credit or debit cards — these are like an ATM for criminals.
- Your garage door remote control — this and your home address allow thieves to steal items from your garage and then your home.

Sidestep speeding tickets. Obviously, the best way to avoid a speeding ticket is to obey the speed limit. But if you do get pulled over, here's what to do.

- Do not speak first. Respond "No" if the officer asks if you know why he pulled you over. Never admit any wrongdoing, argue, or try to make excuses.
- Make notes at the scene. Details like the location of the stop, weather conditions, traffic conditions, names of any passengers, and any distinguishing characteristics of your car could come in handy later if you need to cross-examine the officer.
- Show up in court and plead not guilty. That's half the battle. Many times, especially in the summer months when people take vacation, the officer will not show up — and you'll get off.
- Be prepared to defend yourself. You can't count on the officer not showing up, so you should have a Plan B. Maybe the officer's view was obstructed, maybe he pulled over the wrong car, maybe his radar gun wasn't calibrated right, or maybe his recollection of the incident was foggy.

Even if you lose, you'll pay the same fine you would have paid in the first place. Fighting the ticket will only cost you time — and may cost you nothing.

Protect yourself from carjacking. When driving, you need to be alert for pedestrians, other vehicles, traffic signs — and carjackers. These car thieves can sneak up on you if you're not on the lookout. Follow these tips to reduce your risk of being carjacked.

- Park in well-lit areas.
- Do not park near walls, dumpsters, woods, or large vehicles that obstruct your view.
- Use valet parking or a garage with an attendant.
- Keep your doors locked and windows rolled up.
- Be especially alert when you slow down or stop at garages, parking lots, intersections, self-service gas stations, car washes, highway ramps, and ATMs.
- As you walk to your car, take note of suspicious people sitting in cars, handing out flyers, or loitering in the area.
- If someone approaches you on your way to your car, change direction or enter a busy store.
- Do not turn your back while loading packages into your car.
- Look under, around, and inside your car before getting in — then start it and drive away immediately.
- Do not stop to help someone who looks like they're having car trouble. Call the police instead.
- If you're bumped by another car filled with young males, wave the other vehicle to follow you to a gas station or busy place before getting out.

- Try not to drive alone, especially at night.

Most important, if an armed carjacker confronts you, do not resist. Give up your car. It's not worth losing your life over a vehicle. Get away as quickly as possible and call the police. If you are forced to drive, consider crashing your car at a busy intersection where bystanders can call for help.

Steer clear of skidding. The calm before the storm can be deadly. A recent study found that the more days between periods of precipitation, the more accidents take place when it finally rains or snows. That could be because oil on dry roads turns slick on the first day of rain, but it gets washed away with more rain. Or people could just drive more carefully after a day or two of wet weather. Whatever the reason, here's how to cope with poor conditions.

- If your car starts to skid, turn the wheel in the direction you want the front of your car to go. Lay off the gas and brakes unless you have anti-lock brakes. In that case, brake firmly as you steer.

- If your car starts to hydroplane, do not brake or turn suddenly. Ease your foot off the gas. Pump your brakes gently if you need to brake. If you have anti-lock brakes, you can brake normally, and your car's computer will do the pumping.

- To prevent hydroplaning, slow down and stay away from puddles. Try to drive in the tire tracks left by the cars in front of you. Make sure your tires have good tread and are properly inflated.

Cleaning: quick and easy techniques

7 ways to clean your house quicker. Stop spending all of your spare time cleaning. The key is to work smarter, not harder. These seven tricks will slash the time it takes to tidy up your home. Get started and use the extra time to do anything you want.

- Remove kitchen grease without scrubbing. Soak a towel with hot water and lay it over the stuck-on gunk for 10 minutes. Then use the same towel to wipe off the softened mess.

- Run your shower on the hottest water possible for several minutes before you clean it or the tub. The steam will loosen the dirt, so you can do less work.

- Wash tough-to-clean items in the dishwasher — glass globes from light fixtures, the grille from the exhaust fan, soap trays, plastic hairbrushes, scrub brushes, dish drainers, and more. Turn off the heated dry, so nothing melts accidentally, and place delicate items like glass light globes in the top rack. Wash household items separately from your dishes.

- Clean rooms by moving in one direction, either clockwise or counterclockwise. You'll use fewer steps and be less likely to get sidetracked.

- Wear a tool belt or apron with pockets while house cleaning. Stash a dusting cloth, sponge, scrub brush, cleaners, and other tools in them. You'll have everything on hand as you work through a room and make fewer trips to fetch supplies.

- Dust last, after you have vacuumed and finished your normal cleaning routine. Cleaning, especially vacuuming, stirs up dust. Let it settle for a few minutes then wipe down surfaces.

- Wipe hard-to-dust places like the baseboards with a dryer sheet. The sheets will grab existing dust and repel it in the future, so you won't need to dust as often.

Leave dust at the door. Your shoes are the source of most of the dust and dirt in your home. An incredible 80 percent of the dirt in your house travels in on your shoes. Cut down on dirt and clean less with a few simple steps.

First, institute a no-shoes rule in the house. Have everyone remove their shoes as soon as they come in. If that's not an option, then designate one or two pairs as indoor-only shoes. Take off your outside shoes as soon as you walk in the door and slip into your inside shoes to avoid tracking in dirt.

Second, invest in a commercial-quality walk-off mat, the kind of doormat you see at the entrances to grocery stores and office buildings. These are specially made to trap dirt and water. Look for them at janitorial supply stores. If that's not in the budget, at least buy a good carpet runner for indoors, and place a doormat outside each entrance to your home.

Scent your house with homemade air fresheners. Store-bought air fresheners are loaded with chemicals and artificial fragrances. They're also expensive. Why spend money on costly air polluters when you can make natural air fresheners at home?

Gel fresheners are as easy to make as jello. Boil a half cup of water, and slowly stir in two packets of unflavored gelatin. Once mixed, add one teaspoon of salt and a half cup of water. Mix thoroughly and remove from heat. Stir in 10 to 15 drops of your favorite essential oil, then pour the gelatin into a mason jar. Once it cools, place it in a room that could use a boost of fresh air.

Here's an even simpler recipe. Pour a half cup of baking soda into a mason jar, add 10 drops of essential oil, and mix well. Cover the mouth of the jar with fabric to match the room, and tie it on with a ribbon. Or punch holes in the metal lid with a hammer, and nail in a decorative pattern. Give the jar a shake every week or so to boost the scent.

For fresh scent on demand, make your own room spray. Mix together one part vodka, three parts distilled water, and 10 drops of essential oil. Pour into a pretty spray bottle and shake, then spritz. Add more oil for a stronger fragrance. Remember to shake the bottle well before spraying as the oil and water will separate between uses.

Add pizzazz to your cleaning routine with citrus peels. Save your citrus rinds and make your own fresh-smelling cleaning solution. Put rinds from oranges, lemons, limes, or grapefruits in a jar of white vinegar and seal. Let brew four weeks, then strain the liquid. You can use this brew to clean your home just like regular vinegar.

10 ways to clean with vinegar	
windows and mirrors	Mix one part white vinegar and three parts water, spray on windows, and dry with newspaper.
toilets	Pour one cup undiluted white vinegar into bowl, let stand five minutes, and flush. This white vinegar formula makes any toilet automatically spic and span.
dishwasher	Place a cup containing white vinegar on bottom rack of dishwasher and run through full cycle to remove soap buildup in your machine.
tile mildew	Spray on equal parts white vinegar and water, wipe with a sponge.
bathtub film	Wipe down with white vinegar and rinse with water.
stainless steel, ceramic sinks, chrome, and appliances	Dip sponge or cloth in white vinegar and wipe clean. Polish to a shine with soft, damp cloth.
clogged shower heads	Fill a watertight plastic bag halfway with white vinegar, place over shower head so head is submerged in vinegar, and secure with a rubber band. Leave on overnight, then rinse with hot water.
vinyl floors	Pour half a cup white vinegar into one gallon warm water and grab a mop.
white rings on wood furniture	Rub with equal parts olive oil and white vinegar.
foul odors	Boil one tablespoon white vinegar in one cup water to banish bad smells. Set a cup of white vinegar in a room to absorb the smell of stale smoke.

The 5 cleaning products you should never be without. You don't have to spend a fortune on cleaning products to keep your house spotless. The only five you need cost less than $10 for the lot of 'em.They'll help you repair, clean, shine, and protect everything in your home for pennies. Even better, you probably have everything you need in your house right now.

- Baking soda, also known as bicarbonate of soda or sodium bicarbonate, is made up of fine particles. That means if you mix it with a bit of water to form a paste, you can scour pots, pans, sinks, bathtubs, and ovens. And because it's absorbent, it's famous for soaking up odors.

- Liquid hand dishwashing detergent contains surfactants — organic chemicals that actually change the properties of water. They help quickly wet the surface of whatever you want to clean, make dirt easier to loosen and remove, and trap oils so they can't settle back on the surface and are easily rinsed away. Most hand dishwashing detergents cut grease and are biodegradable.

- White vinegar is often called a household wonder cleaner. It's inexpensive, nontoxic, and useful for dozens of chores. It's the acid in vinegar that cuts through grease and germs and inhibits bacteria and mold.

- Bleach is simply a chemical mixture of chlorine gas, sodium hydroxide, and water. It's the chlorine that makes bleach such a great disinfectant. This one inexpensive household product kills disease-causing bacteria and viruses in your bathroom and kitchen, gets rid of mildew, and makes your laundry whites whiter. Why bleach is a great stain remover is a little more complicated, but it has a lot to do with a chemical reaction that removes color.

- Ammonia can be a tricky product to use because of the important safety measures you must take. The vapors can irritate or even burn your skin, eyes, or lungs, so you always want to work in a well-ventilated area. And never use ammonia with bleach. This mixture produces a dangerous gas.

Mask the sharp smell of vinegar

Cleaning with vinegar can be an unpleasant chore only because of the odor. Breathe easier and leave a room smelling great by adding a few drops of your favorite essential oil to your vinegar cleaning solutions. Oils such as rosemary, lavender, eucalyptus, and grapefruit may even give your cleaner a germ-killing boost.

Amazing ways to use dryer sheets. Clean window blinds, TVs, and computer screens, add a fresh scent to luggage and closets, and even shine your shoes — all with a dryer sheet. You would normally throw it away after using it just once, but fabric softener sheets have many lives.

- Dust window blinds and TV and computer screens with dryer sheets. They grab dust easily and help repel future dirt.

- Clean caked-on food by placing a sheet in a dirty pan, filling with water, and soaking overnight.

- Place a new fabric softener sheet in the vacuum cleaner bag to freshen a room while you sweep. Change the sheet every few weeks or when the scent starts to fade.

- Keep thread from tangling by pulling a threaded needle through a dryer sheet before sewing.

- Stick them in stored luggage to ward off musty odors.

- Tuck a sheet in a smelly shoe to banish bad odors, then use it later to buff that boot or pump to a nice shine.

- Replace old scented sachets with a dryer sheet in dresser drawers, closets, and stored, out-of-season clothing.

Kill the germs on mops and sponges. Cleaning your cleaning tools is just as important as cleaning your house. After all, they spend their lives picking up dirt and germs. Don't spread bacteria and viruses around your home with a dirty mop or sponge. Disinfect them regularly, and do it the right way.

Sponges have a special "ick" factor — they're both dirty and germy. Start by washing off as much grime as possible, then sanitize them in the dishwasher. Secure them to the top rack with a large binder clip, so they don't fall into the heating element below. Then run the dishwasher on the longest, hottest setting possible, and use the heated dry cycle. The U.S. Department of Agriculture found that this method kills 99.9 percent of bacteria in sponges.

Don't have a dishwasher? Wet the sponge thoroughly, and pop it in the microwave for one minute on "high." Handle the hot sponge with tongs or let it sit until cool. Never microwave a dry sponge or one that contains metal. They may start a fire.

Sanitize sponge mops with removable heads the same way as sponges — in the dishwasher. Mop heads made of string or strips of cloth, on the other hand, can go in the washing machine with bleach and hot water.

Clean mops with stationary heads in a bucket with one gallon of hot water and one cup of hydrogen peroxide. Let soak for 10 minutes then wring out and air dry. Bleach will also do the trick. Soak the mop for one minute in one cup of bleach mixed with one gallon of warm water. Then rinse, wring out, and air dry.

Whip up your own wipes. Why buy expensive cleaning wipes when you can make your own for pennies apiece? First, get a roll of good, strong paper towels. Cut the sheets in half, and fold to fit in a plastic storage container. For general cleaning, pour in one part white vinegar and one part water. For disinfecting, make a solution using your favorite liquid cleaner. Check the directions on the bottle. Gently pour over your towels, seal the container, and let sit overnight.

6 secrets to faster kitchen cleanup. Minimize kitchen messes with a few simple tips.

- Leave your dishwasher open and the racks pulled out while cooking. Drop in each dirty dish and utensil as soon as you finish using it.

- Measure out dry ingredients first, then wet ones so you only need one measuring cup.
- Marinate meats in sealable, disposable, plastic bags.
- Measure over wax paper to keep spills off your counter. Pour the dry ingredients that spill back into their containers.
- Line your produce drawer with paper towels, so juices are easier to clean up.
- Tear open produce bags but leave the produce in them. If food goes bad, it's less messy to toss.

Breathe better air at home. You try to keep your home clean and smelling fresh, but you may be doing more harm than good. Air fresheners, candles, cleaning products, disinfectants, aerosol sprays, paint, and dry-cleaned clothing can release toxic chemicals called volatile organic compounds into your home — compounds linked to cancer, as well as heart, liver, nervous system, and breathing problems. You can improve the air in your home with five simple steps.

- Keep the humidity level between 40 and 50 percent during very cold weather and between 40 and 60 percent the rest of the year to minimize pollutants.
- Always use commercial cleaners and disinfectants, aerosol sprays, and air fresheners with lots of ventilation. Open windows or run exhaust fans that vent outdoors.
- Switch to more natural cleaners. Baking soda, vinegar, liquid dish soap, and plain old water are safer, less toxic, cheaper, and just as effective as most commercial cleaners.

- Avoid imported candles. They are more likely to have lead wicks, and burning them can cause unsafe lead levels in your home. Scented candles, on the other hand, are more likely to produce potentially harmful soot particles.

- Leave windows open to let in fresh air when burning incense. Incense can release large amounts of pollutants, including compounds linked to contact dermatitis, asthma, and cancer.

Stop allergies cold with a houseplant

Are you breathing in mold, or something even worse? Chuck the air purifiers and pot some English ivy instead.

When researchers put ivy a sealed container with mold and dog feces, this beautiful plant removed 78 percent of airborne mold and 94 percent of dog fecal particles in the air. And that was after just 12 hours.

Make English ivy your houseplant of choice, and you could cut back on allergies and keep the air in your home fresh for free. It's a simple, natural trick to keeping allergens to a minimum. Remember to keep the plant away from small children and pets because it's toxic if eaten.

The dirt-cheap secret to perfectly clean mirrors. Toss the glass cleaner and paper towels. Not only are they expensive, but they can literally ruin your mirrors. One day you'll finish spraying and wiping, spritzing and rubbing, and stand back to admire your handiwork. That's when you'll notice the scratches. And wait, what's that black stuff along the edge?

Blame the scratches on rough paper towels. They are meant to be abrasive — the better to scrub away stains and spills. Not so good for mirrors or glass, though. What's worse, a tiny drip of glass cleaner behind the mirror's edge can make the backing lift from the glass, leaving an ugly, dark rim.

The solution is cheap and easy. Clean your mirrors with a soft microfiber cloth dampened with warm water. Wipe and then dry quickly with another cloth for a streak-free shine. For stubborn spots, spray cleaner on the cloth — not the mirror — and avoid the edges.

Beware of hidden hazards in household cleaners. Household cleaners are responsible for thousands of calls to poison control centers every year. Although two-thirds of those calls involved young children, accidents and mistakes with cleaners harm adults, too.

For example, a simple cleaner like bleach can create toxic gases if it's mixed with other cleaners, including ammonia and vinegar. Many cleaners contain ingredients that can irritate your eyes and lungs. What's more, some cleaners put volatile organic compounds (VOCs) into the air. VOCs are chemical gases that can cause headaches, dizziness, fatigue, nausea, and throat, eye, or nose irritation. And they can remain in the air for a while after you finish cleaning.

To help avoid serious problems, take these precautions.

- Read household cleaner labels carefully. Pay close attention to the instructions and information about hazards.
- Do not mix bleach with other cleaners.
- Open a window or door and turn on the vent fan when cleaning your bathrooms.
- Keep people out of recently cleaned bathrooms and kitchens for 30 minutes.

Clean toilets and tubs without scrubbing. Why scrub and scrub your toilet and tub when you can just spray and walk away? Discover just how much easier cleaning can be with these clever tricks and tips.

White vinegar alone can be enough to remove those irritating waterline marks on your toilet. Just pour one cup into a spray bottle, spray around the inside of your toilet bowl, and leave overnight. If you have hard water, pour in an extra cup of vinegar. The next morning, simply flush the toilet to rinse the marks away.

For an even stronger cleaner, drop two denture cleaning tablets into your toilet bowl, and let them spend all night attacking the stains. The next morning, you shouldn't need to scrub. Just run your toilet brush over the stains, and flush them away.

If your toilet requires major cleaning power, flush the toilet, and sprinkle one cup of borax all around the bowl before pouring one cup of vinegar around the bowl. Let sit overnight. If you have particularly heavy stains, a little scrubbing may be necessary the first time you do this. But you probably won't need to scrub again if you use this powerful cleaner regularly.

To clean your tub, mix one part warm vinegar with one part dishwashing liquid, and pour in a heat-tolerant spray bottle. Spray on the tub, and walk away. After one hour, return to wipe away any grime and rinse off the tub. Some people who use this method claim you won't get the best results unless you use the original, blue Dawn dishwashing liquid.

For a no-scrub shower cleaner, pour 8 ounces of rubbing alcohol into a 32-ounce spray bottle and top it off with water. Spray the walls and door right after a shower. You don't even have to rinse. Do this daily, and you may never need to scrub.

Unclog your drains with vinegar. Clear clogged drains like a Roto-Rooter with this three-ingredient drain opener. It's natural, safe, and won't damage pipes, either. Pour half a cup of baking soda down the drain, followed by a cup of hot vinegar. Let the two bubble and break apart the debris. After a few minutes, flush the drain with a quart of hot water. Try these other natural remedies for nasty clogs, too.

- Sweep sink drains clean by dropping three Alka-Seltzer tablets down them followed by a cup of white vinegar, then flush with hot water.

- To remove grease buildup in drains, dump half a cup of salt and half a cup of baking soda down the drain, then a kettle of boiling water. Allow it to sit overnight before rinsing.

- Maintain free-flowing pipes with this weekly treatment. Combine 1/4 cup of baking soda, 1/4 cup salt, and 1 tablespoon cream of tartar, and stir thoroughly. Pour the mixture down the drain, then immediately follow with a cup of boiling water. Wait a few seconds, then rinse with cold water.

Banish rust rings from your bathroom. Put an end to rust rings and rust stains on your porcelain sinks and tubs. To get started, pick up some cream of tartar from your supermarket spice aisle. For a quick cleaning, make a paste of cream of tartar and hydrogen peroxide. Cover the ring or stain with this paste, and scrub with an old toothbrush. Rinse thoroughly.

For more stubborn rust rings, mix the cream of tartar with lemon juice, apply to the stain, and let sit for up to two hours. Rinse with warm water, and the stain should be gone.

To prevent future rust rings on your counters, sinks, and tubs, save low-rimmed plastic lids from your kitchen. Place all your rust-forming containers on top of lids from now on. Just as coasters help protect your coffee table, these lids help prevent rust rings on your counter, sink, and tub surfaces. Problem solved.

Prevent nasty toilet tank problems. Even if your toilet bowl is always spotless, it's easy to forget the power behind the throne — your toilet tank. But over time, mold, germs, mineral deposits, and even sediment can build up in your tank, leading to mechanical problems or even health concerns. That's why it pays to clean your tank every once in a while. Here's how.

- Remove the toilet lid. Don't panic if you see a small amount of dirt or sand in the tank. It will be gone soon.

- Turn off the water supply control to the toilet using the valve at the back of the toilet near the floor.

- Flush once or twice to empty the toilet tank. If you saw sediment in the tank, this should help clear it out.

- Make sure the bathroom is well-ventilated, and then spray chlorine bleach on the inside walls and floor of the tank. Let sit for 30 minutes.

- Pour in two gallons of water or enough to nearly fill the tank. Flush to remove the bleach. Keep adding water and flushing it away until the bleach is gone.

- Pour a few cups of vinegar in the tank, and let sit for a few hours. Keep in mind the bleach must be completely gone before you add vinegar. Bleach and vinegar can produce a toxic gas.

- Scrub the inside walls of the tank with your toilet brush. Be careful to avoid dislodging any tubes, chains, or connectors.

- Flush once or twice to remove the vinegar.

- Turn the toilet's water supply back on, and flush to rinse the toilet tank.

Make your bathroom mirror shine. Don't fret if you're out of glass cleaner. Just look for your bottle of rubbing alcohol, or brew some tea.

To clean foggy hairspray deposits off your mirror, dampen a lint-free cloth with rubbing alcohol and wipe. If your bathroom is well-ventilated, you can spray the rubbing alcohol on your mirror and wipe it with a coffee filter.

For an all-purpose mirror cleaner, brew regular black tea, and chill it in your refrigerator. Pour some of the tea in a spray bottle. Spray a small section of your mirror, and wipe away stains, spots, and smudges with a coffee filter or lint-free cloth. Keep spraying and wiping until your entire mirror is clean. You'll give your mirror a sparkling shine that might just put chrome to shame. Be sure to wipe any tea residue off counters and fixtures below the mirror. Use any leftover tea to clean other glass surfaces.

3 smart ways to fight mildew. Turn your bathroom into hostile territory for mildew. You can even make the room look and smell better while you do it.

- Save and clean several berry baskets and their lids, and spray paint them with a color that matches your bathroom decor. Line the lower half of the basket with aluminum foil and drop in a piece of charcoal. Distribute these baskets around your bathroom to absorb the moisture mildew loves. You'll find the charcoal will absorb odors, too. Change the charcoal regularly, and you'll help keep your bathroom moisture-free.

- If you already have mildew, make a mildew-fighting spray by adding one drop of tea tree oil to one cup of water. Spray directly on mildew to kill it.

- Put a timer switch on your bath fan to remove moisture from the air after you shower. It will shut off automatically when the moisture is gone. You can even find switches that turn on automatically when humidity is high.

Simple solution for grimy grout. Clean your bathroom floor grout without smelly, toxic cleaners. Mix seven cups of water with one-half cup of baking soda, one-third cup of lemon juice, and a quarter cup of vinegar. Pour into a bowl, and apply directly to grout with an old toothbrush. For dirtier grout, pour the mixture into a spray bottle, spray your floor grout, and let sit for up to 10 minutes before scrubbing. Although you will love the citrus smell, be sure to rinse thoroughly, and wipe up any residue.

To get rid of mildew stains on tub or shower grout, make a paste of hydrogen peroxide and baking soda, apply to the grout, and let sit for 30 to 45 minutes before scrubbing.

Insider secrets to removing carpet stains. The biggest mistake you make when cleaning your carpet is probably overwetting it, says David Tassa, a Certified Master Cleaner and owner of Diversified Cleaning Systems.

Do-it-yourself carpet cleaning machines use hot water extraction, the method most carpet manufacturers recommend. But overzealous homeowners end up soaking their carpets in too much water. "Overwetting actually breaks down the glue between the two backings and causes what's called delamination," he explains.

Another problem — using too much soap. You end up with soap left in the carpet, which attracts more dirt. "The carpet gets dirty faster, so they clean it again, and again, getting it too wet every time. In two years' time, the carpet is shot."

Instead of cleaning the whole carpet regularly, spot treat messes as soon as they strike. You don't have to buy expensive stain removers, either. Tassa says, "Patience will remove more spots than anything."

"Remove as much of the spill as you can. Scoop up excess amounts, blot off as much as possible, then apply some water." He suggests wetting the spot and agitating — but not scrubbing — it with your finger or a damp rag. "Throw the rag on it, let it sit for 15 minutes, then come back and blot it." You'll be amazed at how many stains you can remove with water alone, he says. And if that doesn't do it, "Put a couple of drops — not squirts, just drops — of dishwashing detergent in a cup of warm water," then wet and blot with that.

Keep curtains out of the way

Stop sucking your curtains into your vacuum cleaner. Slip the end of each panel over a hanger, and hang this over the curtain rod until you finish cleaning.

Get the bug, not the stain. Stop — if you squish that bug, it will leave a nasty stain on your wall, carpet, or curtain.

Instead, roll up a piece of packing tape or regular tape around your fingers, and press it on the bug. The bug sticks to it and can be disposed of — without the leftover mess.

Put an end to pet hair. Fluffy's fur sticks to everything, which is why manufacturers hawk vacuums made especially for pet hair. Save your money and try these tips instead.

- Mix one part liquid fabric softener and three parts water in a spray bottle. Spritz your rug or carpet and wait for the solution to dry, then vacuum. The fabric softener squashes static electricity, making pet hair easier to pick up.

- Lightly mist the dust bunnies hiding in corners with the same solution, then sweep. They won't be able to blow away and escape your broom.

- Drag a dry sponge or the rubber edge of a squeegee over upholstery to pull pet hair off sofas and chairs.

Brew up polish on the cheap. Dust your wood furniture to a stunning shine without using an expensive brand-name polish. Just brew several cups of strong unsweetened black tea, let it cool, and pour it into a small bowl. Dip a cloth in the tea, wring it out, and use it to dust your wood furniture. Not only will the wood look beautiful when you're done, but the tannins in the tea may help fend off dust mites.

You can also use brewed, black tea to clean dark hardwood floors, but you'll need one or two quarts of unsweetened tea to get the job done. To start, dampen one microfiber cloth with tea, wipe a section of floor, and immediately wipe dry with a dry, microfiber cloth. Keep cleaning sections until the entire floor is gleaming clean.

Take care of your wood for good. Your home is filled with wood furnishings. With proper care and maintenance, your wood-made goods can last a lifetime. Use this handy table to know how to preserve these five popular woods.

Type of wood	Characteristics	How to care for
Cherry	Strong, durable, resistant to shock and wear and tear	Wipe with warm water and nonabrasive soap. Rinse, then wipe dry. Use lemon oil occasionally and a thin coat of paste wax annually. Avoid exposure to direct sunlight.
Mahogany	Heavy weight, even texture	Apply a solution of warm water and vinegar with damp cloth. Avoid abrasive cleaners and exposure to direct sunlight.
Maple	Dense, resistant to shock	Dust daily and wipe smudges with a damp cloth. Polish weekly. Oil annually.
Oak	Durable, resistant to wear and tear	Avoid direct sunlight. Maintain a room humidity level between 25-35 percent. Dust often. Use coasters and place mats to protect.
Pine	Lightweight, great for paint and varnishes	Avoid direct sunlight. Maintain even room temperature. Use coasters and place mats to protect. Wipe with a damp cloth. Apply wax periodically.

Say "so long" to scuff marks. Scuff marks don't have to stain your floors forever. Here are three ways to rub them out.

- For vinyl or linoleum floors, poke a hole in a tennis ball, insert a dowel or old broom handle, and rub the scuff mark with the ball.
- Erase scuff marks on tile with a clean pencil eraser.
- Remove them from tile or vinyl with a damp cloth and a little white toothpaste or baking soda.

Knock out furniture nicks and rings. Chances are your furniture has taken a beating over the years. But before you cart off your dining room table, try these simple ways to fix — or at least cover up — nicks, scratches and water rings.

For scratches on oiled, waxed, or unfinished pieces, a fresh coat of oil or wax should do the trick. Furniture coated with shellac, varnish, or polyurethane needs a bit more TLC. Apply one part shellac and one part denatured alcohol with a watercolor brush. Allow to dry.

Hide minor nicks by rubbing them with a shelled pecan, walnut, or Brazil nut. The nut's natural oils disguise blemishes. Or steep tea to the same color as your wood and apply to scratches.

Consider an option from your medicine chest — petroleum jelly. Coat your small scratches and allow to sit for a day. Then rub the jelly into the wood and wipe off any excess. Polish like you normally would.

To tackle white water rings, allow the stain to dry, then cover with a lubricant like paste wax or petroleum jelly. Or rub in nongel toothpaste.

Clean couches for keeps. Spills happen. So when one happens on your sofa, you need to act quickly. Blot the stain — don't rub — with a clean, white cloth. Then look for the manufacturer's tag with cleaning instructions, often hidden under the couch. The tag will include one of four codes. Use the table below to interpret the codes and follow their instructions.

Codes	Cleaning instructions
W	Use water and a water-based detergent.
S	Use a solvent. No water.
SW	Use either a solvent or water-based detergent.
X	Must be professionally cleaned.

To keep your sofa looking spiffy longer, vacuum your couch weekly and rotate cushions periodically. Mend loose threads and buttons. Consider spraying your sofa with a soil retardant, but always read the manufacturer's label first to make sure this is safe.

Keep closets smelling fresh. Keeping closet doors closed may lower your heating and air conditioning bill, but it can also lead to musty closets. If you notice an unpleasant smell in a closet, leave the door wide open to let it air out for a few days.

To prevent future odor problems, try one of these deodorizers. Don't forget to replace them regularly.

- Grab a few unused tea bags, or tie up loose tea in a coffee filter, and place in your closet. You may be surprised at how well the tea absorbs odors.
- Save a large metal coffee can, and poke at least 15 holes in the plastic lid. Fill the can with charcoal briquettes or clay kitty litter, put the lid on, and place it in the closet.
- Tuck an open box of baking soda in a shoe box or large, clean can. Hide it away on a closet shelf.

Smooth out scratches with baking soda

Before ordering a new piece of glass to replace a scratched-up table top, try this easy solution. Mix about a teaspoon of baking soda with nongel toothpaste, and rub it on the table with a clean, damp cloth. Wipe dry and check the scratch. If it's smoother, keep working on it. It may take a few attempts to buff it out completely.

How to care for fine feather pillows. Pacific Coast Feather Company, a leading maker of feather pillows, offers these tips to make yours last for years to come.

- Check to make sure your pillow is machine washable. If it is, wash with a mild detergent in warm water on the gentle setting. Washing two pillows instead of one can help balance the load.

- Put pillows through two rinse cycles, then two back-to-back spin cycles to remove as much water as possible.

- Dry on low heat. Keep drying until you don't feel lumps. These mean the pillow is still wet inside, even if it feels dry to touch. Fluff the pillows by hand between cycles.

In between washings, fluff up flattened down pillows by popping them in the dryer on air-dry with a couple of clean tennis balls and a dryer sheet. Be warned — the tennis balls will make quite a racket.

The 3 biggest no-nos when cleaning jewelry. According to Gerald Golech, instructor for the Gemological Institute of America, "Using harsh chemicals or abrasives that could damage certain gemstones or scratch the metal" is the biggest mistake people make when cleaning their jewelry. "Diamonds are very durable, but you have to be very careful with other gemstones, like emeralds or pearls," he cautions. His three biggest no-nos:

- Think twice about lemon juice. "I've heard people say, 'clean pearls with lemon juice.' That's the opposite of what you want to do." Lemon juice is highly acidic. "It can actually dissolve the material pearls are made of."

- Avoid chlorine bleach at all costs. "It can actually damage some of the metals and more fragile gemstones."

- Don't use ammonia, also found in jewelry cleaners, on porous organic gems like pearls or turquoise.

What should you do? A mild soap, like dishwashing liquid, and a soft-bristled toothbrush will often do the job. "Use a new toothbrush, because toothpaste often has abrasives in it that could scratch the metals," Golech advises. Commercial jewelry cleaners sometimes contain metal brighteners that can shine-up dulled metals.

Don't clean your jewelry over the sink without plugging the drain. "That's a common problem. People accidentally drop their pieces down the drain." And have a professional inspect pieces you wear about once a year to find loose stones and thin prongs before they become a problem.

Shine up silver without polishing. Don't spend your precious time polishing your silver. Get silver jewelry and serving pieces gleaming again, no polishing necessary. Pour one tablespoon each of salt and baking soda into an aluminum pie pan, or line a bowl with aluminum foil. Cover with hot water, and stir until the mixture dissolves. Drop your silver into the solution, and leave until the tarnish has disappeared, usually just a few minutes. Heavily tarnished pieces may not come completely clean. For these, you may need to follow up with a little polishing.

Of course, it's even easier to prevent tarnish in the first place with a sneaky household trick that costs just pennies. Buy a box of white blackboard chalk. Break the chalk into pieces, and slip them into your jewelry box and wherever you store silver. They will absorb the substances that cause tarnish. Replace with fresh chalk every two months.

Wipe out rust and tarnish. Rub out the rust spots on plated silverware with this all-natural remover. Make a paste of three parts salt to one part lemon or lime juice. Rub it on rusty areas with a dry cloth, then rinse with warm water and buff dry.

Polishing copper and unlaquered brass is even easier. Cut a lemon in half, and press the cut side onto a plate of salt. Rub it over the tarnished spots, rinse well, and wipe dry. A paste will handle stubborn stains on uncoated brass and copper. Dissolve one teaspoon of salt in a cup of vinegar, and mix in enough flour to form a paste. Apply this and let it work for 15 minutes, then rinse it off with warm water and buff the items dry.

Banish bothersome bugs with lemons

It's easy to wipe out fleas and have a spotless, fresh-smelling house when you finish. Here's how — add the juice from four lemons to a half-gallon of hot water and mop your floors.

Or make a homemade spray to chase fleas out of fabric. Put 10 drops of lavender, rosemary, or eucalyptus essential oil in a spray bottle with water, and lightly mist pet beds, upholstered furniture, and carpets after vacuuming.

Clever trick cleans cast iron skillets. Scour away food in your cast iron cookware with a cup of coarse Kosher salt. Pour the salt into your skillet while it's still warm, then rub it in with a hand towel or paper towel until the food loosens. Rinse the pan briefly under hot water, and heat it over medium-low heat to dry it thoroughly. Prevent it from rusting by placing a clean coffee filter in the pan when you store it.

Follow 4 steps to prevent pesky pests. Bugs and rodents are always looking for food and shelter. Make your home a no-pest zone by following these helpful guidelines.

Step one — clean. Don't give pests a meal of leftovers or a comfy spot to nestle.

- Sweep and vacuum your floors regularly.
- Keep bathroom and kitchen areas dry.
- Take out garbage daily and keep garbage cans clean.
- Clear out stacks of newspapers, magazines, packing material — all good hiding places for pests.
- Wipe up spills immediately.
- Keep ripe fruit in the fridge.
- Don't leave dirty dishes in the sink.
- Make sure all food and drink containers outside the fridge or freezer are tightly sealed.

Step two — deny access. Keep pests out by making a barrier they can't get past.

- Interior. Cockroaches and mice often enter homes through holes around the plumbing under the kitchen or bathroom sinks. Plug these tightly with rags or steel wool to stop them in their tracks.

- Exterior. Mice, rats, squirrels, and bugs can all get in the house through holes and gaps. Stop them with copper mesh, expanding foam, or caulk in the gap — whatever best fills it. Keep vegetation, firewood, and other debris away from the exterior of your house so pests can't climb up and in. Put screens on the front of vents, or repair holes in any already there.

Step three — repel. Try these natural methods to keep those creepy creatures away.

- Eucalyptus and pennyroyal oils — a teaspoon of each in a spray bottle of water is a good, all-purpose repellant.

- Mint — ants and flies both dislike the smell. Grow a plant or leave sachets out.

- Cucumber peel — ants hate cucumber. Leave peels out to send them running.

- Cinnamon — sprinkle on the floor or surfaces to block the ant trail. They do not like to cross it.

- Basil — keep a plant growing in your kitchen. Flies hate the smell and will stay away.

- Peppermint essential oil — put a few drops in a spray bottle of water. Spray to keep mice and spiders away.

- Build a moat. Put the pet bowl into a pan of soapy water to stop ants going after pet food. And don't leave pet food out during the night.

Step four — exterminate, but avoid highly toxic, harmful chemicals.

- Use your vacuum cleaner for individual bugs — they'll usually suffocate in the bag.

- A mixture of baking soda and salt will kill ants.

- You can also put small piles of cornmeal where you see ants. They can't digest it so they die after eating it. Be patient as it can take about a week to be effective. Cream of Wheat and Minute Rice also work the same way.

- Borax mixed with powdered sugar will lure ants and roaches and poison them. But don't use it if you have children or pets.

Food strategies: eat better for less

4 ways to make money-saving food choices. Get the ingredients and foods you need for less just by visiting a different part of your grocery store. It's easier than you think, and you can experiment with techniques like these to see which ones you like.

- Replace expensive ingredients with cheaper substitutes. For example, try switching from cardamom to equal parts ground cinnamon and ground cloves, or use canned salmon when recipes call for fresh or frozen salmon. You can even replace part of the meat in a recipe with cheaper ingredients like beans or oatmeal. For more tips, check the cookbooks in your local library or log on to *www.foodsubs.com*.
- Buy fresh fruits and vegetables when they're in season. For out-of-season produce, compare the price of the fresh version with canned or frozen options. Buy the one that's cheaper.
- Choose the most natural and least-processed version of the food. Buy whole meats, cheeses, fruits, and vegetables instead of pre-sliced or precut versions. Skip prepackaged salad greens in favor of washing and chopping your own. Choose rolled oats instead of instant oats. Some people even make their own condiments, mixes, snacks, and sauces from scratch, and claim to save hundreds every year.
- If you buy organic produce, you may have another option. According to the Environmental Working Group,

fruits and vegetables with the least amount of pesticide residue include avocados, pineapples, cabbage, onions, corn, asparagus, mangoes, papayas, kiwi, cantaloupe, eggplant, grapefruit, cauliflower, and sweet potatoes. Consider buying conventional versions of these foods instead of their pricier organic siblings.

A+ way to choose organic

Some types of produce have especially high levels of pesticides inside that can't be washed off. Here's a list to help you choose where to spend your money.

Highest in pesticides	Lowest in pesticides
apples	bananas
cherries	blueberries
imported grapes	grapefruit
nectarines	kiwifruit
peaches	mangoes
pears	papayas
raspberries	pineapples
strawberries	plantains
bell peppers	plums
celery	watermelons
hot peppers	asparagus
potatoes	avocados
spinach	broccoli

— adapted from Vegetarian Times

Find a hidden opportunity for savings. Take this test the next time you go shopping. Make a grocery list of what you need. When you return from shopping, compare your grocery list to your supermarket receipt. Notice which items appear on your receipt that were not on your list. A couple of these may be things you simply forgot to list, but the rest may be impulse buys. Add up the cost of your impulse buys to see how much money you can save on future grocery trips. Take this test every time you shop, and you'll be surprised at how easy it becomes to resist impulse buys.

3-minute task saves you $1,000 a year. School kids aren't the only ones who brown bag their lunch. Lots of adults do, too. Packing your lunch the night before, if you work or plan to leave the house for the day, can save you both time and money. Eating lunch out can easily cost you $5 a day, but you can make your own at home for about $1. Add it up, and this three-minute task can save you more than $1,000 a year. That's like getting paid $54 an hour for your time.

Slash food spending with a grocery price book. You may be surprised at how much you can save by writing down and comparing grocery prices. Even if you don't spend much time on it, a price book can help you:

- recognize which bulk discounts save the most money and which ones don't.
- spot pricing trends and recognize regularly recurring sales you can count on seeing again.

- avoid the frustration of stocking up at one sale only to find a better sale a few weeks later.

- uncover which store offers the cheapest price on an item.

Some people have even discovered that sales with seemingly big discounts really saved less than a nickel.

To see what a price book can do for you, start with the high-efficiency version. Pull out your grocery receipt, and choose the top seven items you want to save money on. Circle or highlight these products.

Get a pocket-sized tablet or notebook, and divide it into food categories such as meat, dairy, beverages, fruits and vegetables, and so on. Write each of your seven items in the appropriate category. Include the purchase date, the price, and the store where you bought it. If possible, calculate the unit price, and write the unit size nearby. Otherwise, take a calculator with you when you shop, and add the unit price then. Finally, leave space for future entries because you will write down a lower price the moment you find it.

As you shop, check the prices on each of your seven items at each store you visit. Update the price book when you find a better price than what you paid in the past. You'll soon find you don't need to look at your price book very often because you'll already remember the best prices. Not only will you avoid overpaying for your seven items, you'll know when to stock up so you can save the most money.

For even bigger savings, add seven more products to your price book, and start saving on those, too.

When to find the cheapest produce. With the high cost of fuel, shipping out-of-season fruits and vegetables from afar is even more expensive. Get better taste and lower prices by buy ing produce at its peak season.

Month	Best bets
January	oranges and other citrus fruits, cabbages, broccoli, cauliflower
February	oranges and other citrus fruits, papayas, broccoli, cauliflower
March	pineapples, mangoes, broccoli, lettuce
April	pineapples, mangoes, zucchini, rhubarb, asparagus, artichokes
May	cherries, apricots, okra, zucchini, asparagus, artichokes
June	watermelon, cantaloupe, strawberries and other berries, peaches, apricots
July	watermelon, cantaloupe, strawberries and other berries, tomatoes, summer squash, corn, green beans
August	watermelon, cantaloupe, strawberries and other berries, apricots, plums, cucumbers, corn, tomatoes
September	grapes, pomegranates, eggplant, pumpkin, tomatoes, spinach
October	grapes, cranberries, apples, pomegranates, sweet potatoes, pumpkins, winter squash
November	cranberries, oranges, tangerines, pomegranates, sweet potatoes, pumpkins, winter squash
December	pears, oranges and other citrus fruits, pomegranates, sweet potatoes, mushrooms, broccoli, cauliflower

Beware unit pricing traps. Be careful when you compare unit prices. Make sure both prices are based on the same size unit. For example, one bottle may be measured in liters while another is labeled in fluid ounces. To help solve this problem, carry a calculator with you to the grocery store, or use the calculator in your cellphone. You can also copy this quick reference to help convert prices based on different units.

- 1 liter = 33.8 ounces or 1.06 quarts
- 1 fluid ounce = 2 tablespoons or 29.57 grams
- 1 gallon = 3.78 liters or 4 quarts or 128 fluid ounces
- 16 fluid ounces = 1 pint or 2 cups
- 1 dry ounce = 28.35 grams
- 1 pound = 16 ounces or 453.6 grams

Many people automatically assume the economy-size version of a product is always cheaper. Don't make that mistake, especially if you're shopping at a warehouse store. Whip out your calculator, and check the unit price to find out whether bigger really is better — or if the product is cheaper at another store.

Spend less time on coupons to save more. Coupon queens report massive savings on every trip they make to the supermarket, but those savings may require hours of time spent hunting, reviewing, and organizing coupons. Use these three rules to get the most savings for the least amount of work.

- Only cut out coupons for items you planned to buy anyway. Otherwise, your coupons may cost more than they save. To find the right coupons more easily, glance over the packaging of products you regularly buy. You may find one hidden behind a label.

- Don't clip a coupon unless it can save more money than buying the store brand. In many cases, your grocery store's house brand may be cheaper than buying a name brand item with a coupon.

- Aim to use your coupon when the item is on sale or when you can combine a store coupon with a manufacturer's coupon. Look for store coupons in the store's weekly ad flyer and manufacturer's coupons in the Sunday paper. It should tell you at the top of the coupon which one it is. Just be sure to ask whether your store allows them to be used together before you try this trick.

Have you caught the coupon craze?

You should! Using coupons to save just $20 each week adds up to $1,000 saved in a year. Redeem dollar-off coupons on double-coupon days, and it's not hard to reach that $20 in savings. One careful shopper reports paying $240 for $900 worth of groceries by using coupons, cashing in on her store's preferred-customer card, and watching the specials.

Weigh options for best deals. One supermarket in your town may have the lowest prices on frozen foods, while another has lovely fresh produce. Maybe a third store offers the best specials on canned goods. There's no such thing as a perfect supermarket, so you may need to visit several stores to find the quality you want at the best price. But once you're familiar with each store, don't spend your weekends making the rounds. Plan ahead and check store flyers for specials so you can take turns at your favorite stores yet still limit your shopping to once a week or less.

Time your shopping for extra savings

Drop by your grocery store in the evening, and you may find that morning's fresh baked breads marked down drastically. This is known as a manager's special, a sale that happens when perishable items won't last much longer. Keep an eye out for these sales, and learn what time of the day or week they are most likely to happen. If you can shop at the right time and use the product right away, you may pay a lot less for that food than everyone else does.

You can get even more bargains right after a holiday. For example, find Christmas baking ingredients at deep discounts on December 26, buy turkey and canned pumpkin on sale after Thanksgiving, and stock up on bargain-priced mustard, ketchup, and other barbecue foods right after July 4.

5 questions to ask before joining a food co-op. Food co-ops can be a great way to get discounted foods, fruits and vegetables fresh from the farm, organic foods, or items your grocery store doesn't carry. But before you join, ask these questions to see if the co-op is right for you.

- Do I have to join to get bargains? Co-ops are owned by their members, which includes both the farmers who grow the food and the people who buy it. Some co-ops allow nonmembers to buy from the co-op, but only members get discounts. Other co-ops sell only to members.

- Is every member expected to volunteer? To join the co-op, members may be required to pay a fee, volunteer part time at the co-op, or both. If you work, you may prefer a co-op that does not put demands on your time.

- Will I save money? Some co-ops claim to save as much as 40 percent off your grocery bill, but savings may vary from one co-op to the next. If the co-op requires a membership fee, make sure you can save more money than the fee costs. Also, check each product's prices and unit prices to see how co-op discounts compare to prices at other places where you shop.

- Do I have to buy in bulk? Ask if your co-op only offers discounts on bulk orders or if you can get price breaks on smaller orders, too. If you must buy in bulk, determine whether you have enough cash for the bulk buy, whether you can use the food before it spoils, and whether you can make space to store or freeze it.

- How do I shop at the co-op? Some co-ops are open most anytime you need to buy, while others have limited hours or require you to shop or pick up your order within a limited time. Find out how your co-op wants you to buy and whether you can be available at the right times.

Find a food co-op near you

You may be living right on top of a food co-op and not even know it. Ask at local food stands or farmer's markets to see if they know of any food co-ops in the area. If you have a computer, you can go online to the website *www.coopdirectory.org* for more information and to find the closest food co-op.

Make haste without wasting dollars. Nobody likes spending a lot at the supermarket — either time or money. But finding the best deals seems to take all day. Try these tricks to speed up your bargain hunting.

- Make a list, and check it at least twice. Look at the store's weekly ads before you leave home so you won't spend time standing at the shelves comparing prices. You can find supermarket weekly sales fliers online or in the newspaper.

- Swim upstream. Most people move counterclockwise through the grocery store. If you go in the opposite direction, you'll spend less time waiting behind slowpokes in the aisles.

- Get there early. If a sale starts on Sunday, you may find items sold out by Friday. You may get a rain check on the sale item, but that means another trip to the store.

- Stay home. You can order all kinds of groceries, including specialty items your local store doesn't carry, by shopping online. Your goodies will be delivered right to your door. See what's available at *www.freshdirect.com*, *www.schwans.com*, *www.shopfoodex.com*, or *www.amazon.com*.

Don't be fooled by product placement

Don't be fooled by product placement. Supermarkets count on catching your eye with items that earn them the most money. Favorite brands placed at eye level on the shelf are typically the higher-priced choices. Look to the top and bottom shelves for better deals.

And here's a shopping secret that may shock you. You can't assume that items in the sale bin are always the best bargain. Compare unit prices to be sure.

4 ways to choose a cheaper package. Even if you don't like to buy food in bulk, make these package picks to save money.

- Buy frozen vegetables in bags rather than boxes. You can then pour out a serving or two of vegetables and reseal the bag for another meal.

- Stay away from prepared single-serving juice, pudding, and gelatin. Your grandkids will like what you mix up just as well.
- Instead of buying tea in bags, buy it loose and use a tea strainer or infuser ball. You'll save money and be able to brew up a wide variety of flavors.
- Skip the single-serving packets of instant oatmeal. You'll save more than half the cost by buying quick oats in a can.

Speed shop through the grocery store

Shopping in the same grocery store each week gives you a benefit you may not have thought about. You know exactly where everything is. Take advantage of this when making your grocery list, and write down the items in the order you will pick them up in the aisles. Put your coupons in the same order. To save even more time, shop when the store is less crowded. You'll be amazed at the difference in time small changes like these can make.

Find good bread on the cheap. You can buy the staff of life — even a popular brand — for nearly half its regular price at bakery thrift stores. Check packages, since items are probably nearing their expiration dates. But if you do it carefully to avoid crushing, you can freeze your bargain bread, rolls, buns, and tortillas to use later.

Be a cheese whiz — shred your own. Nothing says convenience like a package of shredded cheese — especially when you're throwing together a last-minute meal. But you really pay for the time savings. Get the best of both worlds by buying a big block of cheese and shredding it yourself. Freeze small portions in individual freezer bags, and they will be ready whenever you are. And don't shy away from soft cheeses like mozzarella and fontina, which usually make a mess on your grater or food processor. Simply stick these in the freezer for a few minutes before you shred.

Fancy oils on the cheap. Flavored oils give your cooking an extra kick and your bread a tasty dip. Making your own is easy and saves you from paying fancy prices. Make a garlic-flavored oil by combining a quarter cup of extra virgin olive oil with two cloves of crushed garlic and the zest of one lime. Let it stand for 15 minutes. For a spicy southwestern flavor, use two crushed chile peppers instead of the garlic cloves. Strain the flavored oil through cheesecloth. Store your oil in the refrigerator, and use it within a week.

Save hundreds by never tossing out food. The average family of four wastes up to $2,275 of food annually. That means you could save hundreds of bucks a year if you avoid tossing out food. To help you start, try these handy "keep it fresh" tips.

- Place a paper towel in the plastic bag with your carrots to keep them fresh for up to several weeks.

- Keep milk on your refrigerator's top shelf behind your carton of eggs, instead of storing both foods in the refrigerator door. The door temperature is warmer, so moving eggs and milk to the shelf preserves them better and saves them from an early grave.

- When you store bread or other foods in a resealable bag, press all the air out of the bag before it goes in the refrigerator or freezer. You'll be surprised at how much longer that makes foods last.

- To give lettuce as much as an extra week, forget storing the whole head. Rinse and dry completely. Chop the lettuce, place in an airtight container, and store in the refrigerator. Tuck a paper towel over the lettuce to draw moisture away, and replace the paper towel daily.

- Line your vegetable crisper with paper towels, and your vegetables may take longer to spoil. Replace the paper towels once a week.

- Make celery last up to four weeks. Trim the ends, and wash and completely dry each stalk. Wrap the celery in dry paper towels. Store in a plastic bag in your refrigerator's crisper drawer.

- Store whole tomatoes at room temperature with the stem end down.

- To extend the life of cottage cheese or sour cream, close the tub, make sure the lid is on firmly, and slip a rubber band around it to secure that lid. Keep the tub upside down on a paper towel in the refrigerator.

Freeze bulk buys from the farmer's market. You can't believe the amazing deal you've found at the farmer's market, until you realize you must buy in bulk to get that deal. But if you can freeze part of your bulk-bargain produce, you can enjoy spectacular savings. Use these tips to help.

- Be careful to select produce that's not too ripe for freezing. If you must accept some overly ripe items, use them right away, and freeze the younger produce.
- Make sure you have enough freezer space before you buy, and invest in some high-quality freezer bags to store your produce in.
- Check with the seller, the library, your local cooperative extension office, or online sources to determine whether you must blanche your produce before freezing, and for how long.
- Label each freezer bag with the name of its contents and the purchase date. Use your frozen produce within six months. Mark a deadline on your calendar just to be safe.

If the vendors are only offering small amounts of fruits and vegetables, don't be afraid to negotiate to see if you can get a bulk deal for the items you want. You have nothing to lose and potential savings to gain.

Spend less on milk, juice, and soda. Forget "no pain, no gain." You can save money on milk, juice, and soda without feeling deprived.

First, stop using fresh milk in cooking. Buy less-expensive nonfat dry milk to use instead. To replace one cup of skim milk in a recipe, mix one-third cup of nonfat dry milk with seven-eighths cup of water. To replace one cup of whole milk, use one cup of reconstituted dry milk.

You can also use nonfat dry milk to stretch the milk you drink. Mix up the nonfat dry milk according to the package directions. Fill your glass with three parts fresh milk and one part of the dry milk mixture. Gradually work up to equal parts fresh milk and dry milk. You can even try drinking the dry milk mixture on its own, but chill it first for best results.

Some veteran skim milk drinkers say they save money by watering down 2 percent or full-fat milk so it tastes like skim milk. But keep in mind, this may also affect your intake of calcium, vitamin D, protein, and other nutrients, and it only saves money if higher-fat milks are the same price as skim milk.

Stretching juice and soda is easier than stretching milk. Just start by mixing the beverage with a small amount of water. Gradually increase the amount of water over time, while reducing the amount of juice or soda. If you don't like the combination, replace the water with another beverage that is less expensive than the soda or juice. You may discover a delicious new flavor combination — and you'll still save money.

Keep berries fresh for a week. Love fresh berries, but hate that they can go bad or get moldy in just a few days? Here's an easy way to make them last more than a week in your refrigerator.

In a large bowl, mix 3 1/2 cups of water with three-fourths cup of white vinegar. Drop the berries in the bowl, and swirl them around to wash them. Drain them in a colander, and rinse under cold, running tap water.

Spread the berries out on a paper towel spaced well apart. If possible, place the paper towels on racks or screens before spreading the berries across them. Let the berries dry for one to two hours. Be careful to dry the berries thoroughly, or you will taste vinegar when you eat them. Store your berries in a loosely covered container lined with paper towels, and place that container in the refrigerator. Most berries will last at least one week. Try it and see for yourself.

And to make sure you're getting the freshest berries, sniff that basket of strawberries before you buy it. The ones that smell the best will also taste best.

Free $ with Upromise account

Help send your favorite grandchild to college just by buying groceries. Get started by opening a free Upromise account at *www.upromise.com.* Then register your store's preferred-customer card, and you'll earn 1 to 5 percent when you buy certain participating brands. We're talking favorites like Nestle, Lysol, and Tylenol. The money goes into your Upromise account, then you can deposit it into your grandchild's 529 college savings account.

5 surprising foods that last for months in the freezer. Freeze these foods before they go bad, and you'll have plenty of time to find another use for them.

- Eggs. Break eggs into a bowl. Add either one tablespoon of sugar or one-third teaspoon of salt per cup of eggs, and stir until the yolks and whites are blended. Measure three tablespoons — the equivalent of one egg — into each cup of an ice cube tray. This makes your frozen eggs a great size for baking. Let the mixture freeze solid, slip the egg ice cubes into a freezer bag, and keep in the freezer for up to six months. Thaw in the refrigerator before using.

- Avocados. Peel ripe avocados, remove their pits, and mash them. Add one-half to one tablespoon of lemon juice per avocado. Freeze in a container with a little air space. These keep up to five months.

- Cheese. Hard or semi-hard cheeses like provolone, mozzarella, cheddar, and Swiss freeze well enough to work in recipes. What's more, they last four to six months in the freezer and can rescue you from unsavory encounters with moldy cheese. To freeze, cut into blocks up to 1 1/2 pounds, wrap tightly in plastic wrap, and put in a freezer bag. Thaw in the refrigerator, and use within a day. The cheese may be too crumbly to add to your favorite sandwich, but it will taste delicious in your favorite recipes.

- Buttermilk. Freeze buttermilk in small paper cups, a muffin pan, or an ice cube tray. You can freeze in sizes up to a half cup if you use paper cups or muffin pans, but use the ice cube tray for portions of one or two tablespoons. Wrap each cup in plastic wrap after it freezes. Store cups or ice cubes in a freezer bag in the freezer for up to two months. Thaw in the refrigerator or microwave. Freezing may cause solids and whey in the buttermilk to separate, so whisk, stir, or run through a blender before using.

- Nuts. Freeze in an airtight container, or place them in a freezer bag, and press out the air before sealing. Use within six months. You can chop them or toss them whole into a recipe right from the freezer, or thaw them in the refrigerator first.

Don't let nutrients escape

You buy nutritious foods to help you stay well, but those foods may lose plenty of nutrients by the time they reach your plate. Use these techniques to retain more vitamins and minerals in your dishes.

- Steam or microwave your produce instead of boiling. If you don't have a steamer, cook your vegetables in a pan with only a small amount of water. Less water and shorter cooking times help preserve nutrients.
- Keep milk out of strong light. More light means less vitamin B2.
- Don't add baking soda to green vegetables to keep their color. It destroys vitamins.
- Boiling pulls nutrients out of vegetables and into the cooking water. Take advantage of that nutrient-filled water — refrigerate it, and use it to make soup later on.
- Eat both cooked and raw produce. Cooking may reduce the amounts of B and C vitamins but can increase nutrients like lycopene, beta carotene, and minerals.

Condiments and crumbs — good to the last drop. Don't waste the last bit of food in the container. Try these frugal ideas for making the most of what you buy.

- Add some oil and vinegar to that nearly empty mustard jar, sprinkle in salt and pepper, and shake. You just invented a tasty salad dressing.
- Sweet crumbs at the bottom of a box of cookies or dry cereal make a great topping for an ice cream sundae.
- Crusts of bread don't have to be for the birds. Use your food processor to turn them into crumbs, add some Italian spices, then freeze. Next time you need crumbs for breading or to top a casserole, reach for your homemade supply.

Savor the flavor of fresh herbs. Fresh herbs like basil and oregano make your Italian cooking taste marvelous. Too bad you can grow them only a few months out of the year — and have you seen the price of fresh herbs in the supermarket?

This summer, freeze a bumper crop of basil for your winter pesto. Strip the basil leaves from the stems, then rinse them. After they're dry, chop them to the size you like to use. Freeze in small batches in freezer bags, and be sure to label each bag. Your basil will be good for up to six months.

Bypass food-freezing blunders. A bad experience with freezing and thawing food could mean you didn't do it right. Follow these simple rules, and you won't be left out in the cold next time you want to save food for later.

- Banish freezer burn. Air can dry out the surface of your food, causing gray ice crystals to form. That means a bad taste. Squeeze out all the air from around the food when you seal it into bags.

- Keep it small. Divide food into small portions so it freezes more quickly. The faster food freezes, the fresher it will taste later. Also, you're more likely to find a use for small portions of frozen foods than for large ones.

- Bag it right. Freezer bags may cost more than other plastic bags or wrap, but they're worth it. Containers meant for the freezer are durable enough to keep your goodies safe.

Get peak flavor from bulk herbs and spices. Dried spices and herbs in little jars are not cheap, but there is another choice.

"Buying in bulk gives you the opportunity to buy top-quality spices for a third or less of what it would cost to buy them prepackaged," says Ellen Bouchard, bulk herbs and spices manager for Frontier Natural Products Co-op.

Bulk spices should keep as long as the prepackaged variety — as long as you store them correctly. "Store them in glass containers with tight-fitting lids," says Bouchard. "This will prevent oxidation, which deteriorates the flavor, color, and aroma." Keep air away from your spices by putting them in containers that are the right size, without too much extra air. And keep them in a cool, dry, dark place.

"A common mistake is to place the spice rack over the stove," says Bouchard. "While this is certainly convenient, being exposed to all the heat and humidity from cooking will cause the spice flavor and color to deteriorate quickly."

Whole spices and herbs should last about one to three years, while the ground varieties stay good about six months to one year. That varies depending on the type of spice. Peppercorns and others with little oil can last longer, while spices like ground cloves, which have more oils, lose their flavor quickly.

Perfect use for bamboo steamer. Cool, dry, dark, yet with some air circulation. That describes the perfect place to store potatoes, onions, and garlic to keep them from sprouting or getting moldy. Place your unused bamboo steamer on the countertop to create the perfect storage environment, and fill it up.

Best fruits to buy unripe. You buy bananas when they're still green, knowing they'll ripen in a few days. The same goes with some other fruits, like apples, apricots, cantaloupes, mangoes, pears, and plums. That's because these are climacteric fruits, which ripen when they're exposed to ethylene gas. Place them in a paper bag — or just leave them alone — for a day or two, and they'll soon be at their best. But buy nonclimacteric fruits, like honeydew melons and watermelons, when they're at their peak of ripeness.

Avoid waste with first in, first out. Even if you freeze it, food doesn't last forever. Do like the grocers do and rotate your stock. Place new purchases at the back of the freezer, and move older items to the front. You'll be more likely to see and use them.

You can also use this trick in your pantry, placing new boxes of pasta behind old boxes. If you hit the sale jackpot on cereals or canned fruits, mark each package with the date so you'll know when it's time to toss.

How to tell when stocking up is a good deal. Whether you're at the supermarket or the warehouse store, nobody wants a bulk buy that doesn't save money. Follow these steps to be sure you only buy bulk deals that are worth your while.

- Check the unit price. Is this price better than the per-unit price at all the other places you shop? If the item is nonperishable, can you get a better deal and free shipping online? Bigger savings may be available in a smaller package.

- Find the expiration date if the product has one. Calculate how often you must use the item to finish it before it spoils, and consider whether you're likely to use it that often. If you can't use the entire product in time, can you split the cost and the food with a friend or family member? If any of the product will be wasted, don't buy it.

- Determine whether you have enough room to store the item in your refrigerator, freezer, pantry, or root cellar. To make this easier, check your storage spaces before you shop. Clean out any foods that have spoiled, and note how much storage space you have left. If you don't have space in the refrigerator or pantry, can you freeze part of the item until space is available? Is there room for it in your freezer? Don't buy anything you have no room to store.

- Don't stock up on a product you have never bought before. If you try the product and hate it, you'll have paid for a large amount of a product you won't use. Also, think twice about products you don't use often, especially if they are perishable.

Snoop out fake whole grains

If your digestion is less than regular, maybe you're missing out on roughage. Dr. John Johanson, a gastroenterologist in Beloit, Wisconsin, says not getting enough fiber is the biggest cause of poor digestive health. Most people get less than half the recommended amount.

Whole-grain bread should have at least 2 grams of fiber per serving, but labels can be misleading. Words like "multigrain," "7-grain," and "wheat flour" don't mean a bread is truly whole grain. Instead, look for whole wheat, whole rye, oatmeal, barley, or graham flour as the first ingredient listed.

5 smart ways to throw out less food. Use more of the food you buy so you won't spend as much at the grocery store. These tips can help.

- Designate one spot in your refrigerator as the Last Chance Cafe, the place where you put leftovers and other foods nearing the end of their shelf lives. Place a brightly colored tray or the bottom half of a shoe or pizza box in that location to contain those foods and remind you they need to be eaten. Use those foods first, and far fewer of them may spoil.

- Store foods in clear containers so you can see exactly what you have in your refrigerator and pantry. You're less likely to lose track of leftovers and ingredients when they're easy to spot, so they shouldn't spoil before you can use them. When clear containers are not enough, use labels. Either plaster a label where you can clearly see it, or put up a flag. Stick a label on a toothpick or half a straw, and tape it to the side of the package so your label stands high enough to be seen — like a flag on a flagpole.

- Use a permanent marker, a label maker, or a date stamp on food packages to mark down when your food went in the refrigerator, freezer, or pantry.

- Portion out your leftovers and stick them in the freezer if they haven't been eaten in several days. Assign them a "use by" date so they won't overstay their welcome. Visit your library or *www.stilltasty.com* to determine which leftovers you can freeze, how to do it properly, and how long they will keep. Your research may also turn up delicious and clever ways to use those leftovers.

- Every time you throw spoiled food away, write down the name of the food and why it never got eaten. Come up with several ideas for how you could have prevented that waste and what you will do next time. Over time, you will get better at using food before it spoils, and you'll end up spending less on groceries.

Food fraud — what you need to know. Some bottles of 100-percent olive oil may contain soybean oil. Even worse, some honey may include corn syrup, and some milk may be watered down. These are just a few examples of food fraud. Such cases include incidents where:

- food is tampered with.

- ingredients are replaced or removed.

- fillers are added.

- packaging or advertising is misleading.

The number of new cases of food fraud keep rising every year. Some foods seem more prone to this problem than others. A study in the *Journal of Food Science* suggests the most common foods afflicted by fraud include milk, honey, coffee, orange juice, apple juice, olive oil, vanilla extract, maple syrup, and saffron.

At the least, this means you may not be getting the food you're paying premium prices for. Even worse, food fraud may boost your odds of eating expired foods, toxic additives like melamine, or an ingredient you may be allergic to. To help avoid tainted foods, take steps like these.

- Buy from local producers when you can. Good places to try include farmer's markets, local farms, pick-it-yourself orchards, local beekeepers, and co-ops. When you can't buy locally, choose foods that are not imported.

- Grow or process your own. Start a backyard garden to grow some of your own fruits, vegetables, nuts, or herbs. Instead of buying juices, juice your own fruits and vegetables. Buy coffee beans instead of ground coffee, and grind the beans yourself.

- Buy well-known brands made by companies that have a reputation to protect.
- Read the ingredient list on packaged products to be sure it contains what you think it does.

Better baking with frozen berries. Blueberries are an outstanding source of nutrients that help battle memory loss, high blood sugar, heart disease, and cancer. That means you'll want to add them to your menu at every opportunity. Buy a bag of frozen blueberries when the fresh berries are not in season. Then throw a handful into your muffin mix, pancake batter, and quick-bread dough. No need to thaw — they'll defrost and warm right up in the oven. But toss them in a bit of flour before you fold them into the batter to keep them from sinking to the bottom.

Put leftover green tea to work

Your leftover green tea can make meat healthier and more tender. A recent study found that beef marinated in green tea for six hours forms up to 75 percent fewer cancer-causing compounds during pan-frying.

Use unsweetened green tea to marinate either beef or chicken. If your leftover tea was sweetened with sugar, it will make an ideal marinade for barbecued meats and steak.

Turn up the juice on lemons and limes. A few simple tricks can prepare your lemon or lime for maximum juicing.

- Bring the fruit to room temperature.
- Roll it firmly between your hands or with pressure on a countertop until soft.
- Microwave for about 15 seconds.

Of course you can use a traditional juicer or citrus reamer, but there are other kitchen tools that will work as well. First, cut your fruit in half, then pick one of the following methods.

- Position one half between the arms of tongs and squeeze.
- Place both halves in a potato ricer.
- Stick a fork into the cut half and twist.

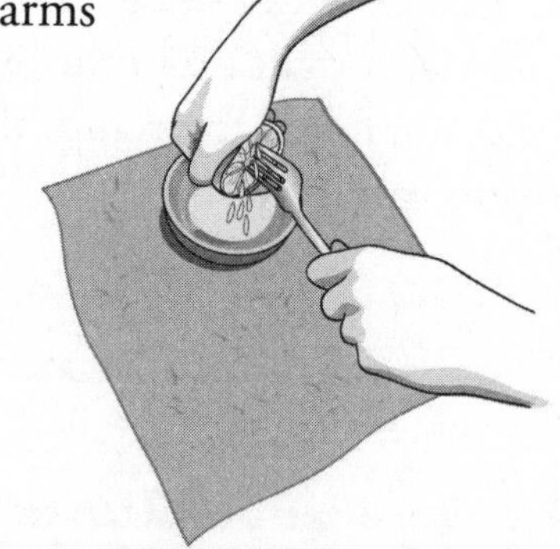

Use this restaurant steak secret at home. Uncover the real reason steaks taste better at a restaurant, and discover how you can get the same results at home without buying more expensive meat.

While your restaurant steak may come with all sorts of specialty seasonings or exotic sauces, it may also come with something anyone can buy from the grocery store — butter. To make the perfect culinary butter for your steak, mix two tablespoons of fresh parsley with a stick of butter. Store the seasoned butter in the refrigerator until needed.

When the steaks are done, remove them from the grill. Scoop out 1 1/2 teaspoons of butter, and drop it in the center of the first steak. Repeat the process for each one. After the last bit of butter melts, serve your delectable steaks, and prepare to enjoy compliments from all your guests.

Simple step to seeded tomatoes. Chop your tomatoes, and drop them into the basket of your salad spinner. Spin until all the seeds are removed. You're left with perfectly seeded tomatoes.

Pop a soda to keep fruit fresh. Slice an apple or pear, and the cut edges can turn brown and unappetizing before your eyes. This happens because an enzyme in the fruit reacts to the oxygen in the air, a process called oxidation. Most people know to pour some type of acidic liquid, like lemon or orange juice, over the fruit to reduce the pH levels and prevent oxidation. But a lemon-lime soda, such as Sprite or Seven-Up, works just as well and has a lighter, less tart flavor.

Prep strawberries for easy eating. Don't let the trouble of preparing fresh strawberries keep you from enjoying these tasty tidbits. Try one of these options for removing the stems and leaves.

- Push a drinking straw through the berry, starting at the bottom and exiting the leafy top. The core and leaf slide into the straw, and you're left with a neatly hulled berry.

- Use the pointed end of a large star tip from a cake-decorating kit by pushing it into the stem end. Twist and pull out.

- A can opener with a V-shaped end — sometimes called a church key — is just the right shape for scooping out the stem.

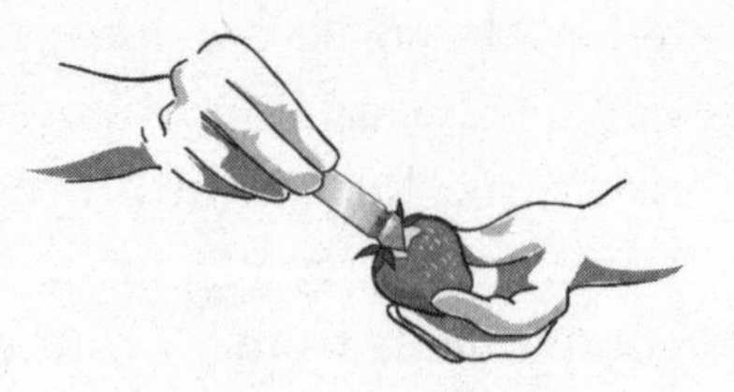

5 ways to avoid onion tears. You'll never shed another tear when preparing your famous homemade salsa if you understand the role science plays in the kitchen. Whenever you slice, crush, or cut an onion, it releases sulfur-containing compounds into the air. These mix with the fluid in your eyes, producing a mild form of sulfuric acid that irritates the nerve endings, producing tears. All you have to do is keep those potent fumes from reaching your eyes. Here are some things you can try.

- Chill your onion for about 30 minutes before cutting.
- Cut the onion under cool running water.
- Chop near a fan, stove exhaust fan, or open window.
- Wear goggles.
- Cut the root end of the onion last.

2 tricks to cut that fishy smell. You're done cutting and preparing fish steaks or fillets, yet the smell lingers on your hands. Try these gentle remedies to get rid of the odor.

- Scrub your hands with white fluoride toothpaste. Use it like soap, then rinse your hands completely.

- Douse your fingers and hands with bottled lemon juice. Then wash your hands as usual.

Keep food fresh and safe

"Check the temperature of your refrigerator and freezer with an appliance thermometer," says Katherine Bernard, acting manager of the USDA Meat and Poultry Hotline. The refrigerator should be 40 degrees Fahrenheit or below, and the freezer should be 0 degrees or below. That way food will stay fresh until you're ready to eat it. Use this information to decide where to store your groceries.

Food	Refrigerator lifespan	Freezer lifespan
Ground meat	1–2 days	3–4 months
Steaks, roasts	3–5 days	6–12 months
Pork chops, pork roast	3–5 days	4–6 months
Whole chicken	1–2 days	12 months
Lean fish (flounder, cod)	1–2 days	up to 6 months
Fatty fish (salmon, perch)	1–2 days	2–3 months
Luncheon meats	3–5 days	1–2 months
Milk	5 days	1 month
Cheese	3–4 weeks	4–6 months
Ice cream	—	2–4 months

Follow this "eggspert" advice. According to the American Egg Board, here's the best way to boil and peel an egg.

- Start with eggs that aren't too fresh. Once they've been stored about seven to 10 days, they'll peel easily.
- Place eggs in a single layer in your pot, and add water to at least one inch above the eggs.
- Cover, bring just to a boil, and remove from heat. Boiling at too high a heat or for too long will make the white tough and rubbery, and turn the yolk hard and a gray-green color.
- Keep the eggs covered, and let them stand in the hot water for 15 to 18 minutes.
- Cool them immediately and thoroughly under cold water.
- Tap each egg gently to break its shell, then roll it between your hands to crackle it all over.
- Hold under running water and start peeling from the large end of the egg.

Some people claim adding a bit of salt or vinegar to the cooking water makes boiled eggs easier to peel.

Trap juicy overflow. Set your cutting board inside a larger cookie sheet whenever you chop juicy fruits or vegetables, like tomatoes, oranges, or watermelon. You'll keep the mess inside the cookie sheet and off your counters.

Tidy mixing is in the bag. You like how meatballs and meatloaf turn out when you mix them by hand, but what a mess.

Try this trick to keep raw hamburger off your hands and out from under your nails. First, put all the ingredients into a large bowl. Then grab two small plastic baggies, and put them on your hands like loose gloves. Your fingers stay clean while they're free to move and mix.

Simple way to prevent pantry pests. Even the cleanest kitchen can be prone to a bug infestation. That's because insects that overrun food can get in while it's in the processing mill, at the store, or during transportation. They may spread from flour, cornmeal, or rice to noodles or cookies, making it all unfit to eat. Avoid the problem by freezing new bags of grain for at least four days. Then store in an airtight container.

4 steps to a safer kitchen. Even the most nutritious food may contain germs. "Bacteria are everywhere in our environment," says Katherine Bernard of the USDA Meat and Poultry Hotline. "Raw meat, poultry, seafood, and eggs are not sterile. Neither is fresh produce such as lettuce, tomatoes, sprouts, and melons. Any of these foods can harbor bacteria." You can't see or smell these dangerous critters. That's why you should follow some basic rules to avoid getting a food-borne illness.

- Clean up. Wash your hands and countertops with hot, soapy water after you handle raw meat. Clean cutting boards and utensils in the dishwasher.

- Separate foods. Use one cutting board for meat and poultry, and use another board for vegetables and breads. When you put raw meat or seafood in the refrigerator, keep it in a sealed container so juices don't spread to other foods.

- Cook thoroughly. You can't always tell when meat is safe to eat by how it looks. Use a meat thermometer to be sure. When you reheat gravy or soup, bring it to a rolling boil.

- Chill food promptly. "One of the most common problems with serving is to leave food at room temperature longer than two hours," Bernard says. Keep hot food hot, at 140 degrees Fahrenheit or warmer, and cold food cold, at 40 degrees or cooler.

Wipe out top 5 germiest kitchen spots. Get 'em where they live — dangerous bacteria, that is. Focus your cleaning efforts on these top five homes for bacteria, and you'll go a long way toward making your kitchen safer.

- Kitchen sponge. Think this is too expensive to replace often? Then kill the bacteria by popping your sponge in the dishwasher. Put it in the silverware basket, and use the hottest cycle.

- Cutting board. First you cut raw chicken on it, then you slice fruit. Bad idea. Tiny cracks in the board let bacteria survive and then move to other foods. It's best to use a separate cutting board for foods like raw meat.

- Sink drain. It's hard to see down there, but a sink drain is a dark, moist place for bacteria to hide. Disinfect it regularly, just as you do the countertops.

- Handles of doors, appliances, and faucets. Everyone touches these, so they're great places to spread bacteria. Use a disinfectant spray or wipe on them every day.

- Hand towels. They're a nice decoration, but shared cloth towels also share germs. Dry your hands using paper towels instead.

Simple step to a spotless drain

Sanitize your kitchen sink, drain, garbage disposal, and connecting pipe to remove trapped food and the growth of bacteria that comes along with it. You can make a solution of a teaspoon of chorine bleach in a quart of water, then pour it all down the drain. Hot water and soap may remove what you can see, but they won't kill the bacteria.

Smart tips for buying bagged produce. After recent scares, when outbreaks of dangerous *E. coli* bacteria were traced to bagged produce, you may be afraid to buy these items. Don't be. You don't need to give up the convenience of buying salads, spinach, or baby carrots in bags. Follow these safety tips from the U.S. Food and Drug Administration to keep your healthy greens from causing harm.

- Keep all fruits and vegetables separate from meat and seafood when you bring them home from the store.

- Put bagged salads in the refrigerator within two hours of buying them, and keep the refrigerator at 40 degrees Fahrenheit or below.

- Read the label of precut, bagged salad or produce to see if it's been washed. If it has, you don't need to wash it again.
- If you buy loose produce or salad in open bags, wash it thoroughly under running water just before you eat it. Wash your hands well before and after you wash the veggies to avoid transferring bacteria to other foods.

Avoid dining-out dangers. Eating out should be fun, not risky. Take these precautions so you don't suffer unpleasant aftereffects from your next restaurant experience.

- Use your eyes. If the restaurant doesn't look clean, don't eat there.
- Order food completely cooked. Just like when you dine at home, your meat, poultry, seafood, and eggs should be cooked thoroughly to kill germs. If your meal arrives cold or undercooked, send it back.
- Skip the citrus. Lemon slices placed on the edge of beverage glasses may not be safe. Researchers tested the rind and flesh of lemon slices in 21 restaurants. Nearly 70 percent of the lemon slices were contaminated by either bacteria or yeast or both.
- Get your doggie bag into the refrigerator quickly. "I would recommend within two hours from the time that the food was prepared," says Mary J. Weaver, technical manager for NSF Retail Food Safety. "In warmer weather, I would recommend within one hour. Bacteria grow most rapidly between the temperatures of 40 degrees and 140 degrees Fahrenheit, so it is very important to keep foods out of this temperature range."

Home fix-its you can do yourself

Free home repair for seniors. No matter what your income, services like legal assistance, home repair, even housekeeping chores can be yours at no cost through your local Area Agency on Aging. Over 35 years ago, Congress passed the Older Americans Act, which created a network of support services to help seniors with:

- household chores, such as laundry, grocery shopping, cleaning, and meal preparation
- transportation for doctor appointments, errands, and shopping
- in-home healthcare for seniors who do not need 24-hour care
- hot meals, delivered
- friendly telephone calls or in-home visits for homebound adults or those living alone
- legal assistance, including advice, counseling, and representation in civil matters
- Medicare benefits counseling

- utility and heating assistance for low-income seniors
- home repair, including roof patches, plumbing repair, and insulation
- pension counseling

Anyone 60 years or older is eligible for these benefits, although some programs give priority to seniors most in need. For more information, or to sign up for services, call the Eldercare Locator at 800-677-1116 or go online to *www.eldercare.gov*.

Savvy tips for labeling breakers. Take time to label the breakers in your electrical panel once. It's easier than you think, and you'll be glad you did.

First, figure out which outlets go to which circuit breaker. Plug a lamp into every outlet in a room, and turn on every light and fan switch. Have a friend stand in the room while you slowly flip each breaker off. Arm yourselves with cell phones, if you have them, so your friend can call you when a light or fan turns off. Or do it the old-fashioned way and yell to each other.

Testing switches works best with two people, but you can test outlets on your own without any leg work. Plug in a radio, and crank up the volume so you can hear it from the breaker panel. When the radio goes silent, you know you've located the breaker.

Number the breakers directly on the panel, then write the corresponding breaker number on the inside of each switch and outlet plate. Work room by room, and remember to test outside lights and outlets, too.

Can't-miss tips for finding studs. A stud finder is not necessarily the easiest way to find the studs in your wall. A lamp or a strong magnet may yield better results with less hassle.

Begin by holding a flashlight or bare-bulb lamp near the wall as you slowly walk its length. Look for the small, rounded shapes of raised nail heads under the paint or wallpaper. If you see several marching straight up the wall, chances are good you've found a stud. Test by drilling a small pilot hole through the drywall. Poke the end of a hanger into the hole. If you hit something solid behind the drywall, you've found it.

A strong magnet can take away the guesswork. Rare-earth magnets work best, especially on plaster walls, but a sturdy refrigerator magnet will do in most cases. Tape a piece of masking tape to the magnet to use as a handle, and slowly drag it along the wall. When it finds a nail or screw, it will stick. Run it up the wall vertically to check for a line of nails suggesting a stud.

Make sure your level is level. The next time you hang a picture, stop and check your level's accuracy. That little bubble is carefully calibrated. A good hard drop can knock it off kilter for good.

Set your level along the edge of a flat surface, like a table or countertop. The surface itself does not need to be perfectly level. Line up one end of the level with the table corner. Make a mental note of where the bubble is.

Turn the level 180 degrees, and line up the other end with the same corner. Finally, roll the level over so that the vial is upside down. The bubble should appear in the exact same spot each time. If it's farther to the left or right, then your level is no longer accurate.

Do the same against a wall to check for plumb. Line the tool up with the outside corner of a wall and take note of the measuring plumb.

Now roll the level on to its other side. The bubble should be in the same place. Don't just check your home level. Use these tricks to test one in-store before you buy it.

Save yourself from sawdust. Always saw, sand, and drill treated wood outside. That way, you'll inhale as little of the potentially harmful sawdust as possible, and none of it will build up in your house. If you can't avoid working indoors, at least wear a dust mask.

Create your own depth stops. You want to drill holes to a certain depth, but how do you know when you've gone deep enough? If you're a clever craftsman, you use a depth stop, and if you're a really clever craftsman, you use a cheap depth stop made of cork. Simply drill a hole smaller than the bit you will be using into a regular cork, then screw the cork onto the drill bit. The cork must be tight on the bit so it won't budge when it hits the wood.

When things get a little screwy. One of the hardest things for the amateur woodworker to do is get a screw to go in straight. Fortunately, one of the handyman's oldest tricks takes care of this problem. Before applying the screw, rub the threads with a bar of soap. The soap helps the screw go into the wood more smoothly and, hopefully, in a straighter line.

Easy fix for a loose screw. Got a screw loose? Get yourself a "twist-tie" or two, the kind used to keep bread fresh. Cut the ties or fold them over so they are about as long as the hole is deep. Next, take the screw out of the wall and insert the twist ties into the hole. When you put the screw back in, it should mash into the twist-ties, and the extra width created should make the screw fit tightly.

Super way to organize nuts and bolts

An old muffin pan makes a perfect organizer for all those odd-sized nuts, bolts, screws, and nails that you accumulate. You can even mount it under a bench top or shelf by securing it with a screw on one end. Use a washer as a spacer, and you'll be able to swing the muffin pan out to find that perfect fastener, and then swing it back under when you're finished.

Never drop a screw again. Do small screws keep slipping from your fingers in tight spaces? A screwdriver with a magnetic tip can be very useful. But if you don't have one, or if the screw you're using is brass or aluminum, use a piece of plastic kitchen wrap to keep the screw on the screwdriver.

Tear about 6 inches of plastic wrap off the roll. Push the screw through the wrap and put the screwdriver in the screw head. Pull the wrap around the shaft of the screwdriver, and the screw is secure. When you're done turning the screw into

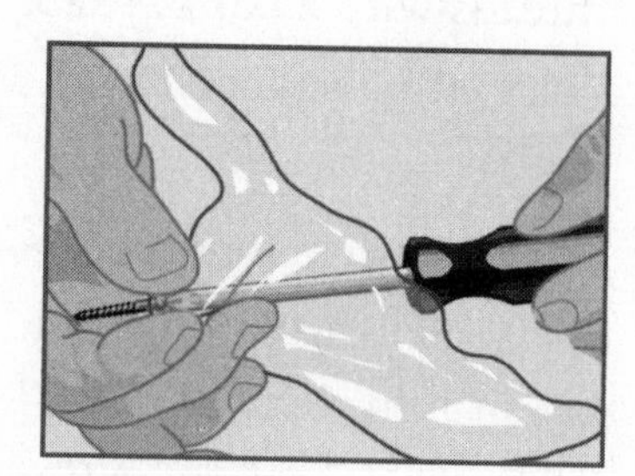

place, just pull off the plastic wrap. Masking tape works, too — push the screw through the sticky side.

Pick the right size nail for your needs. It matters — too long, and your nail will poke through the other side of the wood. Too short, and it could come loose. The same is true with screws. Get it right with this rule of thumb.

Nails and screws are generally used to attach a thin piece of material to a thicker one. Choose a nail around three times longer than the thickness of the thin piece. So if you're nailing a 1/4-inch piece of plywood to a 2x4, use a nail that is three times thicker than the plywood — 3/4-inch. For screws, choose one around two-and-a-half times longer than the thickness of the thin material. That means you'll need a screw 1 1/4 inches long to attach 1/2-inch drywall to a wall stud.

Drive nails straight as an arrow

Avoid the frustration of bent nails and banged thumbs. Drill a pilot hole slightly smaller than the nail to get it started and help it go in straight. Hold the nail in place with a clothespin or needle-nose pliers to protect your thumb while hammering.

You can also stand it between the teeth of a comb or push it through a piece of cardboard to keep it steady while you hammer.

Bang the lid slowly. Tired of putting dents or holes in your wall because you missed a nail with your hammer? Never again. Instead of panicking over the condition of your wall, get yourself a plastic lid off a coffee can or an old Tupperware bowl. Drill a hole in the center that's large enough for your nails to go through, then place this guard around the nails as you pound them home. Now if your aim misses the mark, the plastic shield takes the blow, not your wall.

Never forget another measurement. Remembering a measurement long enough to get to your saw isn't easy. Get it wrong, and you'll be heading to the store to buy more wood. Writing it on your hand can help, but there's a better solution. Paint the sides of your tape measure with black chalk paint, and carry a piece of chalk in your tool belt. Write the measurements on the tape itself and erase when you're done. Even simpler, stick masking tape on the side of the measuring tape, write on it, and remove it when finished.

Camera captures what's hidden in walls

Spread the word — the next time someone you know is about to start a major remodeling job, tell them to snap photos of the open walls before the drywall goes up. Stretch a tape measure along the bottom of the wall or tack a yard stick to one of the studs for reference. Then, if a question comes up later about locating studs, electrical wires, or pipes, the picture will provide all the answers.

Put an end to annoying squeaks. Stop living with squeaky hinges. You have everything you need to silence them for good right in your pantry. Close the door and remove one of the hinge pins by tapping a nail up through the bottom of the hinge. Rub an ordinary candle all over the pin to coat it in wax, then tap it back into the hinge. Do this with each squeaky pin, one hinge at a time.

A dab of petroleum jelly will do the trick, too. Coat the pin lightly, and put a small dollop of jelly in the top of the hinge for good measure. The petroleum jelly will attract dust and dirt, so candles work best if you have them on hand.

Stubborn pins sometimes refuse to come out. Never fear. You can still fix the squeak. Rub a dry bar of soap along the outside of the hinge, working it into every crevice. Open and close the door a few times to spread the soap throughout the hardware.

Pop the lock on interior doors. Locking yourself out of your bathroom by accident is annoying. But frantically trying to reach a loved one who has fallen inside a locked bathroom is terrifying. Fortunately, it's easy to spring most locks in just a few seconds.

These tricks work on doors that lock by pressing and turning the knob or by pushing a button in the center. Look for a hole in the center of the knob. Simply slide a small, straight item, like a tiny flathead screwdriver, into the hole. Fish around until you feel it catch on a slot, then push it and turn the knob at the same time. This should unlock the door. Don't see a hole in the center? Check the knob's stem or plate. The same instructions apply — insert your homemade lock pick, push, and turn the knob.

Anything small, straight, and sturdy will pop the lock. Hex (Allen) wrenches, hairpins, or even a cotton swab with the cotton removed from one end will get you inside.

Erase ugly ceiling stains. You may not need to paint your ceiling to block out a water stain. Try spraying it with bleach water first. Cover the floor beneath the stain with plastic, and don gloves and goggles. Spray light stains with a solution of one part bleach and nine parts water. Let it dry, then mist again if the stain hasn't completely faded. Dab straight bleach on old or dark stains, or spritz with a store-bought mildew remover that contains bleach.

Turn old paint into free primer

Is your basement full of paint you'll never use again? Colors you bought and hated or have outgrown? Don't throw them away. Mix together leftover paint and use it as primer on future projects. Combine similar tones, such as light with light or dark with dark, and types of paint — latex with latex and oil with oil. Sheen doesn't matter. Put a coat of the light mix under light-colored paints and the dark concoction under dark colors in place of expensive, store-bought primer.

How to tell if old paint is any good. Paint stored in a tightly sealed container can last a long time. Latex paint generally has a 10-year shelf life, while oil-based paint can last 15 years. That said, test it before putting it on your walls. Crack open the can and sniff. Good paint will have a chemical odor, while bad paint will smell rancid. Remove any skin that has formed on top and stir. See if you can blend the liquid that has separated back into the paint. Next, brush the paint onto newspaper or cardboard and look for lumps. Lumpy paint is bad paint. If yours passes all of these tests, then congratulations — it's still good.

Cut brush-cleaning time in half. Make paint cleanup fast and painless by soaking your brush in fabric softener. Start by scraping excess paint out of the bristles with a brush comb or old fork. Mix half a cup of fabric softener with one gallon of warm water, or place a couple of used dryer sheets in a bucket of warm water. Let your brush soak in the mixture for several minutes, then swirl it vigorously until it's free of paint. No need to rinse with water afterward. This trick only works for latex, not oil-based, paints.

Prep the brush before painting, and cleanup will be even easier. For latex paints, dip the brush in water all the way up to the base of the bristles. For oil-based paints, dip it in mineral spirits. Blot with a paper towel until the brush is only slightly damp, and get painting.

Help keep the angle on a sash brush sharp by laying it on a glossy magazine page after cleaning. Shake out the extra water, then fold the page around the brush, following the angle of the tip. Tape it closed and hang the brush by the handle to dry until the next time you need it.

Add heat to help tape stick. Painter's and masking tape both lose their stickiness after sitting on the shelf for a while. Before you throw out an expensive roll, try popping it in the microwave for 10 seconds. Heat softens the glue, giving your roll new life. Don't try this trick on duct tape or other plastic tapes, however. They might melt. Warm painter's tape creates a better seal against paint when masking trim, floors, and fixtures. Run a putty knife along the taped section to further prevent bleeding. Heat also helps remove stubborn tape. Aim a hairdryer at the tape as you slowly peel it off.

Clever tips take the pain out of painting. Does the thought of painting make your blood pressure rise? Try these four solutions to the most common problems.

- Protect carpet while painting baseboards. Tear off strips of 1 1/2-inch painter's or masking tape, lay them on the carpet against the bottom of the baseboard, and use a plastic putty knife to push the edge of the tape under the baseboard.

- Stop the bleeding. Run a credit card or plastic putty knife along the edge of painter's tape to create a tight seal between the tape and the wall. Paint won't leak under the tape, giving you a clean line.

- Always remove tape once the surrounding paint is tacky — no longer wet, but not quite dry.

- Reuse old plastic shower curtains as free drop cloths to protect floors.

No-mess way to pour paint. Invest a couple of bucks in a plastic spout that snaps onto the rim of one-gallon paint cans. It will give you a clean pour plus an edge on the inside to scrape excess paint off your brush. Best of all, it's plastic so it cleans up easily with water.

Don't let stairs trip up paint job. When you paint stairs, paint every other step the first day. Do the rest a day or two later, once the first batch has dried, so you can still get up and down the stairs.

Buy exactly the right amount of paint

Take the guesswork out of paint shopping. Three handy websites will calculate in an instant how much paint you need for almost any project. Now if only choosing the colors were that easy.

- *www.paintquality.com/en/tools/paint-calculator*
- *www.behr.com/consumer/products/paint-and-stain-calculator*
- *www.benjaminmoore.com/en-us/paint-calculator*

Silence squeaky floors for good. These four tricks work like magic to quiet almost any creaky floor.

- Generously dust talcum powder between the noisy boards of hardwood floors. Lay down a towel and step on it to work the powder into nooks and crannies. If you still hear a squeak, apply more talcum powder.
- Work liquid wax between the boards of waxed wood floors. Don't try this on floors with a varnish or urethane coating.
- Squeeze a long bead of construction adhesive along the crack where the floor boards meet the joists, for floors where the joists are exposed. Do this from the underside of the floor.
- Buy an inexpensive tool called the Squeeeeek No More to fix carpeted floors when you can't get to the joists. It guides a screw through the carpet into the underlying floor joist. Then it snaps off the screw head so it's totally hidden by carpet. Check your local hardware store for this product or buy it online at *www.squeaknomore.com*.

Smooth sliding for stuck drawers. Remove the drawer and lightly sand the runners with a scrap of sandpaper. Clean off the dust. Then rub a candle or bar of soap along the runners to "grease" them up. For a fresh smell, use scented soap or candles. For metal drawers, spray a little lubricating oil on a soft cloth and wipe along the runners.

Easy way to mend a broken drawer. Is your kitchen drawer falling apart? Did the back fall out or the sides fall in? Fix it fast with a piece of trim. Cut a small piece of quarter-round molding to the same height as the inside of the drawer. Dab a little glue on the two flat sides of the trim, and nestle it in the broken corner. Let the glue set, then nail or drill a screw through the drawer and into the molding.

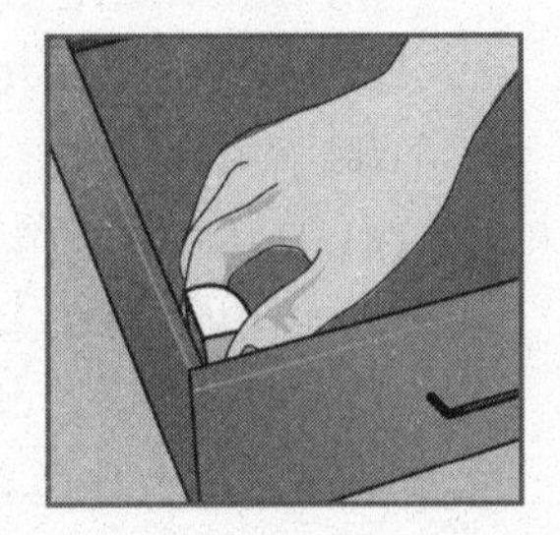

Free fixes for damaged furniture. Before you kick those beat-up pieces to the curb, try some tender, loving care to give them new life.

- Turn the tables. Fix a wobbly table just by turning it. Find the wobbly leg and the one diagonally across from it. Lift the table so that both legs are the same distance off the ground. Begin turning the table around its center until both legs are resting on the floor and — voila! — no more wobble. This trick only works on square or rectangular tables.

- Flatten the warp. Wood tends to warp over time, and varnishing it only on one side speeds up the process. To flatten out table tops and other warped boards, remove the bent piece. Evenly wet the side that curves inward with a damp cloth. Wipe excess water from the other side. Clamp each end of the board or table between two long, flat pieces of wood. Tighten the clamp until the board is flat, and let dry a day or two. Repeat if necessary.

- Mend upholstery. You can sew coarse fabric, but leather and finely woven upholstery will show the stitching. Go thread-free by cutting a piece of canvas or other thin fabric in a shape slightly larger than the tear. Peel back the torn upholstery and use a spoon handle to slide the scrap under the torn edges. Paint latex fabric glue on the meeting faces. Lay the torn flap flat and hold in place with upholsterer's pins until the glue sets.

Secret to reassembling things with ease. Taking something apart is usually easier than putting it back together. You always think you'll remember which piece goes where and in what order, but that rarely happens. The fix is an easy one. Take photos. Each time you remove another part, snap a picture with your camera or cellphone. When the time comes to put things back together, you'll have your own illustrated instructions on hand.

Organize projects with an egg carton. It doesn't do any good to take something apart and fix it if you can't put it back together. An empty egg carton provides an egg-cellent solution to this problem. Just number each of the 12 compartments. When you take something apart piece by piece, put each screw, bolt, or part in the matching egg compartment. Place the first set of screws in compartment one, the next group in compartment two, and so on. When you want to put everything back together, start with the compartment you filled last and work your way back to number one.

Tighten sagging chair bottoms. Cane chair bottoms can lose their charm when they sag too much. To make them taut again, soak two cloths in a solution of hot water and baking soda. Coat the entire surface from the top with one cloth while pushing up from the underside with the other. Dry it with a clean cloth, and put it in the sun to dry.

Quick tricks to fix a stuck sink. Believe it or not, you can free most clogged drains yourself without spending money on plumbers or chemical decloggers. First, make your soda-drinking habit pay off by recycling a 2-liter bottle into a makeshift plunger. Remove the sink stopper and plug the overflow drain with a wet rag. For double sinks, plug the second drain. Next, fill the empty bottle with water. In one fast motion, shove the mouth of the bottle into the drain and squeeze it hard. Water will blast down the drain, blowing apart any clogs in its way.

If you have an old-fashioned, wide-mouth plunger, you can clear a clogged sink as easily as a clogged toilet. Take out the stopper, fill the sink with several inches of water, and stuff wet rags in the overflow or second drain. Wipe a thick layer of petroleum jelly around the rim of the plunger to create a stronger seal. Plunge vigorously for about 30 seconds. Yank the plunger out of the water hard on the final upstroke.

If the sink doesn't begin draining freely, plunge again. Once you clear the clog, run hot water to flush any particles still stuck in the pipes.

You can prevent many clogs in the first place with a monthly flush of the drains you use most often. Pour half a cup of baking soda down sink, kitchen, and tub drains, followed by half a cup of vinegar. Let the mix fizz for half an hour, then chase it down with a kettle of boiling water.

Clear clogs with a coat hanger

Stubborn clogs may need snaking. Improvise your own auger by untwisting a coat hanger. Leave the hook on the end, straighten the middle portion, and bend the other end into a handle, so you don't drop it down the drain. For bathroom sinks, you'll need to remove the rod under the sink that raises and lowers the stopper.

Start by removing the stopper. Then reach under the sink and unscrew the thumbscrew that attaches to the rod. Pull the rod back and out of the drain. Now slide the hooked end of your coat hanger down the drain, twisting and jiggling it up and down as you go. Gently pull it out. With any luck, the gunk causing the clog will come out with it.

Solve plumbing problems with a straw. Put an end to running toilets, and install a new one with ease. All thanks to a simple straw. Toilets often run because the chain on the flapper inside the tank gets kinked. Keep that from happening in the future. Unhook the chain, slide a straw over it, and reattach it. If the straw is too long, just cut it to size.

Straws can also make replacing a toilet much simpler. The hardest part — lining up the holes in the base of the bowl with the bolts in the floor. Do it wrong, and you mess up the wax ring. Get it right the first time by sliding straws over the bolts, then use them as guides when you lower the bowl. Slide the bowl holes over the straws for a perfect fit.

Thaw frozen pipes in a flash. It's a fact of life during winter — pipes sometimes freeze. You should do everything you can to prevent that — drip your faucets during cold spells and insulate exposed pipes, for instance. But if all your efforts fail, you can still thaw them yourself. Just be prepared with a mop, bucket, and dry towels in case the ice has lead to burst pipes.

First, try to locate the frozen section. Look for pipes coated in frost. Those in unheated basements, crawl spaces, attics, garages, and inside kitchen or bathroom cabinets are likely culprits. So are pipes that run up exterior walls. Don't see any frost? Use the process of elimination to figure out which line is frozen. Turn on every faucet in the house, both the hot and cold water, and flush each toilet. A fixture that has very low or no water pressure may be frozen. Shut off water to the area that's iced, or turn it off where the main supply line enters the house.

Chances are, you have everything you need to thaw the pipes yourself. Open the taps nearest the frozen section of pipe. Water moving through it will help the ice melt faster. Wrap a heating pad around the frozen section, rub the area with a hot towel, or aim a hair dryer at it. A space heater nearby can also help defrost the ice blockage. Whatever you do, don't try to melt the ice with a lighter, blow torch, or other open flame. You could damage the pipe or start a fire.

Get perfect caulk lines every time. Caulk is sticky and messy, but laying a smooth bead is essential if you want your work to look its best. Perfect your skills with a few tips from the pros.

- Lay strips of blue painter's tape or masking tape along either side of the line you plan to caulk. Press the tape edges firmly to get a good seal.

- Cut the tip of the tube very close to the end if caulking trim and other woodwork, leaving a 1/16-inch opening. For caulking tubs, showers, or sinks, create a bigger opening, about 1/8 inch.

- Always cut the opening at a 45-degree angle, then smooth any rough edges with sandpaper.

- Squeeze the tube or caulk gun trigger with gentle but steady pressure as you move down the line.

- Smooth caulk with your fingertip for a perfect line. For latex caulk, wipe your finger on a damp rag or dip it in water before touching the caulk. A wet finger makes a smoother bead and keeps the caulk from sticking to you. Wipe your finger off occasionally on a damp rag. To smooth silicone caulk, dip your finger in dish soap rather than water.

If arthritis or tremors make it hard to smooth the caulk by hand, try using an old spoon. Simply run the backside of the spoon's tip along the bead.

5-minute fix for holes in siding. Patch up holes in your vinyl siding with a squirt of caulk. The key to making a nearly invisible repair is to match the caulk color to the siding. Home improvement stores sometimes carry caulk in a variety of colors. If yours doesn't, head to a siding supply store or shop online. Take a spare piece of siding with you, if you have one, to match the color as closely as possible.

Once home, wipe the area around the hole clean so the caulk can seal properly. Squirt it into the hole, filling the space behind the hole, between the siding and the house. Pull the caulk tube back as the hole fills, and leave a small blob sticking out beyond the siding. Let it dry for several days, then shave off the excess with a razor blade or utility knife, leaving the caulk flush with the siding.

First aid for ice dams. Ice dams are like the aches that accompany the flu — they're a symptom, not the cause of the problem. Ice dams form when warm air rises from the house into the attic and heats the roof unevenly. Too little insulation and ventilation in your attic are often the real culprits.

Warm air from the house can warm the attic, too, melting snow on parts of the roof. Meanwhile, the roof's edge stays cold. When water from melting snow hits the edge, it refreezes into an ice dam, blocking the gutters. Melting water then builds up behind the ice. Over time it can find its way under your shingles and into your attic, ceiling, and walls.

The long-term fix is to add insulation, increase the ventilation, and seal the places where warm air in the house leaks into the attic. All three will keep the roof colder in winter, which will prevent snow from melting on the roof and refreezing along the edges.

Until then, treat the symptoms. If you spot leaks in the attic or along exterior walls, act fast. Set a box fan in the attic, and tilt it so it blows air directly at the leak. This will freeze the water fast, stopping the leak until you can clear the ice and snow off the roof. Use a roof rake with wheels to remove snow on one-story homes.

Cut a path through the dam so melting snow has a way to drain. On a warm day, aim a garden hose at the roof to carve out a channel in the ice. Can't catch a warm day? Cut the leg off a nylon stocking, and fill it with calcium chloride ice melt. Tie it closed and lay it atop the ice dam, perpendicular to the roof's edge and crossing the gutter. Use a long-handled hoe to push it into position if needed. Eventually it will melt through the blockage. Keep in mind that calcium chloride may harm plants near the gutter and downspout.

Banish damp smells with cat litter. Next to a haunted basement, a dank, smelly cellar can be a homeowner's biggest nightmare. To scare away moisture and odor, mix 10 pounds of cat litter with 5 pounds of baking soda. Every week, put about 2 inches of litter in shallow pans and place them around your basement.

Don't buy a "hole" new screen. Don't trash that window screen yet. Here are two quick fixes.

- Small holes in a screen can easily be patched using a few thin coats of clear nail polish. Dab it on lightly, letting it dry between coats. This will prevent clumping and dripping, and make the repair job almost invisible.

- If you have some extra screening on hand, you can repair a small hole in a screen by gluing a small piece of screening over the hole. Use a permanent, waterproof glue that dries clear.

Lengthen the life of your air conditioner. Preparing your air conditioner (AC) for winter is a cinch. All you need is a small piece of plywood and a few bricks. Brush away leaves that have collected around the condenser unit outside. Then lay a piece of plywood just large enough to cover the top. Weight that down with four bricks, one on each corner. That's it.

Ignore the advice of anyone who says you should wrap the unit with a tarp. Inevitably, water will find a way under it and become trapped, where it will have all winter to rust your condenser. Tarps also create an inviting home for rodents, that will chew away at the wiring.

Leaving the unit covered but unwrapped protects it from snow and ice, while allowing water to evaporate and discouraging critters. Be sure to remove the plywood before you turn on the AC next spring. If you are worried you'll forget, simply unplug the AC from its power source or flip the circuit breaker that controls it before putting it to bed for winter.

Erase unsightly oil stains. Oil and grease seep into concrete fast, so clean them up as soon as they happen. Stop the oil from spreading by pouring a circle of sand, dirt, sawdust, or cat litter around it. Then pour plenty of cat litter onto the spill itself. Level it with a push broom, and let sit for at least an hour. Sweep it up once it has absorbed all of the oil.

Reach for baking soda to clean up any unsightly stain that's left. Spray a little water over the stain and pour baking soda over it. Let it sit for as long as it takes you to boil a large pot of water. Pour the hot water over the stain and scrub with a stiff nylon brush.

Old oil stains may need special treatment to remove them. Make a paste out of ordinary baby or talcum powder. Mix an ounce of TSP (trisodium phosphate) or TSP substitute with one cup of water and a cup of powder. Smear the paste onto the stain up to half an inch thick with a putty knife. Let it dry for a full 24 hours, then scrape it off with your putty knife and throw it away. Scrub what's left with a nylon brush, and rinse with clean water. Repeat the process if needed.

First aid for cement burns

Take extra care when working with concrete, cement, mortar, plaster, grout, or stucco. Wear gloves and keep a big bottle of vinegar on hand. All of these mixtures contain portland cement, which will suck the water right out of your skin if it gets on you. But worse than drying out your hands, they can all cause serious chemical burns because they are highly alkaline.

If these mixes touch your skin, rinse the area immediately with plain water for several minutes. Don't wait until you finish a job. Alkaline begins killing tissue as soon as it penetrates your skin. You may not feel any pain until hours later, and by then it will be too late to prevent the burns. Follow up by soaking the area with white vinegar to neutralize the alkalinity.

Experts suggest wearing long-sleeve shirts and pants, eye protection, and either butyl or nitrile gloves, not rubber gloves, when working with these products. If they get on your clothes, take off that piece of clothing immediately, and rinse your skin with water and vinegar.

Quick patch for concrete cracks. Hairline cracks in concrete can quickly widen. Fortunately, patching concrete is a cinch. Start by brushing out the loose concrete and dirt with a wire brush. For the patch to stick, the crack must be half an inch deep and wider at the bottom than the top. To deepen or widen it, insert a chisel into the crack and use a hammer to undercut the concrete and widen the base of the crack.

Brush out the debris again and flush out with a hose. Sweep away standing water just before pouring in the concrete patch.

Keep string at your fingertips. For handy string storage, take a clean 2- or 3-liter plastic soda bottle and cut off the bottom. Nail it upside down into the wall and place a roll of string inside. Feed the end of the string down and out the bottle's neck. For even more convenience, attach a pair of scissors to the bottle with a separate length of string.

Extend the life of dull saw blades. That dull saw blade may not need replacing — it may just need a good cleaning. Wood pitch, glue, and other gunk build up on a blade's cutting teeth over time. Even if the blade is sharp, it will cut as though it's dull. Getting the gunk off could restore its bite and save big on replacement blades.

Amazingly, ordinary oven cleaner works best, and it won't harm carbide-tipped teeth. Buy generic oven or grill cleaner and follow the instructions. Be sure to wear gloves, eye protection, and an apron. Cleaners like this may damage Teflon- and plastic-coated blades, though, so apply them at your own risk.

Keep tools in tiptop shape. Prevent rust from forming by cleaning off dirt after each use, then wiping the metal parts with WD-40 before storing them. Keep them in a low-humidity environment to lengthen their working life. To remove light rust from tools, spray with WD-40, then scrub with a heavy-duty sponge. Wipe off the rust and excess lubricant before storing. Don't try to sand off rust. Sandpaper scratches the metal.

Tidy up your tool shed. Straighten up even the worst mess in your garage or gardening shed. Best of all, you can do it for free using scrap materials.

Screw a piece of 1x4 lumber to the wall horizontally, being sure to attach it to studs. Hammer pairs of long nails into the board, but leave them sticking out an inch or two. Space the nails about 2 inches apart so they will cradle the head or handle of the tool.

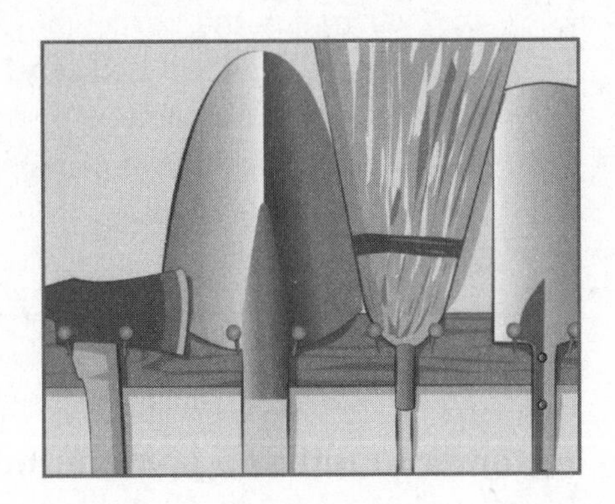

For a fancier look, make holders out of spare PVC pipe. Saw the pieces into 6-inch lengths, cutting both ends at an angle away from the center. Sand off any plastic burrs. Drill pilot holes through the backs of the pieces on each end, and attach them to a horizontal 1x4 or directly to the studs.

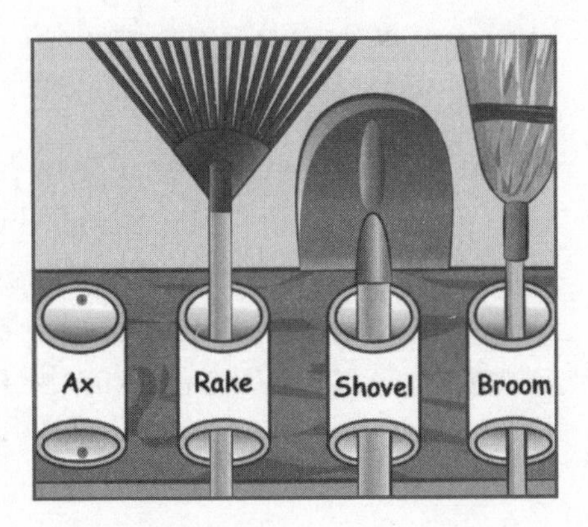

Once you finish, slide your tools handle-first through the mounted pipes. Write the name of each tool on its pipe in permanent marker to up your chances of staying organized.

Personalize your putty

For your next woodworking project, make wood putty that will match the particular wood you're using. Take a spare piece of wood and sand off a pile of the finest sawdust you can manage. Then whip the sawdust into clear epoxy. You'll have personal putty that could make any carpenter envious.

Hammer together a hammer holder. Make yourself the handiest hammer storage rack on the block. Hammer 2-inch drywall nails into a board and hang it on your shop wall. Use as many nails as you have hammers. Then rest the claw of each hammer on a nail as if you were going to try and pull the nail out. This V-notch will fit onto the nail snugly so you won't have to worry about falling hammers. Plus, your hammers will stick out at easy-to-grab angles.

Make a handy scooper. Clean plastic milk jugs can be turned into great scoopers. Hold it so the handle is on top and use a marker to draw a wedge on the diagonal. Cut out this section and you have a great way to dispense cat litter, bird seed, sand, etc. You can keep the cap on for no spills or take it off for filling small spaces like bird feeders — it will do double duty as a kind of funnel.

Home remedies for optimum health

Boost your immune system with yogurt. You want a strong immune system — one that can battle cold and flu viruses before they bring you down. Look to probiotics — friendly bacteria that live in your digestive tract, keeping it healthy. Since two-thirds of your immune system lies in your gut, these good "bugs" perform an essential service, and probiotics help them flourish.

Yogurt is loaded with probiotics. Studies show that two probiotics in particular — *bifido-bacterium* and *lactobacillus* — can reduce the number of colds you catch. Just make sure your yogurt has the "Live & Active Cultures" seal to ensure a favorable amount of living bacteria.

Kefir, a drinkable yogurt, typically packs in even more beneficial bacteria than yogurt. Try mixing this tart beverage with low-fat milk or adding it to a smoothie. Look for kefir in the dairy aisle of your favorite supermarket.

Another way to promote gut health is to consume prebiotics. Prebiotics are nutrients, not bacteria, that stimulate the growth and activity of probiotics. Think of them as probiotic food. To add prebiotics to your diet, graze on oatmeal and other whole grains, leeks, onions, garlic, legumes, raisins, bananas, and asparagus.

2 fabulous foods that can keep you healthy. Nourishing a strong immune system prepares you for cold and flu season like a soldier readies for battle. Take a bite out of these foods to keep viruses at bay.

- Goat milk. Not all milk is created equal. Goat milk, for instance, is brimming with immune-boosting nutrients and anti-inflammatory agents not found in cow's milk. It also prompts your body's cells to attack intruders. If you can't give up your daily glass of moo juice, try goat cheese or goat milk yogurt.

- Lima beans. What do lima beans, pears, and Brussels sprouts have in common? The obvious answer — they're all green. The not-so-obvious answer — they're all great sources of soluble fiber, a potent immune-system supporter. Foods high in soluble fiber act like brooms, sweeping your digestive tract of unwelcome visitors, like germs. Not wild about lima beans? Besides pears and Brussels sprouts, graze on apples, oranges, and legumes like black beans and kidney beans.

Sip sage tea to soothe a sore throat. Your throat is under attack, but drinking sage tea may help you fight back. Sage inhibits the growth of bacteria and decreases mucous secretions. In fact, the U.S. Department of Agriculture says white sage will treat nearly all sore throats. To make a cup of sage tea, boil water and add either 1 teaspoon of dried sage leaves or 1 tablespoon of fresh sage. Allow it to steep for three to five minutes. Now you have two choices — either sip the tea or gargle with it first, then drink it.

Tasty ways to calm a cough

Don't reach for cough syrup the next time you suffer a miserable cough. Try one of these home remedies instead.

- Pineapple juice. For a treat reminiscent of a tropical paradise, drink pineapple juice. Combine 8 ounces of warm juice and 2 teaspoons of honey.
- Hot lemonade. This soothing drink combines the juice from three lemons, 3 cups of water, 1/2 cup of honey, and 1 1/2 teaspoons of grated lemon peel. For a little spice, add cinnamon sticks. Warm the mixture over medium heat in a saucepan. Pour into your favorite mug. Sip and relax.
- Chicken soup. Undoubtedly, you've heard that chicken soup may help fight a cold. But did you know it can help banish a cough, too? The hot liquid will moisturize the back of your throat, while pungent herbs, like garlic, can clear up congestion.

Clear a stuffy nose in seconds. No need to take a decongestant. Your tongue and finger will do just fine, according to a professor at Michigan State University's College of Osteopathic Medicine. Push your tongue flat against the roof of your mouth. At the same time, press a finger between your eyebrows. Hold for about 20 seconds. The pressure will stimulate a bone that runs through your nasal passages to your mouth, causing your sinuses to drain.

Take two aspirins and gargle in the morning. A sore throat can be a real headache. So why not fight it with aspirin? Dissolve two aspirin tablets in warm water and gargle. You'll feel hours of soothing relief. Just make sure you don't use coated aspirin or acetaminophen.

Yummy fruit solves sleep problems. After a good night's sleep, your body and your brain feel refreshed and energetic. But if you're spending every night restless and awake, you might not have enough melatonin, a hormone that regulates your sleep cycle. To raise your melatonin levels naturally, try snacking on a banana an hour or so before bedtime.

Or perhaps you suffer at night from a dry cough that so often accompanies chronic heartburn or acid indigestion. Again, bananas are a great remedy. On top of that, this inexpensive, wholesome fruit has only about 100 calories and is full of potassium, folate, vitamins B6 and C, and fiber.

Tip your cup to ease digestive woes. Irritable bowel syndrome (IBS) is also known as "spastic colon" or "irritable colon," and is actually a set of chronic digestive symptoms. IBS symptoms include abdominal pain, frequent constipation and/or diarrhea, cramping, gas, and sometimes bloating, nausea, headache, and fatigue. IBS isn't life-threatening, but it can make your life more difficult. Luckily, it usually can be controlled with a few diet and lifestyle changes.

Try soothing the discomfort of IBS with one of these natural remedies.

- Peppermint. By far the most effective, this mint can relax the smooth muscles lining your intestines. To make a strong tea, pour two-thirds of a cup of boiling water over two tablespoons of freshly dried peppermint leaves. Let it steep for about five to six minutes and strain. You can also take enteric-coated capsules half an hour before eating. Don't try this with small children. The strong scent can make them gag.

- Chamomile. Like peppermint, chamomile tea soothes muscle spasms. Drink freshly brewed tea three to four times a day for fast relief. Use dried flower heads or buy extracts from reputable companies for best results. If you have allergies to ragweed or daisies, try peppermint instead.

- Ginger. For cramping and indigestion, add fresh ginger to your diet. You can eat it raw, candied, or make a tea. Just steep two teaspoons of grated root in boiling water for about 10 minutes. Strain and sip slowly.

Other herbs that may help IBS are anise seed, caraway, fennel, and coriander.

Help move things along with rye bread. If your internal plumbing clogs up from time to time, eat rye bread. University of Finland researchers found that whole grain rye bread beat laxatives — thanks to a unique fiber — for gently moving food through your intestines. Rye even beat wheat for constipation relief. So the next time you feel the need to go but can't, reach for some whole grain rye bread.

Summer treat soothes sore muscles. Five thousand years ago, ancient Egyptians placed watermelons in their kings' burial tombs to nourish them in their afterlives. Thankfully, you can reap the benefits of watermelon today. A study published in the *Journal of Agricultural and Food Chemistry* found that watermelon juice calms sore muscles after exercise. Watermelon is rich in L-citrulline, an amino acid that ultimately relaxes blood vessels and improves circulation.

While experts agree that more research is needed, you can do your own experiment at home. If you exercise regularly or plan on doing strenuous work around the house over several days, try this — drink a glass of watermelon juice before your workout one day. Go without it the next day, and compare the results. If the juice makes your muscles feel better, keep chugging it before each workout.

Ease leg cramps in a pinch

The next time you wake up with cramps in your legs or feet, pinch your upper lip just below your nose. Hold for 20 to 30 seconds. This "acupinch" technique, used widely in sports medicine, may reduce the pain and duration of muscle cramps.

"Tea" it up to save your heart. Tea, enjoyed around the world for centuries, can do wonders for your heart and arteries.

Loaded with flavonoids, especially compounds called catechins, tea dilates arteries, easing the inflammation associated with atherosclerosis, thereby improving blood flow. It may also make your blood less sticky, lowering your chance of plaque buildup that can lead to heart attack and stroke.

Store green tea in a dark, airtight container, and keep the container in a cool, dry place. Use it within a month or two to get the best health benefits. Because boiling water destroys some of the antioxidants in tea, you should steep it in water that is hot, but not boiling, for about three minutes.

Powerful herb kills germs and fights heart disease. It's been valued for thousands of years for its healing powers as well as its flavor. And now, modern science gives garlic a resounding stamp of approval. Not only can it act as a powerful antibiotic in your body, killing a variety of bacteria and viruses, but specific compounds in garlic keep your arteries soft and flexible, and thin your blood so it doesn't clump. All this means a lower risk of heart attack or stroke. Buy firm bulbs of garlic with white, papery skin, and store them in a cool, dry place. Then add at least one crushed clove to your daily menu.

Put the brakes on arthritis with broccoli. You know eating your greens is good for you. But eating a specific green — broccoli — may help prevent or slow the progression of osteoarthritis. A recent study shows that sulforaphane, a compound found in broccoli, slows the destruction of joint cartilage. It actually blocks the enzyme that causes joints to deteriorate. Sulforaphane is released when you chow down on cruciferous veggies such as Brussels sprouts, cabbage — but most importantly, broccoli.

For a sulforaphane boost, shop for "super broccoli," a specially grown crop with two to three times the amount of glucoraphanin, a compound needed to produce sulforaphane. Look for super broccoli — sold under the name Beneforté — in regional supermarkets such as Ingles, ShopRite, Whole Foods, and Harris Teeter.

Wash away achy joints with wintergreen oil. Nothing feels better than a hot bath to soothe the aches and pains of arthritis. For additional relief, try mixing in one to two drops of the essential oil wintergreen. The wintergreen herb packs a powerful, pain-relieving punch. It contains a chemical similar to aspirin that may help reduce pain and swelling. If you take aspirin regularly or are allergic to salicylates, consult your doctor before using wintergreen oil.

De-stress with magic minerals. As strange as it may sound, eating crab may make you feel less crabby. In one study, participants under physical and mental stress experienced a drop in zinc, iron, and selenium levels. If you are under stress, eat foods high in these minerals — like crabmeat, beans, yogurt, steak, clams, and oysters. And don't forget that poor eating habits during stressful times can weaken your immune system. This makes you more susceptible to illness and can magnify the effects of stress. By choosing nutritious foods, you'll give your body the ammunition it needs to fight off the damaging effects of stress — and that may be enough to help you feel better.

Appealing way to defeat stress. When life hands you lemons, don't just make lemonade. Simmer a lemony stress buster on your stovetop. Scientists say lemons can help fight stress because they contain a powerful compound called linalool. In fact, simply inhaling linalool can reduce the wear and tear of stress.

To put this science to work for you, save the peels whenever you use lemons. When you're ready for some stress relief, throw the peels in a small pot on your stove and cover them with water. Allow the mixture to simmer for several hours on the lowest setting. Add water as needed.

Over time, the lemon scent will spread throughout your kitchen and beyond. When you breathe in that fresh scent, you reap the benefits of stress-fighting linalool. Try this same trick with basil, lavender, or marjoram. They contain linalool, too. Use fresh cuttings from your garden or wilting sprigs from the supermarket. You'll love the relaxing results.

Quell queasiness without drugs

Motion sickness is miserable. But a little acupressure may go a long way toward relieving it. Find a spot on the inside of your forearm, about 2 inches from the crease of your wrist. You should feel two tendons. Press firmly between the two tendons for five to 30 seconds. Repeat until the nausea subsides.

Sweet relief for a burned tongue. You sip on a cappuccino when — Ouch! — you burn your tongue. Don't you hate that? Thankfully, relief is within spitting distance. Reach for a packet of sugar, and sprinkle it on your tongue. The sugar crystals will quickly dissolve, drawing heat from your tongue and numbing the pain.

Drink this to squelch garlic breath. You love the taste of garlic, but hate the bad breath it leaves behind. No problem. Wash away the smell with a glass of milk. In a study published in the *Journal of Food Science*, researchers found that drinking a glass of milk before and during a garlicky meal keeps stinky breath at bay. You can thank the proteins in milk — they mask garlic's unpleasant odor. So go ahead, enjoy your favorite garlic-laced dish, but do so with a glass of milk on the side.

New way to treat a burn. If you think running cold water on a burn is the best way to heal it, think again. A study published in the *Journal of Plastic, Reconstructive & Aesthetic Surgery* suggests otherwise. Experts found that warm water improved circulation and decreased tissue damage. While cold water may zap the initial pain, warm water restores skin in the long run. Consider following one researcher's remedy. Apply cold water first for about a minute. Then, to restore blood flow, use warm water.

Cool a fever blister with aloe. There's nothing cool about fever blisters. They're painful, unsightly, and highly contagious. Caused by the *herpes simplex* virus, the fluid-filled lesions — also known as cold sores — usually erupt outside of the mouth on your lips, chin, and cheeks. Blisters tend to merge then burst, leaving an open sore that crusts over. While there's no cure for the virus, there's no need to suffer the agony of an outbreak. Keep aloe vera gel in your refrigerator for instant relief. With a cotton swab, dab the gel on to the cold sore several times a day. The coolness will provide comfort, and the aloe's polysaccharides will speed up healing.

Dynamic duo calms a canker sore. Canker sores — those pesky little craters that crop up on your tongue or the inside of your cheeks — can cause incredible pain and discomfort. Stress, rough tooth brushing, and acidic foods like oranges or tomatoes are often to blame.

Usually, a canker sore will go away on its own within five to 10 days. But in the meantime, here's a cocktail to help you handle the soreness. Mix a liquid antacid, like Milk of Magnesia, with a liquid antihistamine, like Benadryl. Swirl the solution in your mouth and spit it out. These super heroes will neutralize the acid and numb your pain.

You could also try a rinse with water and baking soda or salt. The salt may sting a little, but it will speed up the healing process. As for over-the-counter mouthwashes, steer clear of them. The chemicals may further irritate a sore.

Simple recipes for younger-looking skin. Start your day with an energizing facial scrub packed with vitamin C — a potent antioxidant used in skin care products to treat the signs of aging. Combine a tablespoon of dried citrus peel — lime, lemon, orange, or grapefruit — with a 1/2 cup plain yogurt and 1 teaspoon raw honey. Blend the ingredients until smooth.

Or try this sugar scrub for a fresh, youthful glow. Combine 1/2 cup dark brown sugar and 3 tablespoons olive oil or raw honey. Add a yummy scent with 1/2 teaspoon nutmeg, cinnamon, or pumpkin pie spices. Mix the ingredients until they form a paste.

Dampen your face, apply your favorite scrub — massaging gently for one to two minutes, rinse with warm water, and pat dry. Place any leftover scrub in your refrigerator for up to a week.

When your face is dragging. If you wake up with puffy bags under your eyes, just brew yourself a pot of tea. If you make it chamomile and wear it instead of drink it, you'll be on your way to smoother skin. How? Chamomile is a naturally soothing herb that temporarily decreases puffiness. Just ice the tea, soak a couple of gauze pads, and place them over your eyes. Bye-bye bags!

Smooth as a baby's bottom. If you're looking for cheap makeup removers, you'll find them right next to the diapers. How about baby wipes? They're loaded with soothing ingredients that will take off your makeup in a flash.

Go bananas to fix dry hair. Sick of monkeying around with dry hair? Mash a banana with a teaspoon of almond oil, and rub the mixture into your hair. Leave it there for 20 minutes, then rinse.

Cleanse your hair with baking soda. Your hair has become a gathering place for old hair spray, gel, and other residue. Strip away the film in your hair with baking soda. Just blend a little baking soda with your regular shampoo. You can also try mixing baking soda with water and massaging it into your hair before you shampoo. Just be careful not to get any baking soda in your eyes.

Revive your hair with beer

Your limp hair could use a lift, but who wants to spend money on expensive hair products? Flat beer strips away soapy film and brings new life and bounce to your hair. Just mix three tablespoons of flat beer in half a cup of warm water and pour it over your head during your shower. Finish your shower and rinse. The beer gets rid of the residue from commercial hair products that can leave your hair feeling heavy and lifeless.

Shine your hair. Put an apple-fresh shine in your hair with an apple cider vinegar rinse. Mix a half cup of apple cider vinegar with two cups of warm water, and pour over your freshly washed hair.

Rock and roll for relief. For cheap and effective relief of heel spurs, place your bare foot on an empty glass soft drink bottle and roll your foot back and forth. Before you begin, make sure the bottle doesn't have any chips or cracks that could cut you. Some people find a frozen can of fruit juice works even better because it offers the doubly helpful combination of cold therapy and stretching.

Tackle athlete's foot. The itch of athlete's foot can drive you crazy. You can cut down on this by soaking socks in a solution of one cup vinegar and four cups of water, then washing them as usual. Soaking your feet in full-strength apple cider vinegar may also help relieve the itching.

Never forget to take your pills again. If a regular pill organizer doesn't help you remember to take your medicine, try these ideas.

- Ask your doctor if you can take a time-released pill, so you won't have to take your medication as often.
- Link your pill taking with another activity you do regularly. For example, you might decide to take your pill after picking up the newspaper each day.
- Set your watch alarm, clock alarm, or cell phone alarm to remind you. If you need an extra alarm, consider buying an inexpensive travel alarm clock.
- Switch to a pill organizer that comes with an alarm.
- See if the manufacturer of the drug you are taking offers a reminder program. Ask your pharmacist for the manufacturer's name and check that company's website for information.

Stop wondering if you took your pill. You can't remember if you took your medication, but skipping a pill or taking one too many can be dangerous.

To prevent this problem, create a chart like the one below. Include the name of the medicine, the color of the pill, directions for taking it, and spaces for each day. In each day slot, write the times you plan to take each pill. When that time rolls around, take your pill and mark through the time on your chart. Here's how your chart might look at 2 p.m. on Monday.

Drug and directions	Sun.	Mon.	Tues.	Wed.	Thurs.	Fri.	Sat.
drug #1 (red pill) 4 times daily with food	~~9 a.m.~~ ~~1 p.m.~~ ~~5 p.m.~~ ~~9 p.m.~~	~~9 a.m.~~ ~~1 p.m.~~ 5 p.m. 9 p.m.	9 a.m. 1 p.m. 5 p.m. 9 p.m.	9 a.m. 1 p.m. 5 p.m. 9 p.m.	9 a.m. 1 p.m. 5 p.m. 9 p.m.	9 a.m. 1 p.m. 5 p.m. 9 p.m.	9 a.m. 1 p.m. 5 p.m. 9 p.m.
drug #2 (pink pill) 3 times daily	~~8 a.m.~~ ~~3 p.m.~~ ~~8 p.m.~~	~~8 a.m.~~ 3 p.m. 8 p.m.	8 a.m. 3 p.m. 8 p.m.	8 a.m. 3 p.m. 8 p.m.	8 a.m. 3 p.m. 8 p.m.	8 a.m. 3 p.m. 8 p.m.	8 a.m. 3 p.m. 8 p.m.
drug #3 (blue pill) before bed	~~9 p.m.~~	9 p.m.	9 p.m.	9 p.m.	9 p.m.	9 p.m.	9 p.m.

Make a large capacity pill organizer for pennies. You might think you take far too many pills to fit into an inexpensive pill organizer. But no matter how many pills you take, you can make a pill organizer that matches your pill regimen exactly. All you need are self-stick labels and two sizes of resealable bags.

Buy one package of resealable bags labeled as "snack size" and another labeled as sandwich bags or pint-size. If you later decide snack-size isn't small enough, check office supply stores or craft shops for tinier bags.

Label each of the sandwich or pint-size bags with a day of the week. Next, write down your pill schedule on paper. For example, you may take nine pills at 8 a.m., six at noon, and five at 7 p.m. Label one snack-size bag for each clock time you expect to take a pill and then fill each bag with the appropriate medications.

Drop this first set of bags into one of your day-of-the-week bags. Then fill all the other day-of-the-week bags the same way. Each morning, pick up your bag for that day and slip it in your pocket or purse so your pills can go wherever you do. Just remember to remove the bag at night and refill your convenient pill organizers every week.

Poultices from your pantry. Feeling the sting of an angry bee? For instant relief, mash some fresh papaya and apply it to the site of the sting. If you don't have any papaya handy, a paste of meat tenderizer and water will offer similar relief. If you don't have any meat tenderizer either, it's probably a good bet you do have baking soda. A paste of baking soda and water will also soothe stings. All of the above will also reduce swelling and relieve pain and itching.

Give bugs the spray. If you don't have bug spray handy when a pest starts buzzing around your head, use hair spray. It will make the bug's wings stiff and sticky. He'll drop like a stone and then you can swat him.

Take the sting out of bug bites

Bees and skeeters can't help it. They love to bite and sting human prey. Often, despite your best efforts, you can't keep them away. To alleviate the pain and swelling from a bite, dab on a little toothpaste. Toothpaste contains glycerin, which dries out the venom in the affected area. Or apply a gauze pad soaked in witch hazel. It will relieve the sting and swelling of any bite.

Smell swell to repel bugs. Sometimes avoiding bug bites is a matter of common "scents." Apply some lavender oil, just like you would perfume. People will think you smell great, but insects won't agree — and they'll leave you alone.

A mitey allergy aid. Do you or someone in your family suffer from asthma or allergies? If so, you know how miserable dust mite droppings in clothing and bedding can make you feel. You can get rid of both the droppings and the dust mites by adding eucalyptus oil to your wash. The *Journal of Allergy and Clinical Immunology* reported that this "recipe" can kill up to

95 percent of dust mites: 1 part detergent 3 to 5 parts eucalyptus oil Make sure the detergent dissolves in the oil. If not switch detergents. Add this mixture to the washer after it's filled with water. Put in the items to be washed and soak 30 minutes to an hour. Wash normally.

Rx for scratched glasses. Seeing the world through rose-colored glasses might be fun, but looking through scratched glasses is anything but. If your plastic lenses are scratched, make them like new again with Pledge furniture polish. Just spray the furniture polish on both sides of the lenses, gently rub it in, and wipe with a soft cloth.

Get more mileage out of your toothbrush. Would you like a clean, fresh toothbrush without buying a new one? How about throwing your old one in the dishwasher? It might sound strange, but the high heat and detergent that kills bacteria on your dishes can do wonders for personal hygiene items. So while you're at it, throw in your nail brushes, loofahs, or other sponges and give them all a new lease on life.

Insurance essentials

Find the best deal on homeowners insurance. Your home is your castle, but without a drawbridge and moat, you need protection from homeowners insurance. Here are some tips for saving money on this essential insurance.

- Shop around. Spend some time searching, and you should find a good deal. Ask friends, consult consumer guides, call insurance agents, or look online to compare prices and service. The National Association of Insurance Commissioners provides helpful information at *www.naic.org*. Narrow your choices down to three and get price quotes.

- Consider complaints. Don't just look at price. Check each company's complaint records. A lower premium isn't worth much if you have to fight for each claim.

- Stay loyal. If you've kept your coverage with a company for several years, you may receive a special discount for being a long-term policyholder. You may save as much as 10 percent on your premium.

- Ask about other discounts. You may pay lower premiums if your home has safety features, like dead-bolt locks, smoke detectors, an alarm system, storm shutters, or fire-retardant roofing material. If you're at least 55 and retired, you may also qualify for a discount.

Insure your home for the right amount. Surveys suggest up to 61 percent of homeowners don't have enough insurance to rebuild their homes after a disaster. This may happen to you if your insurer based your policy amount on the real estate value of your home. Unfortunately, the price tag for rebuilding your home could be much higher than the price it would sell for today.

To fix this problem, tell your insurance agent you want the structural limit of your home insurance policy to be based on a rebuild estimate for your home rather than its market value. Your insurer can provide that rebuild estimate. Some experts recommend you also check with local contractors to verify what it would cost to rebuild a home like yours. Recent disasters have revealed that insurer estimates of replacement costs are sometimes too low. You can also get estimates for a reasonable price from a website like *www.hmfacts.com/homeowners/*.

Alert your home insurer after a car break-in. Your car insurance doesn't cover the loss of items like newly bought clothes if they're stolen during a car break-in, but your homeowners insurance does. Surprisingly, home insurance covers some items that aren't inside your home, including personal possessions in your car. Most people are covered for losses equal to as much as 10 percent of their total personal property coverage. So if your coverage is $100,000, up to $10,000 in stolen possessions may be covered, but check with your insurance agent to be sure. To file a claim for the stolen property, you'll have to meet a deductible and file a police report. Meanwhile, call your car insurance agent as well. If you have comprehensive coverage, that covers damage to your vehicle from the break-in.

Best ways to file claims

Need advice about filing an insurance claim? United Policyholders, a nonprofit organization dedicated to educating the public on insurance issues and consumer rights, can help. Just go to *www.unitedpolicyholders.org* and click on "Claim Tips." Then read about the best ways to file claims for property damage — including fire, flood, earthquake, or mold — as well as tips for auto, health, long-term care, disability, and other types of insurance.

Make renters insurance an even better value. If a fire rages through the apartment or home you're renting, the landlord's policy won't cover your personal belongings, but you can insure them with renters insurance for just pennies a day. What's more, those pennies really work hard for you. They can insure $20,000 to $30,000 worth of your stuff against damage from burst pipes, fire, lightning, windstorms, hail, theft, or vandalism. That's why experts recommend renters insurance as a good value.

But if disaster happens, the only way to replace what you've lost is to provide your insurer with a detailed list of every item and its replacement cost. Try naming all the items in your kitchen from memory, and you'll see how this could be a problem. So before a disaster happens, make a home inventory video showing every item in your apartment or rental house. While making the video, describe each item, and estimate how much it cost. When you finish, store a copy of the video with a friend or family member, or upload it to a cloud storage site like Google Drive or Dropbox.

"Standard" insurance you don't really need. Reliable insurance coverage is a godsend when you need it, but there are some policies you'll probably never use. Here are eight insurance plans experts say you don't need.

- Life insurance if you're single. Life insurance provides money to live on if the breadwinner dies. If you have no dependents, your death won't create a financial hardship. The same is true if both spouses have ample individual income or an adequate retirement plan. Here's a rule of thumb — if your income won't be needed, don't buy life insurance.

- Air travel insurance. If you die suddenly, it doesn't matter if it's from an airplane crash or a heart attack. Your family will still need financial support, so get regular life insurance with full coverage. Besides, most credit cards offer free coverage if you charge the tickets.

- Mortgage-life insurance. These policies protect your lender if you die, since proceeds can only be used to pay off your loan. A better — and cheaper — choice is straight term insurance, which can be used for anything.

- Private mortgage insurance. PMI is a special case because you usually have to get it when you buy a home with less than a 20-percent down payment. The cost of PMI simply becomes part of your loan payment. However, once you owe less than 80 percent of the value of your home, you can, and should, ask to cancel it.

- Credit-life insurance. These are policies attached to bank and credit card loans. They pay off your loan if you die, or make your payment if you are sick, hurt, or out of work. It is very expensive insurance and sometimes you don't even know you're getting it. Buy term life insurance instead and forget about disability or unemployment policies because their payouts are so low.

- Life insurance on children. The death of a child is an emotional catastrophe, not an economic one. When no one depends on them financially, life insurance is little consolation.

- Cancer insurance. Unless you're pretty sure you're going to get hit by a particular disease, spend your money on more comprehensive health coverage. In any case, read the fine print closely. Many of these, and other one-disease policies, are cheap because they don't cover a lot.

- Rental car insurance. This really isn't even insurance. Rental car companies call it a "collision damage waiver." It's very expensive, and your own car insurance or your credit card company probably covers you. Check to be sure, especially if you'll be renting a car in a foreign country.

Choose a cheap add-on that can really pay off. You've just been injured in a car accident by a driver with no insurance. You could be stuck for major medical bills unless you have a special type of coverage on your own policy. Uninsured motorist coverage is one of the cheapest kinds of car insurance you can buy, and it could save you a bundle in the long run, experts say.

One out of every seven drivers on the road has no car insurance, and this coverage will pay the medical costs if one of them injures you or your passengers. It may also pay if you're the victim of an underinsured driver who doesn't have enough insurance to fully cover the medical costs. Experts recommend you buy uninsured motorist coverage if you don't already have it. Talk to your auto insurance agent to learn more.

Can driver monitoring save you money? Yes, say some insurers. You may save up to 50 percent on your car insurance if you install a "black box" device in your car that records your driving habits. But actual savings vary depending on what your insurance company measures, the kind of driver you are, and several other factors. That's why it pays to ask questions and learn as much as you can about your insurer's program. Here's where to start.

When you sign up for one of these programs, you agree to provide information on your driving habits to your insurance company so they can evaluate your driving. Whether you get the discount and how deep it is depends on how well you meet your insurer's definition of a low-risk driver.

Some programs mostly look at how many miles you drive, while others may also record your speed, the times of day you drive, where you drive, how hard you accelerate or brake, and how you take corners. Of course, you can't win the discount game if you don't know the rules your particular insurer uses, so ask questions like these before you sign up.

- What does the device record besides mileage?
- What driving habits help me get a bigger discount?

- What driving habits would lower or prevent my discount?
- If my spouse or someone else drives my car, how does that affect my discount?
- Can I lose any of my other discounts due to information the device provides?

Be ready if the unthinkable happens

You can't think straight right after a car accident. That's why you should have expert help on hand to help you report the accident for your insurance claim. Ask your insurance agent for an accident form to keep in your car and fill out at the scene of the accident. If your insurer does not provide a form, visit *www.dmv.org/insurance/post-accident-checklist.php* for a form you can print out.

If you have a smartphone or iPad, apps are available to help you through the reporting process. For example, USAA offers an app for the iPad, and Nationwide has one for your Android phone or iPhone. Check with your insurance company to find out whether they offer their own app for accident reporting.

Win a fair payout for your totaled car. Your car may have been declared a total loss, but you can still take steps to avoid a low payout check. Confirm the exact make and model of your car, its age, and its mileage. Visit the library or the web to check sources like Edmunds (*www.edmunds.com*), the Kelley Blue Book (*www.kbb.com*), and the National Auto Dealers Association (*www.nadaguides.com*) for estimates of the market value of your car just before the wreck. Print or make a copy of your findings, and average the figures from all three sources. If you have the receipts, add the price of any customizations or extras installed after you bought the car — including the dealer-installed ones.

Because you'll have to pay the sales tax, registration, title and other fees for a new car, insurance allows you to add those figures to your payout. So call your state's department of motor vehicles or visit its website to learn what fees and taxes you'll pay for a new car with the same value as your old car. Add that to your car's value and subtract your deductible to get your final payout number. If the amount your insurance agent offers is significantly lower, show her your findings and calculations, and campaign for an estimate closer to yours. She may agree to cut you a bigger check.

Nab the best long-term care. If you need to spend time in a nursing home or assisted living facility, you'll need help paying for it. Just one year in a nursing home can easily cost more than $50,000. Don't get caught off guard.

You may be surprised to find out that Medicare doesn't cover long-term care, including help with activities of daily living like dressing, bathing, or using the bathroom. That's where long-term care insurance comes in. When considering long-term care plans, America's Health Insurance Plans — an association of nearly 1,300 insurers — says to keep these questions in mind.

- What services will be covered? Options include nursing home care, home health care, assisted living facility, adult daycare, alternate care, and respite care.

- How much does the policy pay per day for the above services?

- Does the policy have a maximum lifetime benefit? If so, what is it for each type of long-term care?

- Does the policy have a cap on length of coverage for each period of confinement?

- What is the waiting period before a pre-existing condition is covered?

- How many days must you wait before your benefits are available?

- Does the policy require assessments of daily living activities or cognitive impairments? Is a doctor's certification of need required? Does the policy require a hospital stay before coverage is allowed?

- Is the policy guaranteed renewable?

- Does it offer inflation adjustment?

Of course, you should also ask how much the policy costs. Prices vary and depend on your age, the level of benefits, and how long you are willing to wait until benefits begin. Most policies also come with a 30-day "free look" period. If it does not meet your needs, you can return the policy and get your money back during that time.

Lawn and garden smarts

7 bargains and freebies for gardeners. You could spend loads of money on planters, plants, and garden supplies, but you'll probably like these bargains and freebies better.

- Ask your county extension agent how late you can plant spring bulbs so they still bloom this coming spring. If the right time is after the New Year, buy during spring bulb closeout sales when you could get up to 75 percent off.
- Don't buy garden tools or equipment if you only need them a few times each year. Instead, borrow or trade tools with other gardeners. For larger, rarely used items, renting may be cheaper than buying.
- Check local dairies, horse farms, and other farms for free manure.
- Don't buy fresh annuals every year. If you live in the southern half of the country and your annuals don't reseed, dig them up, pot them, and keep them in your garage until replanting time. Get advice on overwintering annuals from your local county extension agent.
- Don't spend loads of money on a composter. Make a compost pile in your backyard instead. If pests or other

problems make a composter necessary, check with your local trash company. They may sell quality composters at far more reasonable prices than your garden supplier.

- Organize a plant swap to trade plants you don't need for new plants you want. Seed swaps can work equally well.
- Shop flea markets and yard sales for plants and garden supplies. Also, try the bargain bins at home improvement stores. Just be sure to check the health or quality of the product carefully before you buy.

And don't forget reusables. "Items like older pots, colanders, or pitchers that you no longer use in the kitchen can easily be planted up to find new life as whimsical, inexpensive planters," says Colleen Vanderlinden, freelance writer and creator of *www.inthegardenonline.com*.

Spend less for quality trees and shrubs. Get the best deal possible if you're buying from the plant nursery. Bypass that tree in the 10-gallon container and buy the smallest size available instead. Not only will you get a dramatic discount, but your tiny tree will probably be the same size as the 10-gallon version in just a few years.

That may sound unlikely but consider this. Because a 10-gallon tree is container-bound for several years, it can't grow as rapidly as a younger tree planted where roots can spread out. So buy small when shopping for trees, shrubs, and perennials. Your new plant may become just as big and impressive as its older brothers in a few years, but you'll save big today.

Free plants for your garden. There's no need to make a big investment in plants if you're just getting started in gardening. Here are some sources to consider when looking for something to grow. Be flexible, and see what's offered.

- Online. Check out the "free" section and the "farm and garden" sections of Craigslist. And go to *www.freecycle.org* — type in your general location and browse through the free offers for trees and plants.

- Landscaping crews. They often toss perfectly good plants when they change displays or redesign someone's yard. Ask nicely, and you may be able to adopt some.

- Garden club. Consider joining a local or online gardening club, which may host plant swaps among members. Or ask a neighbor about a trade.

- Membership. If you want trees, consider joining the National Arbor Day Foundation for just $10. You'll get 10 trees in return, along with access to advice and a support network for your tree-growing adventures.

- Nursery. If you're at a nursery buying and asking for advice, don't forget to ask if they have any plants they're throwing away. You may get some that need a little extra care, but when the price is right, a little added effort is worth it.

- Volunteers. Be on the lookout for volunteers — plants that come up unexpectedly — and make the most of these happy accidents.

Guide to gardening through the seasons. Knowing what to do and when to do it is the key to a beautiful lawn and garden.

Spring

- Prepare beds and borders for new plants by mixing in 1 to 3 inches of compost.
- Put fresh mulch in flower beds and around shrubs and trees.
- Lightly fertilize lawn. Aerate, dethatch, and overseed if needed.
- Apply a pre-emergent herbicide to kill crabgrass and other lawn weeds.
- Plant your summer-flowering bulbs and perennials.
- Divide perennials that have grown too large.
- Prune spring-flowering shrubs and climbers that have already bloomed.
- Prune rose bushes, butterfly bushes, and deciduous shrubs and climbers that flower in late summer.
- Fertilize established shrubs, including roses.
- Plant evergreen trees and shrubs.
- Prune away dead, broken, or diseased branches. These become easier to spot as plants leaf out in spring.

Summer

- Rebuild your compost pile, and water it to keep it moist.
- Mow the lawn regularly, but let grass grow a little taller during the hottest months.
- Mulch any garden beds you missed in spring with grass clippings or compost to keep weeds down and water from evaporating.
- Water lawns when nature doesn't provide enough rain. Grass needs 1 inch of water per week, rain and sprinklers combined.
- Water new trees and shrubs each week, with enough water to reach 1 foot deep.
- Prune the last of spring-flowering shrubs and climbers.
- Trim fast-growing hedges after their spring flush of growth. Wait until late summer to trim evergreen and conifer hedges.
- Divide cluttered clumps of irises and primroses after flowering.
- Deadhead flowers.
- Prune herbaceous plants and rambling roses once they bloom. You may get a second round of blossoms.
- Plant daffodil bulbs in late summer.

- Prune back fruiting shrubs.
- Prepare cold frames for fall vegetables.

Fall

- Rake leaves off the lawn, and add them to the compost pile.
- Add a layer of leaves over beds to crowd out weeds and feed the soil.
- Plant (or transplant) trees, shrubs, and certain perennials to give them a head start come spring. If they are deciduous, wait until after their leaves have fallen.
- Prune the roots of any shrubs and trees you hope to transplant in spring.
- Cut back flowering perennials, including rose bushes, to prepare them for winter.
- Divide cluttered clumps of hardy perennials, and replant them.
- Turn off and drain outdoor water lines and sprinkler systems.
- Store hoses and sprinklers for the winter.
- Clean up overgrowth in your yard, and add it to your compost pile.

- Fertilize the lawn again, and top-dress with a layer of compost. Overseed thin spots.
- Get spring-flowering bulbs like tulips into the ground.
- Dig up and store cannas, dahlias, and gladiolus after the first frost, in cold climates.
- Remove rotten fruit from the ground around fruit trees to discourage disease.
- Apply compost to vegetable beds.

Winter

- Begin planning next year's garden and landscape. Pre-order plants and seeds.
- Check your stored bulbs, and toss out any that are soft with rot.
- Prune woody shrubs and trees, especially fruit trees, while they are dormant. But don't prune plum and cherry trees.
- Plant bare-root roses.
- Apply a light scattering of nitrogen fertilizer to green winter lawns.
- Knock snow off tree limbs and hedges to guard against broken branches.
- Coppice shrubs in late winter, if you like the unique look.

- Keep adding kitchen scraps and leaves to your compost pile.

Make a garden kneeler for pennies

Buy a slab of 3-inch foam and wrap it in thick plastic bags. Some of the thinner discount store bags won't hold up well, so stick with department store bags or outdoor garbage bags. Consider putting one inside the other for added durability. When you're done, use duct tape to secure the bags snugly around the foam.

Keep cut flowers fresher longer. Your cut flowers can look lovelier and last longer with these secrets.

- Snip most flower varieties in late afternoon or early evening. Not only will each flower be thoroughly supplied with water and food when you cut it, but you'll also get a longer-lasting display. Cut roses and irises while they're still buds.

- Don't cut with scissors. They crush the stem and cripple the flower's ability to drink. Use a very sharp knife, pruning shears, or florists' shears instead.

- Make a slanted cut. A flat cut rests against the bottom of the vase so the stem can't easily take in water.

- To help flowers retain their beauty and freshness, mix one cup of regular lemon-lime soda with three cups of very warm water and one-quarter teaspoon of bleach. Add one-quarter teaspoon of bleach every five days. For a simpler solution, mix one-quarter cup of Listerine mouthwash with a gallon of very warm water.

Seed starting for tightwads. You can make most seed-starting kits cheap or free. Here's how to create a seed-starting station that provides warmth, light, humidity, and the best odds of success.

- Don't waste your money on plastic pots. Instead, poke holes in the bottom of cleaned out avocado skins or eggshells. Now you have free "pots" for your seeds.

- Seeds thrive on humidity, so place your "pots" inside clamshell plastic containers. Once closed, these containers keep humidity inside. You get these containers any time you order take-out food. Just save them and rinse them out.

- The inside of your refrigerator may be very cold, but the top is nice and warm. Set up your seed starters there.

- Seeds demand light, so place fluorescent lamps above them.

Dig up ideal seed keepers that cost nothing. An empty, plastic pill bottle from your last prescription is an ideal place to store seeds. Unlike seed envelopes, the bottles keep your seeds visible and in one place if the container tips over. They'll also keep your seeds dry and protected. So when you're done using a pill bottle, just clean it out, let it dry, and drop your seeds in. You can even label the bottle. If you don't have enough pill bottles, ask friends and family members to pass along their empty bottles when they no longer need them.

Become a bulb expert. The next time you shop for spring or summer bulbs, keep these tips in mind.

- Make sure the retailer has them displayed in a somewhat of a cool, dry place. If they've been exposed to sun or moisture, they will start to rot.

- Look for bulbs that are firm, never mushy.

- Larger bulbs may cost more, but consider the benefits. You're going to get more plants out of the bigger bulbs. The little bulbs are fine for value. Just buy more of them, and you might get a better deal.

- Make sure spring bulbs have lots of paper-like skin on the outside. And, instead of buying bagged bulbs, look for single bulbs packed in Styrofoam or shredded straw. You get a better quality bulb when you can hand select.

Be careful after buying bulbs, too. Plant them at the right time and the right depth. People make a lot of mistakes because the bulbs become available much too early to plant. Plan on planting spring bulbs by September and October if you live in the colder areas like the Northeast, but wait until November or December if you live farther south. Cold-area gardeners should plant summer-flowering bulbs in late May or June, while Southern growers can plant their bulbs in April.

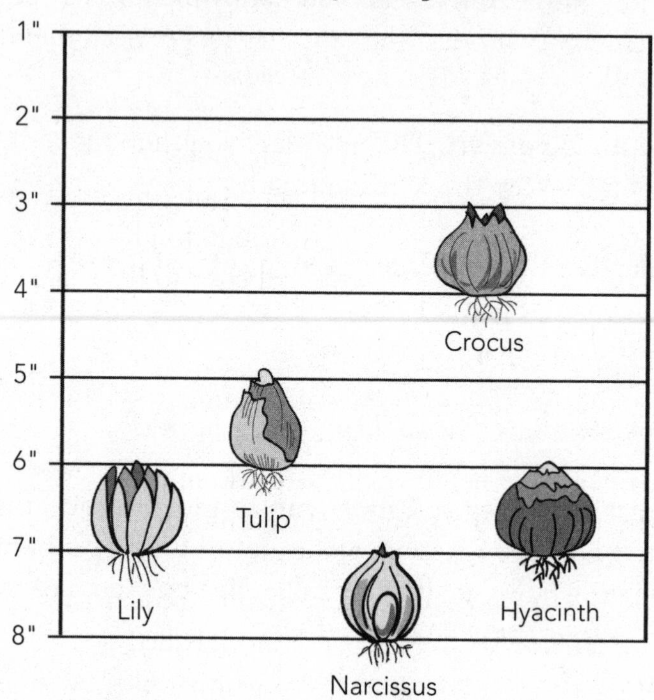

Pick the right tree every time. Buy the wrong tree and you could waste a lot of money on a plant that can't survive. To bark up the right tree, remember this expert advice.

- Decide whether you want quick shade or a slower grower. Fast growth always provides a fast shade, but at the same time, it provides a very brittle tree that is easily blown over or breaks in strong winds and ice. Slow-growers are more likely to survive bad weather.

- Figure out how much sun and shade your tree will get. Do a little research to determine which tree varieties grow well in that light and then eliminate the ones that grow too fast or too slowly for your needs.

- If you're planting the tree yourself, choose a tree with a trunk diameter — called a caliper — of 2 inches or less. Trees with larger calipers can be tough to plant on your own. You may need a professional crew to help you dig the hole and get it in.

- Only choose trees with a straight trunk.

- Bypass trees with scars, exposed bark, or peeled bark. These are signs of damage during unloading.

- Avoid any container tree that has very loose dirt or looks as if it fell out of its container. Check balled and burlapped trees closely, too. Make sure it has a nice size ball. It shouldn't be square or odd-shaped, and the ball must be firm. If the ball is loose, that means it was dropped and soil has moved away from the roots, and the tree probably won't live.

Avoid pruning mistakes that disfigure trees. Don't make the unkindest cut of all. Prune your trees skillfully so you won't lose the extra branches — or the whole tree — to disease. Before you cut, find the node, the place where one branch or twig connects to another. Cut near the node, but don't cut too closely or peel bark off the tree.

These mistakes — called bark-ripping, flush-cutting, and stub cutting — can leave the tree open to damage, disease, and dead branches. But if you prune correctly, the neatly pruned branches make great stakes for flowers and vegetables. Not only do they provide a charming, natural look, they also help you spend less money on stakes.

Bark ripping

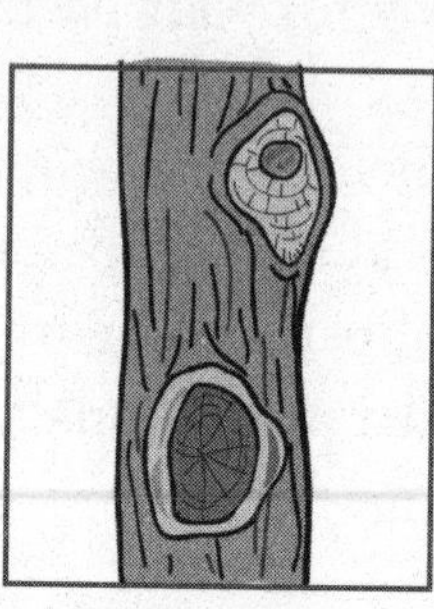

Flush cutting

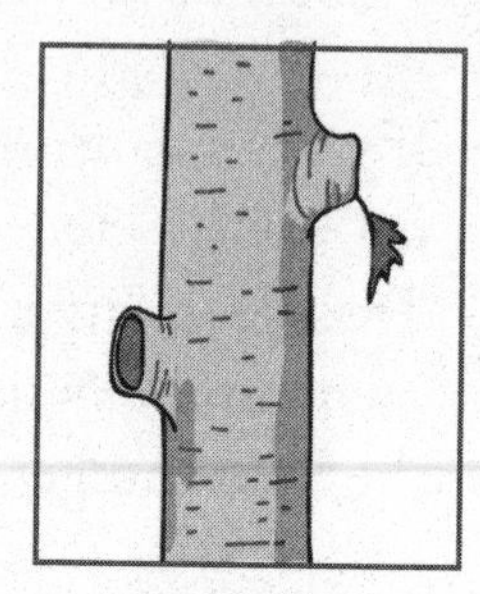

Stub cutting

Make an ugly tree stump fade away

Get rid of an unsightly tree stump without digging it up. This no-fuss method works wonders and saves you a boatload of cash.

Drill large holes deep into the stump, especially near the edges. Fill them with sugar and soak the stump and its holes thoroughly with the hose. Cover with a foot of mulch and wait. Your tree stump will simply decay away. Or drill a few holes in the center of the stump and dump your leftover coals from the barbecue grill after every cookout. You'll burn the stump away from the inside out.

Rev up your roses with a secret ingredient. Brew up your own "liquid gold" for your roses. Here's how. Shop for alfalfa pellets or alfalfa meal. You'll need at least one-third cup of alfalfa for each rosebush, so be sure to buy enough. Pour the alfalfa into a container and add one gallon of water for each bush you'll feed. Let this alfalfa tea brew several days before using it to water your roses. Repeat this process once every three or four months. If you don't have time for tea, push a handful of alfalfa pellets into the soil around your rosebushes instead. Roses will devour it and reward you with luscious blooms.

Get the most blooms from your rosebushes

Before you snip that gorgeous rose, be sure to cut at the right spot. Otherwise, your plant will produce tiny, weak stems that won't hold up your stunning rose. When you're pruning or clipping, cut back to a stem with at least five leaves. Your rosebush will thank you by putting out a stronger stem that can support the weight of more rose blossoms.

Simple steps for safer transplanting. These two key steps will help you keep your perennials happy when moving them to a new location.

- Before — water plants the night before a move. It gives them a boost and helps keep stress away.

- After — keep plants shaded for a few days to let them recover. This is especially important for older perennials or in hot weather.

Successful mulching — the inside scoop. Mulch nurtures the soil, helps it retain moisture, and controls weeds. But be sure the time is right before you spread it. In springtime, give the sun some time to warm the ground before putting mulch around perennials. Too early, and they won't have the heat needed to get them going and growing strong. In winter, the best time to mulch is after the first hard frost. That ensures a stable temperature to help your plants thrive. And remember, if it doesn't get too cold where you live, many perennials are fine without mulch.

Using gravel as mulch can throw off too much heat in warmer climates. It reflects sunlight and can harm surrounding plants. Use darker, less-reflective material in hot, sunny areas. In dry or drought conditions, whatever the usual climate, wood chips can absorb what little rain falls. After the rainfall, the water evaporates from the chips without ever reaching the ground. Use dry grass or pine straw instead, to let the water seep through.

When it comes to mulch for lawns, it's usually best to let cut grass go back into the lawn during mowing. This provides constant feeding of new growth with the old. But there's an exception. If your lawn develops diseased areas, it's better to bag and remove cut grass rather than adding to the problem.

Turn kitchen waste into plant food with no composting. Use banana peels to grow beautiful flowers and tasty vegetables. But don't stop there. You can find many more ways to reuse the things you usually throw away. Start with these.

- Save your banana peels year round. Air dry them on an old window screen until they're slightly crunchy. Then store them in a sealed container until you need them. Spread whole or shredded peels around tomato roots, rosebushes, staghorn ferns, veggies, and more. Their phosphorous and potassium make plants healthier and happier.

- Crushed eggshells are great for potted plants and outdoor plants. Press them into the soil and watch your plants flourish.

- Don't throw out that pickle jar. Pour the leftover juice around your gardenias and other acid-loving plants.

- Save the water from boiling potatoes or spaghetti, let it cool, and use it to water your plants occasionally. Plants adore this "starchy" water.

Free fertilizer from an unlikely place. You won't believe what you can put in your garden soil that works just like organic fertilizer. Come springtime, you may have a good supply of ashes from your wood-burning stove or fireplace. Wood ashes are rich in nutrients plants love, and you can scatter them directly in your garden as fertilizer. For lawns, approximately 12 pounds will feed 1,000 square feet. For flower and vegetable gardens, use around 10 pounds for 500 square feet. A half pound will do the trick for individual shrubs or rose bushes.

Ashes increase the pH level of soil — a good reason to test your soil before you try this. Don't use ashes if your level is 7 or above. Scatter them carefully and keep away from acid-loving plants, such as blueberries and azaleas. Only use ashes from burnt wood, like hardwood trees, not pressure-treated, painted, or stained wood. And never use ashes from burned trash or cardboard.

Beware the dangers of wood ash

Sprinkle potassium-rich wood ash around your flowers, and you might get bigger blooms — but sometimes it can do more harm than good. This ash can turn acidic soil more alkaline in just a few days. But if your soil is already alkaline, it could damage your plants and deprive them of vital nutrients.

On top of that, wood ash adds salt to your soil, which can harm some plants even more. So don't use wood ash if your soil is neutral, alkaline, or already has plenty of potassium. A soil test can tell you whether your soil is acid or alkaline and what its potassium levels are if you're not sure. Consider doing this inexpensive test every other year. Your plants will thank you.

Grow tastier tomatoes and beat blossom end rot. If you constantly battle blossom end rot, you could grow your tomatoes in extra large tomato cages. Caged plants resist blossom end rot better than staked tomatoes. But there's a better solution.

For the sweetest, juiciest tomatoes ever, add powdered milk to their water. It nourishes your tomatoes with calcium, so they're far more tantalizing and delicious. That extra calcium can also defeat blossom end rot before it starts.

Beat damping off and blackspot. Simple ingredients from your kitchen pantry can stop these two fungal bullies from picking on your yard and garden. If damping off is the problem, drink some chamomile tea and drop the used tea bag into 3 3/4 cups of water. After the tea bag has soaked awhile, remove it, and pour the water over your seedlings. For severe cases, use a fresh tea bag straight from the box. Damping off fungi hate it when you do that.

When the problem is blackspot tainting your lawn, fight back by sprinkling cornmeal right over those little brown patches. It's cheap, easy, and you may be surprised at how well it works.

Unleash more power from your fertilizer. Soil that's too alkaline or acid can prevent your plants from absorbing the fertilizer you give them. That's like pouring fertilizer money down the drain. Fortunately, soil testing is easy and inexpensive. Just dig up a few samples and ask your local cooperative extension agent how to get them tested. The test results will reveal whether your soil is acid or alkaline, which nutrients it needs, and how to fertilize or amend it so your plants and lawn flourish.

But remember, your soil test results are only as good as the samples you take, so be careful to do it right. Don't mix samples from the vegetable garden with samples from the flower bed, shrubbery bed, or lawn. After all, the kind of soil that grows a perfect lawn can differ greatly from the ideal soil for veggies. Pick which areas you want tested and take one group of soil samples for each. You'll be surprised how easy it is.

For example, go to your veggie garden, dig up several 5-inch-deep plugs of soil, and mix them together. Remove anything in the soil sample that isn't soil. Drop the sample into the container recommended by the testing lab and label accordingly. Follow the same process for the lawn or any other area you want tested. When you're done, you'll have perfect soil samples that may lead to the most dazzling yard and garden you've ever had.

Shield grass seed from pesky birds. Before you reseed a small patch of lawn, look in your basement or garage for an old window screen — or one that's not being used. Use it to protect your newly seeded area while the grass grows. Place the screen over the seeded patch, and weigh it down with a few stones to keep it secure. Birds won't be able to move it, and your seeds will be safe.

Bypass the No. 1 lawn mowing mistake. Mowing your lawn to a short height may mean fewer mows per season, but it's the worst mowing mistake you can make. In fact, this short cut may force you to spend extra time and money fighting weeds, insects, and grass disease. And here's why.

Lawns that get regular buzz cuts naturally have shorter blades and shallower roots. Because the size of each grass blade determines how much sunlight it absorbs, shorter blades take in less. This sunlight shortage makes your lawn more susceptible to disease and insect damage. Meanwhile, the shallower roots can limit each blade's water supply, making the grass even weaker. As if that weren't bad enough, a short lawn invites weeds to grow because more light reaches weed seeds and seedlings. That gives weeds extra fuel to help them choke out your grass.

You could beat these problems by constantly weeding and spraying during every month your grass grows, but that's hard work. Instead, keep your lawn at a height between 2 and 3 inches and never chop off more than one-third of the blade. Your lawn may reward you by smothering weeds and turning itself into lush green carpet your neighbors will envy.

Say sayonara to sticky grass clippings

You can forget about cleaning your mower. Spray WD-40 on its underside so grass clippings can't stick there anymore. Then, when you're hot and tired after mowing, you won't need to pry clippings off your mower deck. Instead, you can check that deck, smile at how clean it is, and go inside for a cold, refreshing drink.

Defend your turf against drought. You may not be able to end a drought, but you can arm your lawn against it. To help fortify grass so it recovers from drought quickly, start with five simple steps.

- Adjust your standard mowing height upward. Add a half-inch if your mowing height is 2 inches, 3/4 inch if it's 3 inches, or a full inch for 4 inches. You'll encourage a deeper root system and natural chemical reactions that help your grass tolerate drought stress.

- Avoid shallow and frequent watering. Instead, wait until the first signs of wilt show up and then water deeply.

- Keep off the grass whenever possible. The less people and pets walk on it, the better off your lawn will be.

- Keep your mower blade sharp. The rough cut made by blunt mower blades causes grass to retain less water.

- Avoid using pesticides on your grass until the drought improves. They'll just add stress to an already-weakened lawn. By simply storing your pesticides until the drought breaks, you'll buy fewer containers of pesticide and your lawn will be more resilient.

Kill weeds and their seeds naturally. You wouldn't expect a common household ingredient from your pantry to work like an expensive weed killer, but white vinegar does. Just heat it up, pour it in a spray bottle, and take aim. It's cheap, easy, and poison-free.

Expect young weeds to die quickly, but stubborn or well-established weeds may require another round or two of spraying. If that's a few sprays too many for you, try a single dose of pickling vinegar. It's more powerful than household vinegar and hits weeds harder. But aim very carefully or you may accidentally kill nearby plants.

Once you've wiped out your weeds, prevent future weed wars with these tips.

- Raise your mower blade. Taller grass blades keep light away from weed seeds, so they never start growing in the first place.
- Keep weeds out of your beds for good. Cover them with landscape fabric and a light coating of mulch.

Use the power of the sun to get rid of stubborn weeds. Solarizing is an organic, chemical-free technique that harnesses the heat of the sun to get your garden ready for planting. It not only kills weeds, but also gets rid of pests and diseases. You'll need to plan for your plot to be idle for 4 to 8 weeks, then follow these four steps for success.

- Cultivate. After you've chosen your plot, till it thoroughly and remove debris. Take out any bits and pieces that could contain weed seeds.
- Level. Get your rake and break up any clumps left over from tilling. Smooth out the ground, making it as flat as possible. This will allow the plastic a tight fit later.
- Irrigate. Give the plot a good soaking — ideally down to about a foot deep. Be ready to place plastic on top as soon as possible after watering.
- Cover. Use clear plastic — thinner (1 mil) is better for heating, but if you're in a windy area, use slightly thicker (2 mils) so it doesn't get disturbed. Then weigh down

the edges using soil or stones, and wait. How long? Usually, 4 to 6 weeks are enough if it's hot, but if it's cooler, windier, or cloudier where you are, leave the plastic on for 6 to 8 weeks.

Try to disturb the soil as little as possible after removing the plastic. This will help avoid stirring up any weed seeds that could be lurking. Your soil — weed-free and nutrient-rich — is ready for your plants.

No more weeds in driveway cracks. You've finally killed the weeds that set up housekeeping in your driveway and sidewalk cracks, but they'll grow back if you're not careful. Fill the cracks with sand, so the weed seeds can't get enough light to grow. For smaller cracks, try masonry sand, or stone dust. Here's another idea — scuttle weeds in the cracks of driveways and sidewalks with boiling water. Follow up by salting the cracks.

Defend your plants from weed-killing sprays. Whether you're spraying your weeds with vinegar or something more toxic, you don't want to damage the surrounding plants. Here's a simple solution. Trim off the bottom of a plastic 2-liter bottle and do the same to a 16-ounce bottle. Store them both with your garden supplies. When you're ready to spray a weed, pick the appropriate size bottle. Place the bottle over the weed, slip the sprayer nozzle into the mouth of the bottle, and spray. Give the chemicals 30 seconds to sink in and then move on to the next weed. Your plants will remain safe, but your weeds won't live to tell the tale.

Water without wasting a drop. Use the right watering tool at the right time to make sure all the water gets to your plants.

If you water with a sprinkler, do it in the morning. Up to 40 percent of the water can be lost to evaporation if you run the sprinkler during the warmer, sunny afternoon hours. On top of that, morning watering allows leaves to dry before evening when damp leaves are more likely to "catch" fungal diseases. But if you water with a soaker hose or drip system, do it at night so the water has more time to sink into the soil.

Make tomato stakes that water roots. You could install both tomato stakes and root-watering pipes, but you'll like this clever two-for-one trick much better. For every tomato plant you plan to grow, cut a 5-foot length of 2-inch PVC pipe. Make a mark about 10 inches away from one end of each pipe. Next, use a post hole digger to make holes near each spot where you plan to place a tomato plant. Dump the displaced dirt on a plastic bag near each hole.

Drop the first pipe into one of the holes. Push it down into the soil as far as you can. Place a 2-inch thick piece of board over the top of the pipe. Hammer the board directly above the PVC pipe to push the pipe further into the soil until the mark on the PVC pipe is even with the ground. Roughly 4 feet of PVC pipe should remain above the dirt. Fill in the space emptied out by the post hole digger and dump any leftover dirt back down the pipe. Repeat this process for all the other poles. When you're done, you'll be ready to plant tomatoes. Just make sure each tomato plant is only a few inches from a pipe.

When you're ready to water, turn the hose on extra low and put the nozzle end in the pipe. Allow the pipe to fill and move on to the next pipe. Check back on the first pipe a few minutes later. If the water drains quickly, you may need to refill the pipe a few times. As the tomatoes grow, tie them to your PVC stakes. Wrap your tie around the stake first, knot it in place, and then tie the remaining lengths to the tomato plant.

Stretch your growing season

Extend your growing season farther into autumn with this easy-to-make hot cap. Cut the bottom off a 2-liter plastic bottle, soak the label to remove it, and place it over the plant you want to protect. Push it down into the soil a little to keep the wind or animals from pushing it over. If the plant is too bushy for a two-liter, try a bottomless plastic milk jug.

Unlike some hot caps, you don't need to remove these bottles from your plants every day. Instead, just remove their caps. This lets hot air vent up and out of the bottle so your plants don't overheat on warm, sunny days. Just be sure to put the caps back on at sunset to keep your plants toasty all night long.

Plot the perfect garden layout every year. Find an empty squeezable ketchup or mustard bottle or an empty drink bottle that has a pull-up "sipper." Clean it out, let it dry, and fill it two-thirds full with flour. Now, go out to your garden bed and use this squeezable marker to mark where each plant should go.

For best results, "draw" a shape that matches the plant's mature size and leave a gardener-size working space between plants. You can even mark spaces for walking paths or garden art. When you're done, you'll have the perfect garden layout for your space. This clever trick also saves money because you'll never buy more plants than your garden can hold.

Grow a salad bar in your yard. More vegetables mean more nutrients and a healthier life. The simplest, most cost-effective thing you can grow is salad. Start with a simple mixed salad — put lettuce, radish, and carrot seeds together in a container with sand to help it spread. Mix well and scatter them on a prepared bed and cover with a thin layer of dirt. As the veggies sprout, thin them for space, then let them mature. The mixture of plants helps keep both weeds and pests away.

Cool weather is especially kind to salad greens, so think about a fall planting of your favorite lettuce, as well as spinach, kale, Swiss chard, raddicchio, and arugula. A great trick for getting a constant supply of your green leaf of choice is to sow a lot of seeds in trays to get them going, but wait to transplant them in intervals of two weeks or so. Then instead of piles of lettuce all at once, you'll get a steady supply for your salad bowl. And you'll save loads compared to what you'd pay at the supermarket, especially if you like the more exotic leaf.

Another great bargain is growing your own tomatoes. Heirloom cherry tomatoes are an especially good value. They have a longer growing season and a larger overall crop. Plant basil with them for added flavor. And consider growing other flavor enhancers — dill, parsley, and scallion — to complete your bountiful harvest of good-for-you salad.

Extend gardening season for pennies. Imagine making a season-extender that won't blow away or break the bank — no matter how many you use. All you need are 2-liter bottles and duct tape. Place one bottle as your center marker and form a circle of bottles around it. Wrap duct tape around the outside of the circle to bind all the outer bottles together. Then remove the center bottle, and you have a new cloche.

For best results, position the cloche around the plant in the morning and fill each bottle with water and a pinch of salt to help hold the heat. The sun will heat the water during the day. That will keep your plant warmer during chilly nights because water retains heat better than air does. For extra protection from frost, throw a sheet of clear plastic or a transparent old shower curtain over the cloche.

Get rid of bugs and slugs with plastic bottles. Recycle your plastic drink bottles to make tidy traps for annoying pests. To make the basic trap, start by cutting off the top of the bottle about a third of the way down. It will look sort of like a funnel. Then turn the top upside

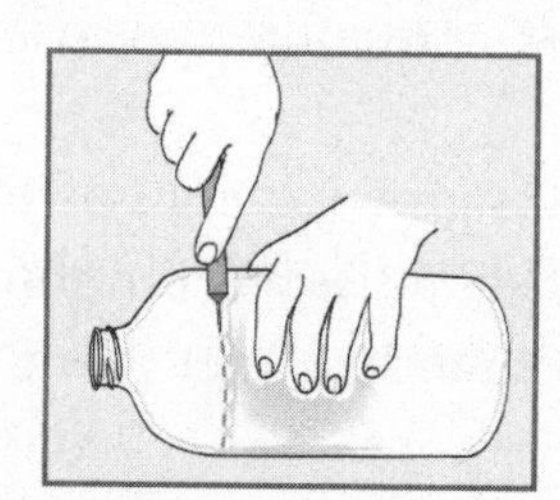

down and put it back inside the bottle, neck first. Tape the edge if necessary.

- Slugs. Put beer in the trap and lay it on its side in the garden. Slugs will slip inside for a drink, but they won't be able to get back out.

- Flies. Make the same basic trap, but poke a hole in the bottle cap and leave it on the bottle. Mix some sugar with water to make a sweet syrup and put it in the trap. Stand the trap upright to attract and catch flies.

- Mosquitoes. Do everything the same as the fly trap, but add a little bit of yeast to the sugar water. The yeast gives off carbon dioxide — a strong lure for mosquitoes.

If you have a row cover in your garden, there's an even simpler bottle trap. Put some sticky stuff — Tanglefoot or petroleum jelly — on a bottle full of water and place it upright under the row cover. The sun will warm the water during the day, then bugs will be attracted to it later as the air temperature drops. They fly to the warmth and stick to the bottle.

Clever containers help you pot your plants for pennies. Don't spend all your fun money on fancy containers for your garden. There's a treasure-trove of potential pots all around — if you just know where to look. Here are a few ideas for turning normal household items and yard sale finds into charming planters.

For each project, prevent your potting soil from spilling out the bottom by lining the container with a piece of fine mesh screening, a bit of moss, or even a large coffee filter.

- Glass lampshades. Turn the shade upside down so the narrow opening is at the bottom. Add soil and your plants. What a bright idea.

- Colanders. These are already designed for drainage, and the old-fashioned metal or enamel ones will add a nostalgic touch to your porch or patio. Place them on the ground, or add chains to the handles and you've got a hanging planter with loads of personality.

- Cinder blocks. These hollow building blocks are perfect for filling with plants. But don't stop with just one. Build a wall or tower by stacking them into any shape or design that fits your space. Leave as many blocks exposed as you like and fill with your favorite flowers. For tall structures, consider securing the blocks to each other with a concrete adhesive.

Lighten heavy containers the easy way. "You can use plastic grocery bags to fill space in the bottom of a large flowerpot or window box, which will save you soil and make the container lighter and easier to move," says Colleen Vanderlinden, freelance writer and creator of "In the Garden Online" at *www.inthegardenonline.com*. If you're short on plastic bags, use leaves or packing peanuts instead. Fill the bottom third of the container and then add soil. Your back and your wallet will thank you.

Quick cures for common houseplant problems. The same troubles show up in houseplants time and again. You don't need a degree in horticulture to put them right. Use these commonsense solutions to solve common complaints — and keep your houseplants healthy.

- Yellow leaves. Either too much or too little water or a nitrogen deficiency. Improve drainage by making sure the pot has good soil and enough drainage holes. Don't add gravel or sand. It's a myth that it helps. In fact, it makes the problem worse. Wait till the soil dries to water. Add fertilizer to boost nitrogen in the soil.

- Brown tips. Salt burn from too many minerals in the soil or from hard water. In the shower, flush the soil until the water runs clear.

- Stunted growth, small brittle leaves. Too little water. Water immediately, then again as soon as the topsoil dries out.

- No growth, dull leaves. Too much water. Improve the drainage, and wait for topsoil to dry before you add water again.

- Curling leaves. Too hot. Water and move to a shaded area.

- Tan or brown splotches. Sunburn or too cold. Move to a sheltered spot.

- White crust on soil. Salt buildup from too much fertilizer. Flush until water runs clear, and reduce fertilizer. For a lighter hand in applying fertilizer, try putting some in an old saltshaker and sprinkling lightly.

Water your plants while on vacation. Water your house-plants while visiting Europe or enjoying the beach in Jamaica.

You can do it if you start a few days before your departure. You'll need a bucket, a stool or crate, and an old mop head made of rayon or another synthetic fabric. Fill the bucket with water, put it on the stool, and place your plants in a tight circle around it. Turn the mop head upside down and put it in the water.

For each plant, take one mop strand and bury its end deep in the soil near the roots. Keep the plants lower than the mop head so water can seep down the strand. Also, make sure that part of the mop head will stay beneath the water while you're gone. Check your plants once each day until you leave to be sure they are getting enough water. If they are, just add extra water to the bucket before you go. Your well-watered plants will be waiting when you come home.

Rescue your houseplants from softened water. You've finally installed a water softener, but now your potted plants are struggling. That's because softened water is saltier than hard water even if you can't taste the difference. To fix this salty problem, find out whether your outdoor hose faucets are attached to the water softener line. If not, collect hose water for your houseplants. Otherwise, try one of these.

- Buy gypsum from your garden center. Before watering your plants, thoroughly mix one-half teaspoon into a gallon of softened water.

- Replace the soil once a year and scrub away any salt deposits you find on the pot.

- Collect rainwater to water your plants.

Grow herbs indoors even in poor light. You'd love a window herb garden during winter, but your windows don't let in enough light. Instead of expensive grow lights, tack a fluorescent light fixture to the underside of a shelf. Stock it with one "warm" fluorescent tube and one "cool" one and place your herbs 5 inches beneath it. Give your herbs about 16 hours of this "daylight."

If you used a fluorescent light fixture that has a cord and plug, attach it to a light timer, and you won't have to turn the lights on and off yourself. Just keep in mind that your herbs could use a few hours of real daylight, too. If you can't fit all the herbs you want under your lights, move your chives and parsley to an indoor windowsill permanently. They accept less light than other herbs.

Keep squirrels out of your bird feeder permanently. Feed the birds, not the squirrels, by using these clever tips.

- Find a Slinky that a child no longer wants. Using staple or wire, fasten the top of the Slinky to the underside of your bird feeder so it surrounds the pole from top to bottom. Squirrels will be completely frustrated by this simple barrier.

- Cut the bottom off a 2-liter soda bottle or 5-gallon water bottle. Drill holes through the neck of the bottle and use part of a coat hanger to hang the bottle from the bottom of the bird feeder. The resulting umbrella shape makes pole climbing impossible for squirrels. You can also get the same effect with an old bucket. Just cut the bottom off and drill holes through the sides of the bucket near the base. Use the coat hanger to attach it to the bottom of the bird feeder, and squirrels will seek easier pickings elsewhere.

- Ask someone at the home improvement store to help you find an HVAC reducer. This is a short metal cylinder designed to connect a small duct to a larger one. You'll also need screws and small pieces of wood — called shims — to fit between the inner wall of the reducer and the bird feeder pole. Slip the reducer over the pole, jam the shims in the empty space between the pole and the reducer, and attach the entire contraption to the bird feeder pole with nails or screws.

Tote yard tools with ease. Turn a plastic outdoor garbage can into standup storage for rakes, hoes, and any tool with a long handle.

Fill the inside of the can with a bag of sand to keep it from tipping over. Then drill large holes through the lid with a spade bit,making them big enough to slide tool handles through. Roll your tool caddy around the yard by strapping it to a hand truck.

Prevent container stains on your deck

Before you put containers on your deck, try this inexpensive stain preventer. Check recycling centers, yard sales, flea markets, and other secondhand stores for burner grates from old gas stoves. Ask friends and family to keep an eye out for these, too. Once you collect a few, you'll have charming "stands" to rest your containers on.

Even if the containers drip on the wood, the water won't stay long enough to cause a stain. If the grates look unattractive to you, check your local home improvement store for spray paint that can be used on metal. Turn your grates a bright, modern silver; a country-style copper; or any other color that suits your taste.

3 ways to tame your garden hose. No need to buy something expensive — these free solutions will tame the tangle and keep your hose handy.

- Rake. Replaced your garden rake? Give the old one a clever update that's both useful and ornamental. Secure the handle firmly in the ground — no wobbling — then use the head of the rake for hanging a hose. Loop the hose loosely, and the spaces between the tines of the rake will keep it neatly in place.

- Wheel rim. Got an old car tire sitting around? Take off the metal rim, and attach it securely to your house or a fence. Your hose will curl up nicely around the rim and will unroll easily without tangling. Paint the rim to match your house, and it will blend right in.

- Bucket. Use a sturdy, metal bucket mounted securely to your house or shed, with the open end facing outward. Wrap your hose around it, and inside you can stash items such as gloves, sprayers, and nozzles. Even less work? Just coil your hose inside a plastic 5-gallon bucket and carry it where it's needed.

Put that holey hose back to work

Don't get rid of a leaky garden hose — transform it into a multipurpose soaker hose. Simply puncture the underside of the hose at regular intervals with a hot ice pick. Lay it, pinpricks down, in your garden bed between the plants. Attach one end to your new hose. Plug the other end with a plastic end cap. Cover your soaker hose with mulch and turn the tap on. Water will drip out of the small holes and thoroughly soak your flower or vegetable bed.

Take the strain out of carrying tools. Let your garden tools do the work for you — not the other way around. These clever ideas help make heavy tasks light.

- Instead of carrying around a weighty pump sprayer, put it on your golf bag cart and wheel it around your garden. The pull cart is designed for use on grass, and the sprayer should sit well on the base of the cart. Depending on the cart, you might need some duct tape or a bungee cord to help secure the sprayer.

- An old golf bag makes a terrific caddy for your long-handled garden tools, such as rakes and shovels. What's more, your gloves and hand tools fit neatly in the side pockets. You can put the golf bag on a golf bag cart for easy movement around your garden. After all, they're made for each other.

- Use a 5-gallon bucket to carry your small gardening tools. As a bonus, you can flip it over and sit on it as you weed, plant, or just take a breather. Add an S-hook to the bucket handle, and hook it on to your wheelbarrow, and you won't even have to carry the bucket.

- Attach a plastic window box to your wheelbarrow for a more permanent tool holder — just a couple of screws will do. Drill through the window box into the handles of the wheelbarrow, or use the drainage holes if they line up right. Pop in the screws, and off you go. Keep small tools, your water bottle, even your cellphone, close by and easy to get to.

Leisure time: more fun for less

Claim more senior discounts. The next time you go to an outdoor craft fair, a fast food restaurant, or even the Goodwill store, ask about a senior discount. You will probably get one if you meet the age requirement. Other surprising places where a senior discount may be available include your cellphone service provider, greeting card stores, major and minor league baseball stadiums, outlet malls, fitness centers, amusement parks, theaters, zoos, beauty salons, museums, rental car services, and stores where you fill your prescription for eyeglasses. Just remember, many of these places won't give you the discount unless you ask for it, so be sure to speak up.

Frugal way to learn a new hobby. Spend less learning more about your favorite pastime or taking up a new hobby. For example, if your first love is cooking, visit your local Williams-Sonoma store and ask about their classes. You may discover several free classes you like. Just be sure to confirm that they're free before you sign up. If you have internet access, check out *www.Epicurious.com* for great cooking lessons.

If cooking isn't your thing, check with your favorite hobby stores to see if they offer free classes, demonstrations, or workshops. Also, check *www.youtube.com* and websites dedicated to your hobby. You may find free videos, lessons, or classes there.

Eat out for less

Eating in a restaurant doesn't have to be expensive. Here are eight ways you can dine for less.

- Clip a coupon.
- Go out for lunch rather than dinner.
- Find an early-bird special.
- Drink water — it's free.
- Share the entree.
- Order food to go and skip the tip.
- Search out a kids-eat-free night.
- Try a hospital cafeteria.

Super alternatives to pricey gyms. The high price of a gym membership may seem smart during January snows, but always consider your options. You might save a lot of money.

- Check with your local hospital, community center, or senior center and you may discover exercise rooms, classes, or fitness programs available to the public. Ask about prices to see if the cost is less than a gym. Don't forget to include the expenses of gas and parking when you compare costs.
- Find out if your church or a friend's church offers free or inexpensive workout rooms, a gym, or exercise classes.

Some churches allow nonmembers to take classes or use equipment for a small fee.

- Your cable television company may offer on-demand videos of fitness classes. Find out whether your cable provider offers this service, and ask if it costs extra or is already included in your current cable subscription.

If you need something more specialized, such as tennis courts or an indoor pool, check nearby colleges, high schools, or universities to see if you can use their facilities at a discount.

5 ways to see a movie for less. You'll shell out $15 to see a movie at the theater in some cities. If that price seems excessive, try one of these easy ways to enjoy great movies without going bankrupt.

- Get in early. A matinee showing is usually about 25 percent cheaper than a movie that starts after 6 p.m. But have a snack before you go, so you don't end up blowing your savings on high-priced drinks and food.

- Watch at home. Keep an eye on cable TV listings for a movie you want to see. Record it early in the week, then save it to watch on weekend movie night.

- Borrow for free. Look for movie DVDs you can borrow for free from the public library or a collection at church.

- Be patient. If you can wait just a few months, you'll probably be able to catch that blockbuster for a dollar or two at a local discount theater, sometimes called a "late run" theater.

- Find discounts. Membership in clubs and organizations has its rewards, including cheap tickets.
    - Ask about discount tickets at a warehouse club like Sam's Club or Costco.
    - Look for a loyalty program at your local theater chain.
    - Ask for a senior discount at the box office.

Join the club for movie savings

Don't spend $30 every time you take your honey to the theater. AMC Theatres offers a free MovieWatchers reward card. Show it every time you buy movie tickets and you can earn points for free concessions and tickets later on. Sign up online at *www.moviewatcher.com*.

Regal Cinemas has a similar program, the Regal Crown Club. You can get your free membership card at *www.regalcinemas.com*. Check your local theater to see if it's owned by Regal, AMC, or another company.

High-tech way to save money on music. Instead of paying for CDs or downloads of your favorite tunes, try internet radio for free. You can listen on your computer, tablet, or smartphone, if you have a connection to the internet. Even better, getting started is easier than you think.

For example, if you decided to try the internet radio service, Pandora, you'd create an account. Then you would pick your "radio stations" by choosing an artist, group, song, or type of music. You can find everything from the latest hits to golden oldies. What's more, you can start streaming music to your listening device almost immediately.

But choose wisely. Be sure to select the free version of an internet radio service, and make certain it's compatible with your smartphone or other device. Also, if you stream to your smartphone, track how much data you use so you won't go over your cell plan's data limit. To learn more about your internet radio options, visit these sites:

- Pandora at *www.pandora.com*
- Spotify at *www.spotify.com*

Get instant entertainment without spending a dime. Internet streaming services you pay for, like Netflix, may offer a wide range of choices. But before you pile on the subscriptions, take a quick peek at these free online options for watching movies and more:

- Crackle (*crackle.com*)
- Popcornflix (*popcornflix.com*)
- Snagfilms (*snagfilms.com*)
- tubitv (*tubitv.com*)

These may not have as much variety as the paid services, but if you're looking for a quick fix, they'll do the trick.

And don't forget about network websites like *abc.go.com, nbc.com, cwtv.com*, and *cbs.com*. You probably won't find entire seasons of TV shows, but if you miss an episode, you can often watch it on the website within a few days. Some even allow you to view broadcasts live, depending on your location.

Here's the catch though. Not all networks have apps that will stream to your TV, so you might have to watch on your tablet or computer. But hey, you can't argue with free.

Books for a buck — or free. Some people swear by their local Goodwill store as the best place to find books for a dollar or less. Other thrift stores may also offer top-flight books at bargain basement prices.

Want more options? Watch for yard sale signs, and you may find paperbacks for a quarter or hardback books at deliciously steep discounts. But that's not all these sellers have to offer. If you are willing to dig a little at yard sales and thrift stores, you may uncover great reads and timeless treasures you just can't find in regular stores.

You'll discover treasures much closer to home if you start a small neighborhood library. In fact, you may have already seen this at work in other neighborhoods. The wildly popular "little free libraries" often resemble charming, super-size birdhouses, but you'll find books inside if you look closely. These boxes are also a great way to protect books from the elements.

To start a neighborhood library, check local ordinances, and work with your neighbors to decide where to put the box and who will care for it. For information on how to buy or build a library box, and instructions on starting and maintaining your neighborhood library, visit *littlefreelibrary.org* on the web, or talk to someone in a neighborhood that already has a library.

The website also offers useful information on finding sponsors who may help pay for a box. To kick off your library, ask everyone in the neighborhood to donate a book. This should offer enough books to expand everyone's reading options for weeks or months to come.

How to be a frugal golfer. Jim Bishop, famous American journalist and author, once said, "Golf is played by 20 million mature American men whose wives think they are out having fun."

If golf is your idea of fun, but paying top dollar for equipment and tee times is not, try some of these money-saving strategies.

- Play a cheaper course. Search out public courses and pay less per round.
- Find part-time work at a golf course so you're eligible for free rounds.
- Buy equipment in winter or whenever it's the off-season in your area.
- Look for used equipment from secondhand shops or from online sellers.

- Play with used or recycled golf balls but not refurbished balls, which are usually of lower quality.
- Schedule twilight or early morning tee times. These are often discounted.
- Look online for discounted tee times. Websites like *www.golfnow.com* help you play more for less.
- Practice your putting and chipping for free on a public golf course.
- Pay less to play on nine-hole courses while still getting a good golf workout.
- Walk don't ride. You'll save a lot in cart fees.
- Bring your own food if the course permits, and always carry a water bottle.
- Don't subscribe to golf magazines. They are expensive and most are chock-full of tempting ads promoting high-priced equipment.

When to invest in a club membership

If you're retired and play golf almost every day, it may be cost-effective to join your local club. Do the math to make sure you'll play enough to break even, and check to see if they have any special offers. For example, some clubs allow you to pay less for a weekday-only membership.

Frugal storage ideas for savvy crafters. Spend your limited craft budget on supplies — not on containers to store these treasures. Longtime sewer and quilter Alice Jewell saves money by inventing new uses for old items. "I like clear shallow boxes that are sold to fishermen," she says.

"The small compartments can be customized for almost anything. I use one for various machine needles. Another is set up with the supplies I carry to workshops. One division is large enough for scissors and rotary cutter. Handles make it easy to carry." Jewell points out these fishing tackle boxes are cheaper than similar organizers made just for crafts and sewing.

Don't throw away candy boxes with dividers — they work to separate small items in a drawer or on a table surface. "Reusing a bedroom chest of drawers for sewing-room storage works well," Jewell says. Other great organizing items come from the hardware store and office-supply store.

"I use a desk organizer carousel to separate pencils, marking tools, seam rippers, and other items I want to reach from my sewing machine but have out of the way," she says. "By far my favorite organizer is a pegboard hung within easy reach of my chair. I like this especially for hanging my scissors and having easy access to them."

Moneymakers: ingenious income ideas

Make a fortune on the junk in your attic. You want to sell all the junk in your attic, but you don't feel comfortable having people come to your home for a yard sale. Fortunately, the answer may be as close as your computer. Just sell your stuff on eBay, and you could make good money. One woman reported making more than $1,500 in one year, mostly from selling items she already owned. Some people also say you'll make more money selling certain goods on eBay than you would by selling them in a yard sale. These include electronics, quality clothing, shoes, kitchen appliances, and select household goods.

To get started, visit *www.ebay.com*, and review their tutorials and advice for sellers. Then register for an eBay account, and choose "casual account" to get 50 free auction listings every month. eBay is famous as an auction site, where people bid on an item offered for sale. For each item you sell by auction, you'll pay roughly 10 percent of the sales price to eBay. You can choose to sell at a fixed price instead, but you'll pay additional fees. Before putting an item up for sale, check eBay's completed sale listings to see what prices similar items have sold for. Compare that price to the total cost of shipping your item and paying the eBay fees to sell it. Only sell items that can fetch a higher price than those costs.

When you put an item up for sale, write a clear, accurate description including the item's condition, and plenty of high-quality pictures. This will help you sell your items and start making money.

Transform unique skills into gold

Sometimes the key to making extra money is to put your more unusual skills to work or use common skills differently. Here are several ideas you can try.

- Offer sewing skills with a twist. Find out which doll is the most wildly popular among today's kids, and take orders to make clothes for those dolls. You can also offer to make matching outfits for doll owners.
- Turn repairing electronics from a hobby into a career. Buy and repair broken electronic items, and sell them for a profit.
- Consider selling bagged lunches to friends, busy parents, and large families, especially if people compliment you on the lunches you make for your family.
- Become a garden sitter. Tend and water the gardens and plants of vacationers and business travelers while they're away.
- Transform your years of experience into a DVD or series of booklets you can sell if the physical demands of a service job, like landscaping or hairstyling, have become too much.

Boost consignment shop profits on your stuff. Earn more money from selling your used clothes, furniture, and other things to consignment stores. Start by choosing the best store for your merchandise. Check your local phone book or go online to see which stores are available. Choose several stores to visit, including any that specialize in the items you want to sell. Stores that specialize in a particular type of clothing or in particular categories like furniture or sporting goods may offer more.

When you visit, notice which stores are busiest and which ones sell the items you want to offer. Ask questions about what goods they accept and how the sale process works. Narrow your list, but don't pick just one store. Instead, set appraisal appointments with several stores; show them your clean, used items in good condition; and see what each one offers. This helps you sell each item to the store that offers the most for it.

Clever way to sell things you make. You may be able to get shelf space for crafts, jewelry, clothing accessories, or other things you make at a consignment or thrift store. To help you persuade the store owner, try this first. Find several school or church events where you can set up a table or booth to sell your stuff. Once you get the hang of selling your wares and have several successful events under your belt, you'll be ready to approach a store manager about shelf space.

Visit several consignment or thrift stores to see which one you'd like to approach about a shelf-space agreement. Ask whether the store will allow you to reserve shelf space in exchange for some of the profits. If they're interested, you can show them samples of your products and tell them about your sales. You may discover that if you provide the goods, they'll do the selling for a cut of the profits, and you'll have extra money to take home.

Make more bucks on a garage sale. Get creative when you plan your garage sale. Use these insider secrets from garage sale gurus to boost your profits.

- Ask your neighbors to hold their sales the same day as yours. Advertise a streetwide or neighborhood sale, and you'll all get many more customers.
- Group your merchandise into departments like a store would, and you may double your sales. Clean each item so it looks its best, and display it with the original box.
- Place your most exciting items and any products that appeal to men close to the street. More people will stop at your sale.
- To boost sales even higher, tack a large sign marked "Free" to one box, and fill the box with things to give away.
- Advertise in your local newspaper, but also advertise for free on www.craigslist.com. If you have plenty of goods in a particular category, advertise with a theme like Christmas in October, kitchen-wide clearance, or book bonanza.
- To dramatically increase clothing sales, show off the clothes on racks. Display everything else on tables or bookshelves. Borrow extra tables, shelves, and racks if you don't have enough.
- Make extension cords and batteries available to prove electronics still work.
- Instead of guessing at prices, know what your wares are worth. To find used-good prices, check neighborhood yard

sales, thrift stores, *www.eBay.com*, *www.craigslist.com*, and online price guides from *www.satruck.org* and *www.goodwill.org*. Price each item a little higher than its average selling price, so you'll have room to negotiate. For more expensive items, attach a printed page from *www.amazon.com* showing what the item sells for new. That way, customers can compare it with your lower price tag, or you can simply attach a "make an offer" sign instead of a price tag.

Supercharge sales with super signs

Eye-catching yard sale signs may more than double the money your yard sale makes, claims one expert. But before you get creative, check your local ordinances to learn the rules for yard sale signs. To make an attention-grabbing sign, think big. Make each sign from large, neon-colored poster board glued to a sheet of cardboard. In case of rain, write with waterproof ink, or cover with clear packing tape.

But don't stop there. Use large, bold letters to make the sign easy to read. Include the date and time of your sale and big arrows to guide people to your location. And, if local ordinances allow, attach balloons or plastic streamers to help your signs get noticed. Post signs at major routes nearby, and direct shoppers to your sale location using additional signs. To test the first sign you make, post it at a major route, and try to read it as you drive by.

A job market that loves to employ seniors. Not only is this job market one of the fastest growing in the U.S., it also employs thousands of workers over age 55 — and will be hiring even more with each passing year. So what is it? It's a variety of jobs for direct care workers such as personal care assistants and home health aides. These workers assist older adults and people with disabilities or chronic illnesses, but they may do it in different ways.

Personal care assistants are more likely to help with tasks like cooking, cleaning, or running errands, while home health aides help mostly with tasks like bathing, dressing, meals, and doctor's appointments. Some direct care providers visit people's homes to do their jobs, while others work in hospitals, adult day care, or nursing homes. These jobs are low-wage, come with a higher-than-average injury rate, and can be physically demanding. Yet, they are also a great way to assist people who genuinely need help, and you can usually work part time. Training and education requirements vary by state, so check what's required before you apply.

Play a pretend patient for real rewards. If you live within easy driving distance of a medical school or teaching hospital, contact them and ask how to apply for their Standardized Patient (SP) program. As an SP, you play the patient in a simulated doctor's office visit that helps train medical students. You won't need any acting experience to qualify, but a good memory and the ability to think on your feet helps. You could be assigned the role of a fictional patient with severe knee pain. Like an actor, you'll have lines to memorize, and you may even be trained on how to play some parts of the role. The medical student must ask you the right questions and perhaps do a little poking and prodding to make the right diagnosis. After the office visit, you fill out a checklist to evaluate things like the medical student's bedside manner and communications skills.

In exchange for these patient performances, you'll get hidden extras like free medical information and contacts, and you'll learn what to look for in a doctor and how to recognize the difference between good medical practices and bad ones. Your experiences also teach you how to work with your doctors — helpful questions to ask and what they may look for during an office visit. If all this makes you want to become a standardized patient, plan for a work day between two and six hours and pay rates around $10 to $25 an hour.

Part-time jobs that improve your health. You can get paid to grow healthier during retirement. Today's retirees can work part-time as dog walkers, child care workers, crossing guards, housecleaners, and tour guides. Jobs like these often provide health-building exercise on every working day. That's important because exercise comes with plenty of good side effects. Don't be surprised if it helps:

- boost your endurance.
- control your blood sugar and weight.
- give you energy.
- protect your brain and memory.
- ease arthritis and back pain.
- lower your risk of hip fractures.

In fact, studies show sustained exercise is linked to better health, even if you start exercising late in life. So check with your doctor to find out what exercises are safe for you. Then look for part-time jobs that require plenty of doctor-approved exercise. A job that requires lots of walking may be a good choice. You win two ways — when you start working in a job that requires exercise, you'll boost your bank account and your health at the same time.

Handy moneymakers you can do in your spare time. The best and fastest way to make an extra $300, $500, or even $1,000 a month is to start a business based on skills you already have, suggests author Loral Langemeier in her book, *Put More Cash in Your Pocket.* These skills can come from your job experience, hobbies, volunteer work, or even chores. For example, if you already have skills and experience in:

- Calligraphy. You can be paid for work on wedding invitations, party invitations, and more.

- Transcription or speedy typing. You can be hired to transcribe locally from audio or videos or from material provided online via the Web.

- Bookkeeping. If you're also certified as a CPA, small businesses may pay you to do their bookkeeping.

- Cooking. You may offer classes to neighborhood children, high school kids, or college students. If you have extra skill with baked goods or cake decorating, you can consider a side business in treats like decorated cakes and cookies, pastries, or specialty breads.

Be smart and choose wisely. If you want to quickly turn your skills into cash, Langemeier suggests you shouldn't waste your time on these ideas:

- introducing an innovative product or service that is new to customers and hard to understand
- starting a business that requires you to borrow a lot of money
- launching a business based on skills that are new or unfamiliar to you

Start a specialty cleaning business for more perks. House-cleaning can be a good way to earn extra income. But before you start a housecleaning business, check how many companies you'll compete against and what they charge. If you'll have to charge ultra-low prices because so many businesses already compete for the same customers, consider a specialty cleaning business instead.

Organic or green housecleaners only use nontoxic cleaners and cleaning methods. This kind of cleaning business could mean you face fewer competitors and can charge higher rates. What's more, you won't need to spend a lot of money to get started, and you might even have an opportunity to work part-time so you can enjoy more leisure during your retirement.

Organized living: from chaos to calm

15-minute trick keeps clutter under control. This is the one cleaning tip you can't live without. Set aside 30 minutes a week, and you'll always have a clean, clutter-free house.

Do a quick, de-cluttering sweep twice a week. Set an egg timer for 15 minutes, grab a laundry basket, and go. Move through each room, putting items in the basket that don't belong in that room and taking out items that do. When the timer goes off, stop. You may not make it through the whole house in 15 minutes, but with twice-a-week sessions everything will eventually return to its rightful place.

Give your back a break by using a wheeled wagon or cart instead of carrying a basket. For two-story homes, place small baskets at the top and bottom of the stairs. Drop items that belong up- or downstairs in the appropriate basket, and always take an item with you when you make a trip.

Start slow to let it go. Are you ever torn between keeping things or giving them away or selling them? There's a simple process that will answer that question for you every time, with complete confidence and no regrets. To get started, you'll need a few boxes, trash bags, and a camera.

Pick an item that, for whatever reason, you can't seem to part with, but you no longer need. Handle it only once while you make a decision about it. Consider whether or not you like the object, if it still works, and when you used it last.

Then, make a decision. Either toss it in the trash, give it to someone who will enjoy it, or store it in a box with the date. If the object is sentimental, take a photo of it first. If you don't use it or miss it after six months, don't take it out. Let it go and move on to the next item.

5 steps help you face the day. Wake up ready to face the day and all set to go when you do these 5 little things the night before. You won't believe how much better you'll feel in the morning.

- Load dirty dishes in the dishwasher and clean the sink.
- Prepare your morning coffee. Measure out the coffee grounds and pour water in the holding tank. Come morning, all you'll have to do is flip the "on" switch.
- Pack your lunch for tomorrow.
- Walk around with a basket and pick up all the out-of-place items. While you're in each room, put back the items that belong there.
- Sort the mail into bill, junk, and other piles, then file in the appropriate places.

10 smart uses for a shoe organizer. This handy tool can be hung from a door or wall and makes cleaning up clutter a breeze. Check out these ideas for using a pocket shoe organizer in every room in your house.

- kitchen closet — store bottles of cleaners and sponges. Or hang one in full view and display utensils like spatulas and measuring cups.
- bathroom — store toiletries, hair accessories, and medicine bottles.
- bedroom — corral belts and socks.
- garage — put up cans of spray paint and coiled extension cords.
- craft or sewing room — stash skeins of yarn, spools of thread, and rolls of ribbon.
- linen closet — roll up washcloths and hand towels.
- pantry — stock boxes of rice, seasoning packets, and canned goods.
- home office — organize pens, paper clips, and printer cartridges.
- coat closet — round up winter gloves, caps, and scarves.
- garden — plant herbs and flowers in a cloth organizer to provide drainage.

Cheap storage for every room. Inexpensive melamine shoe cubbies make terrific storage for almost any room in the house. Stack them on a shelf, set them on the floor, or attach them to a wall. Use them to hold:

- scarves, gloves, hats, and galoshes in your hall closet.
- yarn, rolled-up fabric, and sewing notions in a craft room.
- paired socks, sweats, stockings, or pajamas in your bedroom closet.
- toys and stuffed animals in a child's room.
- washcloths, hand towels, and pretty bottles of bath salts in your bathroom.
- bills, catalogs, and incoming and outgoing mail in your home office.

Surefire way to stay organized

You can organize your whole house just by taking it in small bites. Pick a manageable project you can tackle in 30 minutes, and do a new project every day — 30 minutes a day, every day. Break bigger projects, like organizing the hall closet, into smaller bites. Take on your home one drawer, door, and floor at a time. Once you're organized, keep it that way by spending 10 minutes straightening up before bed every day.

Play a de-cluttering game. Kids are hard-wired to play "pretend." Adults are not. But if you want to get your clutter under control, a little bit of make believe may go a long way.

Just pretend you're moving to a smaller home. Knowing you can't fit everything may give you extra motivation to keep only what you truly love.

Gather five bins or boxes and label them "sell," "give away," "recycle," "keep," and "trash." As you handle each object from a room or closet, ask yourself, "Do I really want to pack this? Will I have room for this in my smaller space?"

When you consider that most people only use 20 percent of what they own, giving items away to a worthy cause or a beloved relative will make you feel good about your decision. Don't focus on the money you spent on an old treadmill you never use. Think of how good someone else will feel using it, or how it might benefit a charity.

Turn your junk into cash. Are you ready to stop "hoarding" all that stuff around the house? You can turn it into cash or get it removed for free. Here's how.

Take a good look at the stuff that's overcrowding your home, and start tagging the items you no longer want, need, or can't remember why you purchased in the first place. You could start by holding a garage sale or participating in a community yard sale, pricing items dirt cheap. But if a yard sale is too much work, you can move the stuff out without the hassle of a sale and still make money. Try eBay or Craigslist. List your things on either site, and see if you get a bite. Consignment shops will also sell your items for you and split the profit. Or you could donate to charity and take the tax deduction.

If you just want to get rid of your stuff and aren't looking to make a quick buck, check out *www.freecycle.org*. Membership is free. To use the site, list an item, share the details, and wait for someone to respond. Then make arrangements for the person to pick it up. It's that easy.

Give your clutter to a good cause. When you de-clutter or remodel your home, you are bound to end up with a garage full of stuff you no longer want. You can't lose by donating it to Habitat for Humanity.

This nonprofit organization accepts donated appliances, furniture, rugs, plumbing and electrical fixtures, and more through its ReStore. Your gift will either go into a family's Habitat home or help raise money to build a home, says Sharon Hazel, Manager of the Newnan-Coweta Habitat for Humanity ReStore in Georgia. "Any donated item we're not able to use directly in building a Habitat home, we resell to generate money to purchase the building materials and services to build Habitat homes."

Everything you donate should work and be in good condition. "When it comes to upholstered furniture, we'd prefer there be no tears, snags, animal hairs, smells, or stains." Slight scratches are fine, she says, if they can be painted over. "Appliances must be less than 10 years old and in 100 percent working order." Even used toilets, sinks, showers, and tubs are welcome, says Hazel, "as long as the porcelain is not cracked and someone can reuse it."

Call your local Habitat for Humanity and ask if they have a ReStore. Find out which items they accept and if they pick up. Some offer free pickup, others ask for a small, tax-deductible donation to pay for gasoline. When you donate, you'll get a receipt for the tax-deductible amount of your gift.

Cut out catalog and credit card clutter

Don't send one more catalog to a landfill. The website *www.catalogchoice.org* can help you put an end to unwanted catalogs. Simply log on and create an account for free. Enter the name of a catalog in the search field, and type in the information from your mailing label.

If you don't have the label, you can still have your name taken off the mailing list. The website also lists credit card companies, charitable organizations, and data brokers that buy mailing lists from other companies. Cancel just about any piece of unwanted mail.

Foolproof plan prevents mail pileups. Go through your mail as soon as you carry it inside. Decide right then what to keep and what to toss, then take action. Write that check, file that letter, or pitch that catalog. Do it now, and you'll take a load off your mind — and your kitchen counter.

No-fuss filing ideas. Ever file something away, then need it, but you've forgotten what you filed it under? There's a way to keep that from happening — and it makes your filing much easier and quicker to boot. Use colored hanging files.

Start by assigning one color to a broad category. For instance, pick green for your financial files, red for permanent records, yellow for insurance papers, and so on. Label your green hanging files with subcategories like "bank" and "retirement accounts." From there pick even smaller categories and alphabetize. For example, your labels might read "bank: checking," "bank: money market," and "bank: savings."

Use clear tabs for your hanging files, and arrange the tabs in a straight line per broad category and color. Affix white, adhesive labels to your file folders. Write legibly on all of your labels with the same color ink, or use a label maker.

To keep your new filing system orderly, place only three file folders in a hanging file, and don't place more than an inch of documents in a hanging file or a file folder.

Smart record-keeping tips. You can organize your financial records the easy way. Use this guide to determine what to keep, what to toss, and where to put it all. For short-term filing, keep:

- ATM receipts and bank deposit slips until you check them against your monthly statement.
- credit card statements and paycheck stubs until you receive your W2.
- expired insurance policies, utility bills, and mortgage papers until the start of a new calendar year.
- loan documents until the loan is paid off.
- investment forms until you receive your year-end statements.

- home improvement records until you sell your home.

You can let go of receipts for minor purchases after you've used them a few times or the warranty has expired. But keep receipts for major purchases.

Keep tax returns and tax-related receipts for seven years. After seven years, you only need to hold on to your tax returns. Never get rid of wills, marriage licenses, divorce papers, birth and death certificates, life insurance policies, property deeds, social security cards, and military discharge documents.

Create more storage space in your closet. You can make the most of your closet by looking at the space in a new way. Here's how.

- Dedicate two-thirds of your closet for hanging clothes. Get rid of the long closet rod that's in your closet now and install two rods. Mount one rod high for dresses and coats. Mount another about 3 feet off the floor for tops and folded pants.

- Store folded clothes like T-shirts and sweaters on shelves. Adjustable, wire shelving is inexpensive and easy to install. Separate socks, scarves, belts, purses, and undergarments into their own baskets. Hang the baskets on a wall.

- Put a small dresser in your closet for additional storage if you have extra space.

Expert advice for fixing closet disasters. Diana Auspurger knows closets. President of both the Association of Closet and

Storage Professionals and her own custom closet company, Creative Storage, she's seen almost every type of mistake. Here's her guide for getting it right.

- Size your shelves. "Shelves in the closet don't really need to exceed 16 inches deep unless it's a linen closet." Make them too deep, she says, "and you end up with a jumbled mess." Measure the folded garments or objects you plan to store, and size your shelves accordingly.

- Hang at the right height. "If your dress is 60 inches long, you want your rod at 65 inches. If you allow too much space for long hanging, you've cheated yourself out of extra shelf space."

- Let it go. People keep clothing they never wear, often out of guilt. "So often, people hang on to clothes because they can't forgive themselves for buying something that didn't suit well. Forgive yourself for making a bad buy," advises Auspurger, "and let it go."

- Get real. Along the same lines, be realistic when buying new clothes. "People gravitate to wearing ultra-comfortable things," she points out. If it doesn't feel good when you try it on in the store, "don't buy it, because you probably won't wear it."

- Match, don't mix. "Using the same item in a closet over and over again — the same hanger or shoe box, for instance — creates a sense of uniformity. And uniformity renders a sense of organization." Create an instant aura of order simply by storing items in similar containers.

Foolproof storage for tight closet spaces. Closets were made for clothes, but not necessarily shoes. Create well-heeled shoe space instantly with these three ideas.

- Got plenty of rod space but no shoe space? Shop for shoe cubbies that hang from your closet rod.
- Invest in a shoe rack that mounts to the inside of your closet door. These are sturdy, solid racks made just for shoes.
- Leave them in their boxes. Tape a photograph of each pair on the outside of the box and stack them on shelves, or buy clear plastic shoe boxes to see at a glance what's inside.

Handy trick for hanging handbags. Get purses off closet floors and shelves with this nifty trick. Clip an extra shower ring around the closet rod and loop purse straps through the ring's opening. Do the same with belt buckles and scarves. To save even more space, attach all your belts or handbags to one hanger by clipping several rings onto a plastic hanger.

Free, fast drawer dividers. Make your own free drawer dividers out of cardboard boxes. Simply cut the box into strips to fit in your drawer. Notch the ends so the pieces fit together and interlock. Arrange different-size strips in your drawers to make custom compartments.

Create space for hanging accessories. Pegboards don't belong only in the garage. Cut one to fit on your closet door, then paint it and hang. Insert tool hooks to hold scarves, jewelry, ties, and other accessories.

Old tie racks help organize your kitchen. Hang scrub brushes and towels from a small tie rack on the inside of your kitchen sink cabinet. Mount another on a wall near the stove for cooking utensils.

Divide and conquer kitchen clutter

Look at your kitchen. No doubt you do different things in different areas — wash dishes in one part, prepare food in another, and make toast or coffee in another area. These are your zones. Divide your kitchen into zones, and organize your cabinets and drawers based on what you use most in each. Cookbooks go in the meal prep area, while mugs go in the coffee-making zone. Baking pans and nonstick sprays should be in your baking area.

Sort your spices in a snap. Hang a tension rod inside a kitchen cabinet for an instant spice rack. Lightweight yet durable, a tension rod will hold small spice containers that would otherwise get lost in a pantry filled with canned goods and bottles. And you can't beat the price — $2 to $3 at the dollar store. Pick up a few extra rods, and use one under the kitchen sink to hang spray bottles, and the others as dividers in messy kitchen drawers.

Safer storage for Rx

Straightening your medicine cabinet is as much a matter of safety as neatness. Follow these guidelines for storing prescription and over-the-counter drugs.

- Clean out your medicine cabinet every six months and remove medications that are expired, dried out, discolored, or crumbling.
- Check eye and ear drops, too. Once these expire they may start breeding bacteria and fungus.
- Remove the cotton in pill bottles. Cotton absorbs moisture, which can affect medicine.
- Store drugs in a cool, dry place — not in your bathroom or near the kitchen stove. Most bathrooms are too humid, and areas by the stove get too warm.
- Keep your medicines on a different shelf or in a different cabinet from your spouse's so you don't accidentally take the wrong ones.

Instant bathroom storage secrets for tiny spaces. Tiny bathrooms hold tons of storage space. You just need to think creatively. Try these ideas on for size.

- Horizontal towel bars waste space. Go vertical with towel hooks, one for each person who uses the bathroom.
- Screw a sturdy cup hook into the side of the vanity, and hang your hair dryer, curling iron, or hand towels.

- Glue long magnetic strips to the inside of your medicine cabinet doors. Use them to hang small, metal grooming tools, like tweezers, scissors, and eyelash curlers.

- Screw smaller cup hooks on the inside of vanity doors to hang brushes.

- Lift reading materials off the top of the toilet tank. Place a stand-alone magazine caddy by the toilet or mount a hanging one on the vanity or wall.

- Stand a coat rack in the corner for bathrobes if more than one person uses the bathroom.

5 simple steps to a tidy bathroom. Tired of losing your favorite tube of lipstick or pair of tweezers under a pile of toiletries? These five easy storage solutions will keep you organized — at little or no cost.

- Place kitchen utensil trays in your bathroom drawers. Divvy up your grooming supplies into each slot. You'll never have to dig through a mountain of toiletries again.

- Repurpose a utensil caddy — the kind you use at a picnic to separate spoons, forks, knives, and napkins. Use it to corral your hair dryer, curling iron, hairbrush, and hairspray.

- Create a decorative display with toilet paper by placing rolls in a tall, glass vase; wicker basket; or a paper towel holder.

- Mount a magnetic strip to the back of a medicine cabinet door. Stick tweezers, nail clippers, and bobby pins to it. Never lose them again.

- Make the most of an empty corner in a cabinet with a turntable like a Lazy Susan. Fill it with bottles of skin care or medicine. Spin for easy reach.

Divide and conquer your linen closet. You want to organize your linen closet but don't know where to start. Start with a stopwatch. Set it for a short amount of time — 15 minutes to 30 minutes max. Pick one shelf and sort through it, setting aside items that are in good condition and tossing out the rest. Only work until the timer goes off. Organizing one shelf a day will make the task less daunting.

As you tackle each shelf, place everyday linens at eye level. Use the top or back of a shelf for beach towels and guest room sheets. Separate sheet sets by room by folding each flat sheet, fitted sheet, and extra pillowcases inside one matching pillowcase. Group towel sets by bathroom, or stack washcloths, hand towels, and bath towels separately. Stash extra blankets in clear plastic bins or cases on the floor. Use over-the-door hooks or organizers to hang soaps, bathrobes, or an extra bath mat.

Cut the clutter in your cleaning closet. Mount a thin towel rack on the inside of the door and hang spray bottles from it by their triggers.

Refill station saves you money. Set up a refill station in your utility room and buy soaps, dishwashing and laundry detergents, cleaners, and personal products in refillable containers. Then save money at the store buying bulk refills and pouring into the smaller bottles at home. Store the extra in your utility room, and keep the smaller containers around the house wherever you need them.

Nifty, thrifty way to organize your paint

Your garage is overrun with them — gallons upon gallons of paint. Most of those cans contain very little paint, but you need to hang on to them for touch ups. Here's a simple solution — pour your paint into Mason jars.

They don't take up much space, and you can pick out your paint colors lickety-split. Print labels with the name of each color and its corresponding room or project for additional ease. While you're at it, put a few brushes for touch ups in an empty jar, and store with your paints. Never lose a can of paint or paintbrush again.

Garage storage game plan. Garages are notorious for collecting piles of junk. Deflated soccer balls, broken appliances, and outdated clothing all seem to make their way into a garage's nooks and crannies. Many people can't even park their cars in their garages for all the stuff that's in the way. After tossing out or donating what you don't want, you can take control of what's left with these three simple steps.

- Trade cardboard boxes for clear, plastic bins. If you can see it, you'll use it. And plastic bins are stackable, too.
- Create a sliding storage system on the ceiling. Hang seasonal items that only need to be taken down once or twice a year.
- Designate zones. Store sporting goods in one section, yard tools in another, and cleaning supplies in another.

Get your garage in order with a filing cabinet. Stick that old, rusty piece of office equipment in your garage. Separate sandpaper grades, different-size saw blades, sewing patterns, and tool instruction manuals in hanging folders with labels. Use leftover drawer space for drills, wound-up cords, spray cans, jars of stain, extra light bulbs, or anything else that fits.

Get unruly cords and Christmas lights under control. You can use a cardboard tube to easily store those pesky electrical cords and holiday lights. Just wrap lights around empty paper towel or wrapping paper tubes, then stow away with Christmas decorations.

Another use — keep cords in order around the house with empty toilet paper tubes. Fold up cords on hair dryers and appliances, then stuff the excess inside the tube. Leave enough length to reach the outlet. Slide extra cords into empty tubes to maintain order in your junk drawer, too.

Tangle-free tip for hanging Christmas lights. If you love to light up your house for the holidays, an old garden hose reel will make decorating a snap. Wind your Christmas lights around a stand-alone reel with a handle when you take them down. Cover with a plastic garbage bag to keep the dust off during storage. They'll unwind with ease and go up twice as fast the next year.

Remodeling: home makeover magic

10 low-cost ways to spruce up your home. You want to make your home look its best, but can't afford an interior decorator or home stager. Here are 10 ways to boost the look of your home for next to nothing.

- Make small, adjacent rooms appear larger and seamless by painting them the same color.
- Create a comfortable, relaxing bedroom by removing extra furniture and decorating with neutral colors.
- Replace burned out light bulbs in lamps and light fixtures both indoors and outside.
- Opt for translucent window treatments instead of dark ones. Or consider removing curtains altogether, and leaving your windows bare.
- Add table lamps and floor lamps to dark rooms to make them feel warm and cozy.
- Give each room a single purpose. A guest bedroom that also serves as an office is an instant turnoff.

- Mount curtain rods closer to the ceiling and hang longer curtains. This will make your ceiling look higher, and your room look more spacious.

- Display neutral-colored items in groupings on built-in shelves. Neutral colors will draw attention to the bookshelves.

- Paint your outdated appliances with stainless steel paint. If you plan on painting your stove, use a high-temperature product. And for your dishwasher, cover the front panel with a stainless steel stick-on.

- Hang a white shower curtain and white towels in your bathroom. Accessorize with neutral colors, and paint or replace gold and brass hardware with silver.

Boost your home's value for less. Thinking about selling your home? Or just want to increase what it's worth? You don't need to break the bank with a complete remodel. Here are a few quick ways to add value on a budget.

- Flip through current design books and magazines for do-it-yourself inspiration. Or ask a realtor to spend an hour walking through your home. An agent can provide free counsel on current home improvement trends.

- Transform an empty basement into living space like a home office or media room. More living space equals greater value.

- Upgrade the master bathroom with a window over the tub. Use acrylic block windows to let light in without sacrificing privacy.

- Research ways to cut energy costs. An energy-efficient home is more attractive to a potential buyer. This may mean replacing old windows with new ones.

- Rid your home's exterior of mildew. Kill it with a mildewcide spray, and prevent it from coming back with mildew-proof paint.

- Spruce up your garage by getting as much off the floor as possible. Install extra lights and shelves throughout your garage, and clean or polish the floor.

Curb appeal on a dime. You want to make a great first impression to a potential home buyer, but don't know where to start. Go with easy and economical fixes first.

- Spruce up the outside of your windows. If they're within reach, wipe them down with vinegar mixed with water, then rinse with your garden hose. For windows out of reach, use a long-handled brush.

- Freshen up your front door with paint. Pick a color that contrasts with your home's facade. Hang a decorative wreath or a classic door knocker, and place attractive house numbers on, or next to, your door.

- Affix a sleek kick plate to save your front door from wear and tear along the bottom edge. For as low as $25, you can find them in brass, satin nickel, and oil-rubbed bronze.

- Say hello to a new welcome mat. They're inexpensive, and will make your entry look well-kept.

- Create symmetry by placing potted plants, Grecian urns, or sculptures on each side of your front door.
- Blast dirt and debris off the walkway and driveway with a garden hose turned to its strongest setting.
- Replace outdated light fixtures. Or better yet, spray paint them and save a bundle.
- Tidy up your yard by trimming trees and bushes, and weeding flower beds.

Room design made easy. Choose the look you want for your room with a "decorating diary." Fill the pages of a notebook with ideas you find — paint card samples, pictures clipped from magazines or furniture ads, scraps of fabric, and your own notes and measurements. As you collect images, colors, and textures you love, you'll discover a common theme that becomes the room's "look."

Maximize the space in your home. Revamp your rooms with minimum effort. Simply rearrange your furniture to prime locations throughout your house.

In the living room, move your sofa a few inches away from walls. A bit of breathing room will make the area seem larger. Plus, warm up the ambiance by placing lamps around the room, and divvying up the lighting equally. Split a long, rectangular family room into two squares. Make one square a conversational area with a sofa facing a couple of comfy chairs.

Turn the other square into a space for casual eating or playing games with four chairs around a square or round table.

Make beds the focal point of each bedroom. Choose a light headboard for small rooms, and a heavy headboard for large rooms with tall ceilings. Give yourself a path of at least 2 feet all the way around your bed. For a room with plenty of floor space, place a bench at the end of your bed or a chair in a corner for extra seating.

Dining room tables should be centered beneath a light fixture. If possible, place your table a minimum of 3 feet from walls. Chairs should be placed at least 6 inches apart. A round or square table works best in a square room, while an oval or rectangular table fits the bill in a rectangular room.

For fun and variety, move furniture pieces from one room to another until you find an ideal spot. You never know — a lone dining room chair may find the perfect home in a guest bedroom.

Guard your home against crooked contractors. You've heard the horror stories. A friend hires a contractor to do work on his home. He pays in full and then never hears from the contractor again. It happens. These shady characters love to scam senior adults. But you can protect yourself if you know what to look for.

Stay away from contractors that request full payment up front. Otherwise, the contractor can disappear at any time and never complete the work. And never make a final payment until the work is finished to your satisfaction. Ask for a contract. The contract should include a start date, end date, total cost of the project, and details of the work that needs to be done. It should also include the contractor's signature, and yours.

Make sure the contractor is insured and bonded. Look for that information on their business card. It can tip you off to how reliable and honest they are. If the company is bonded and it doesn't complete the work, you are protected. Shop around by getting at least three estimates. Plus, don't trust a contractor who says he can do the job quicker and cheaper with leftover materials from a previous project. Or a stranger who knocks on your door selling his services for cheap.

Never hire a contractor whose only means of communication is an answering service. You should be able to contact him as needed. Also, steer clear of a contractor whose only address is a post office box.

A good contractor should share a list of references. Better yet, if you have a friend or neighbor whose home improvement project turned out great, find out who did it. A friend's recommendation may be the best reference of all. Your local hardware store may also have some good suggestions.

Give your shower a facelift. Replacing a shower door is a value-packed way to freshen up a bathroom without breaking the bank. "Most older shower doors have soap buildup that is difficult to scrub away," says Scott Cole, a bathroom remodeling contractor. "People also say they can't seem to clean shower doors because of hard water stains. But the glass doors have actually been etched with chemicals and minerals from the water, so they can't be cleaned."

Scott recommends a clear glass door over a frosted one for an updated look. "Clear glass will also make a bathroom look larger," says Scott. He also steers clients away from gold and antique brass trim. Says Scott, "Brushed nickel, oil rubbed bronze, or chrome are the way to go."

Improvements that add the most value

Nationally, adding a deck, replacing siding and windows, and doing minor kitchen and bathroom makeovers earn the most bang for your buck when you sell your house. However, experts warn of a downward trend in the dollar-for-dollar return on remodeling projects.

If you are remodeling to meet your own needs, this may not matter to you. But if you are remodeling in order to sell your home, think twice before sinking lots of money into a major project. Ask a local real estate agent to tour your home and offer advice on which upgrades are worth making.

Update an out-of-date popcorn ceiling. Nothing dates a home more than a popcorn ceiling. But you can easily scrape away this textured relic over a weekend.

Start by removing everything in the room. Next, cover the floor with plastic sheets or drop cloths. For the next few steps, you'll need eye protection, a handheld garden sprayer, a step ladder, and a ceiling scraper, putty knife, or drywall knife.

Spray a 3 foot by 3 foot section of ceiling with water. You can also ask your local hardware store about a solution that will soften the texture. Try scraping off the popcorn. If it's too dry, spray it again and wait a few minutes. Keep working one section at a time until you have scraped the entire ceiling. When you're done, apply drywall mud if needed, then sand the ceiling with a sanding pole and screen. Finish your ceiling with primer and paint.

One word of caution before you get started — if your home was built before 1979, ask a pro to test the ceiling for asbestos.

Whip up a picture perfect wall treatment. Skip the costly wainscoting and create a winsome wall treatment with picture frames. Paint them white, and hang them below a chair rail. For variety, use frames of assorted shapes and sizes. For a uniform look, use identical frames.

Extend the life of your carpet

Your new carpet can last for years or deteriorate quickly depending on the pad you place underneath it. Consider three factors — density, thickness, and material — when shopping for padding. For a combination of cushion and durability, choose a pad with 6 to 8 pounds of density. Make sure your pad meets your carpet manufacturer's specs for thickness. If you don't, you may void your carpet's warranty. Consider going with a rebonded material — it's recycled and reasonably priced.

3 things you need to know about buying carpet. Picking carpet is like shopping for cereal — with so many choices, it's hard to know which one is right for you. If you're in the market for new carpet, the three things to consider are traffic flow, desired feel, and price tag.

For high-traffic areas like hallways and living rooms, go with nylon. It's durable, versatile, and moderately priced. A space with lots of sunlight needs the fade resistance of polyester. This fiber also repels stains easily. Plus, it's easy on your pocketbook. Olefin is a cheap fiber that is easy to clean and fends off the sun's rays. It also gets dirtier faster than the other fibers. Keep it out of high-traffic zones, but it works well in a sunny room. For a soft feel with the durability of nylon and the fade resistance of polyester, go with triexta. Made with corn sugars, a renewable resource, it's also a "greener" option.

In addition to picking the right fiber, consider the carpet type or pile. A twist or cut pile is soft to the touch, looks casual, and works best in a low-traffic room like a bedroom. Loop pile, also known as Berber, offers loads of durability without the softness of cut pile. It's the perfect pile for an active family room or basement. A patterned carpet, which combines cut and loop piles, packs a visual punch and is best served in a formal dining or living room.

Trim tile with ease. You're installing vinyl floor tiles, but can't cut the tiles with a utility knife. Try using your rotary fabric cutter. It's easy on the hands, and works like a charm.

Turn a concrete floor into a work of art. Painting a concrete floor may seem like an over-the-top undertaking, but the payoff is priceless. Experiment with a small section of floor first. Tape off a smaller square or rectangle. With additional tape, create a grid pattern and paint it black and white or two other contrasting colors. Your design will look like tile. If your square is in an open area without furniture, turn it into a large checkerboard or chess board with oversize playing pieces. For the more adventurous, use a stencil with an intricate pattern or paint thick, bold stripes.

Never use regular latex wall paint. It's not formulated to hold up to foot traffic. Instead, pick up paint specially made for concrete floors. Or you can try Chalk Paint — it adheres to most surfaces, and makes a beautiful base for a stenciling project.

Flawless picture placement with a sticky note

Don't put pencil marks on your wall to hang a picture. Use a sticky note to show you where to place the hook. It's a cinch to peel off when you're done, and it will keep your wall clean.

Raise your art to the ideal height. Ever wonder how high to hang your works of art or family photos? Use this quick, step-by-step guide to do what design experts do.

Mark your wall 57 inches up from the floor. Measure the height of your picture and divide it in two. For instance, if your frame is 30 inches tall, the midpoint is 15 inches. Then measure the top of the frame to the wire or mounting hardware. Subtract this number from the midpoint measurement. If the wire is 3 inches below the top of the frame, subtract 3 inches from 15 inches. You end up with 12 inches. Mark the wall 12 inches above your 57-inch point or at 69 inches. Hang your hook at 69 inches. The center of your picture will settle at 57 inches.

These guidelines also work for groups of photos or art work. Decide which picture will serve as the focal point, and follow the above guidelines. Surround your centerpiece with the rest of your photos.

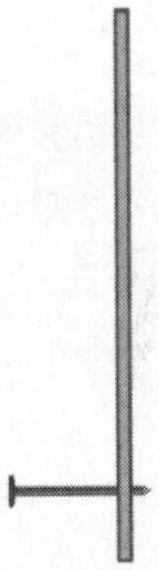

Hang a picture with ease. You need to hang a lightweight item on a wall, but can't quite figure out how to mark the spot. Try making this handy tool. A nail and a thin, rectangular piece of wood — like a ruler or paint stick — are all you need. Drive the nail into one end of the piece of wood, but don't drive it all the way through. You want the sharp end of your nail to just poke through. Hang your picture from the flat end of your nail. Decide where you want to place it on your wall. Gently press against the picture, leaving a small nail mark on the wall. Remove your picture, and put down your new tool. Find the mark on the wall, hammer a new nail into it, and hang your picture.

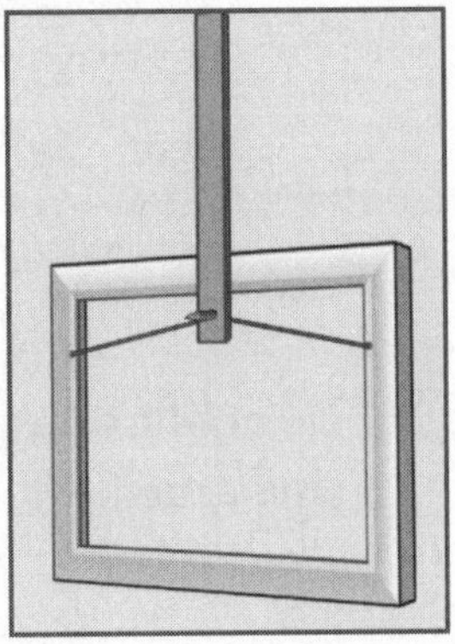

Simple recipe for chalkboard paint. You can make your own chalkboard paint with unsanded grout and flat latex or acrylic paint in any color. The recipe is simple — mix 2 tablespoons of grout for every cup of paint. If you want to paint a larger surface, mix 1 cup of grout with a half gallon of paint. Stir your mixture in a well-ventilated area. Mix it thoroughly to keep it from looking grainy. Then paint away. Allow the surface to dry and cure for two to three days. Rub chalk along the surface and gently wipe it off. Grab a piece of chalk and start writing. Use your custom chalkboard paint for any surface in your home from an entire wall to a kitchen or cabinet door.

Pick the perfect roller for your paint job. No need to hire an expert. You can roll on paint like a pro by following a few easy steps.

- Pick the perfect roller for your paint job by following these guidelines.

Type of surface	Roller nap in inches
smooth	3/16 — 1/4
semi-smooth/ light to medium texture	3/8 — 1/2
semi-rough to rough	3/4 — 1
extra rough	1 1/4 — 1 1/2

- Use a lint roller, vacuum, or the sticky side of painter's tape to remove excess lint from a new roller.

- Paint the edge along the ceiling, shoe molding, and around switch plates and outlet covers with a brush before rolling. You may need a couple of coats to avoid brush strokes.
- Run your roller in a paint tray until it's covered with paint without being over saturated.
- Roll paint on the wall in a "W" pattern, overlapping strokes and covering sections about 3 feet wide.
- Pull the roller away lightly from the wall as you finish each section to prevent painting a noticeable line.
- Rewet your roller, and continue filling in your "W" pattern while starting a new one adjacent to it.

Memory trick for painters

The next time you paint or stain a door in your house, jot down the name of the color on top of the door. If you ever need to repaint or re-stain it, you'll be able to find the color in no time at all. And no one will ever see your handwritten note.

Painting tips for a variety of surfaces. You can't paint brick the way you would plastic or drywall. Each surface needs individual attention. Use these guidelines to optimize your next painting project.

Drywall — Clean drywall with either a trisodium phosphate cleanser (TSP) or a mixture of one cup white vinegar per gallon of water. For drywall with greasy buildup, use a cup of ammonia per gallon of water. Prime the wall to cover water and mildew stains and to keep old color from bleeding through. Apply a coat of paint and allow it to dry completely before applying a second coat.

Brick — Wash brick with a scrub brush and mild detergent mixed with water. To remove tougher grime buildup, try a tablespoon of boric acid mixed with a gallon of warm water. Wipe your bricks with a wet rag, and allow them to dry completely. Brush on a masonry sealer. Apply paint with a long-nap roller, and use a brush to fill cracks and crevices.

Plastic — Most plastic projects require light sanding to help paint adhere properly. After roughing up the surface, wipe it with a clean cloth or TSP to remove excess particles. Coat with a primer and spray paint made specifically for plastic.

Laminate — Use water and mild dish detergent to wash laminate surfaces such as kitchen cabinets. Make the surface gritty with fine sandpaper, and wipe it with tack cloth. To keep your paint from scratching or peeling off, use a primer and allow it to dry completely. Paint your surface then seal it with a protective finish.

Bright ideas for home lighting. Designers divide interior lighting into three categories — task, accent, and ambient. A perfectly lit room combines all three.

Task-oriented light helps define work areas in a room. In a kitchen, for instance, you can hang pendants and install under-cabinet lighting to illuminate work spaces. Pendants should hang about 30 inches above the work surface, and should be fitted with shades or globes that direct light downward. Floor and table lamps with adjustable arms also provide task lighting. Use them to brighten your favorite reading spot in your bedroom or family room. If you're not sure about the size of a table lamp, design pros suggest bigger is better. You can also achieve task lighting by installing recessed ceiling lights and pointing them toward a work space. In bathrooms, shoot for lights that keep shadows and glare away from mirrors.

Draw attention to a focal point in a room with accent lights. A recessed ceiling light aimed at a work of art or family portrait is an example of an accent light. This type of lighting can also shine on architectural features such as interior columns illuminated with candle sconces. The key is to direct light toward an attractive element in a room, and away from unappealing places.

Ambient light fixtures provide mood and general lighting. Torchères or floor lamps with shades that direct light toward the ceiling and then diffuse it throughout a room deliver ambient light. So do recessed lights and dining room chandeliers controlled by a dimmer switch. To pick out a new chandelier for a dining room, go with a classic that won't date your space. Hang about 30 inches above your dining room table.

Buy the perfect ceiling fan. Choosing the best ceiling fan is easier than you think. Start by measuring the length and width of your room to calculate square feet. Next, use the chart on the following page to determine the fan diameter you need.

Room size in square feet	Fan diameter in inches
Up to 75	29 to 36
76 to 144	36 to 42
144 to 225	44
225 to 244	50 to 54

Also, consider the height of your ceiling. Go with a flush mount if your ceiling is 8 feet high. Use a downrod mount for taller ceilings.

Ceiling fans can help you save money on your energy bill. In the summer, run the blades counter clockwise to make your room feel 7 to 10 degrees cooler. And during winter, reverse your blade rotation to keep a room warmer. Don't want to stand on a chair to yank your fan's chains? No problem. Some ceiling fans come equipped with wall controls or handheld remotes. Control your fan from the comfort of your living room sofa, and enjoy the breeze.

Make a splash with an unconventional backsplash. Tin tiles look terrific, but they're expensive. Metal skirting — the sheets used to cover the exposed, lower part of mobile homes — can deliver a comparable look that packs a punch. Pick them up for a fraction of the cost of tin tile from your local home improvement store — then cut and glue in place. The dimpled, block design creates an attractive texture, and metal skirting is durable and easy to clean. For a slick look, affix galvanized metal sheets. They're cheap, sleek-looking, and also easy to install. Don't like the thought of silver metal hanging from your kitchen walls? Prime and paint the metal skirting or sheets to match your kitchen colors.

Old kitchen cabinets get a new look. Spruce up your kitchen cabinets by removing their doors. The open shelves work with any interior design from contemporary to country. Display a collection of china, heirloom glassware, or modern bowls, pitchers, and vases. To spice up the look even more, paint or wallpaper the insides of your cabinets. Keep the doors on a few cabinets to hide stacks of unsightly pots and pans or tacky coffee mugs. The contrast between open and closed cabinets will give your kitchen the update it needs.

Build an entertainment center and save big. You can spend a fortune on an entertainment center. But you don't have to. Give your TV and stereo a place to call home with stock kitchen cabinets. "We did this in our family room," says Kari Cedric. "The bottom 'built-in' cabinets on either side of the fireplace are simply stock upper kitchen cabinets. We topped them with one piece of wood, and then added a few shelves. Big savings!"

Stock cabinets are less expensive than custom-made, but you'll need to assemble them. Measure your space and TV first so you'll buy the right size cabinets. Rearrange them and add shelves above to suit your needs. Finish your custom-built unit with crown molding and filler strips. You can also remove a couple of cabinet doors or replace them with glass-front doors. This idea also works as attractive storage and library space.

Create a cleat to hang heavy items. Here's a great idea for hanging cabinets, headboards, and shelves — anything that's heavy. Create a French cleat out of scrap wood flooring or cut lumber. A French cleat is made up of two pieces of wood, each with an angled edge. Secure one piece to the wall on a couple of studs, angle-side up. Affix the other piece to the object you are hanging, angle-side down. Place the two pieces together to form a snug fit. In addition to giving your heavy object extra support, a French cleat also allows you to slide your item back and forth until it's perfectly placed on your wall.

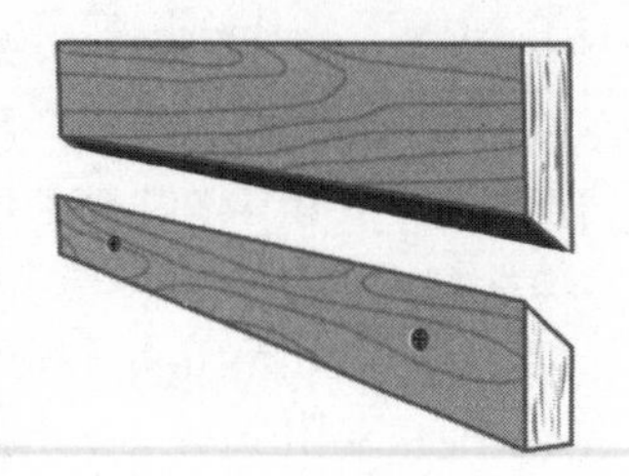

Spruce up tile countertops with paint. You can breathe new life into old tile countertops by painting them. It's easier than you think, and won't cost a pretty penny.

To prep your tile, remove grime with an abrasive tile cleaner, and bleach areas covered in mold. Repair any cracks or chips with caulk or epoxy. Then finish prepping your surface with an epoxy-based primer. Choose an epoxy paint for durability, and carefully apply several thin coats. Allow each coat to dry completely before applying another layer. Once you're satisfied with the coverage, allow two to three days for the paint to cure. Finish your project by protecting it from moisture and scratches with a clear, water-based top coat.

For around $40, you can try a product made specifically for sprucing up old sinks and tile called Homax Tough Tile, Tub & Sink Refinishing Kit. It comes with a cleaning solution, paintbrush, and epoxy paint, and can be used on fiberglass, porcelain, glazed ceramic tile, and countertop laminate.

Clever ways to save on granite countertops. You're ready to redo your countertops, but want to save money in the process. No problem. Start by choosing a common color like an earth tone over a rare one like blue. Pick a square edge over a beveled or curved. Order granite for your countertops only. Choose another option for your backsplash. Shop the remnant section if you need granite for a small area, like a bathroom vanity. Granite remnants are leftovers from bigger jobs, and sell for a fraction of the cost. If these ideas still put you out of your price range, consider granite tile. It costs less than a single slab, and it's cheaper to install.

Two-sided tape helps position strike plate

If you need to install a new deadbolt, stick a piece of double-sided tape to the end of the deadbolt. Make sure the bolt is retracted. Close your door and turn the bolt as if you're going to lock it. Your tape will stick to the door jamb at the precise place you need for your strike plate.

Trendsetting headboard ideas. You can use salvaged doors to create a beautiful backdrop behind your bed. An old barn door evokes a rustic feel. A newer door with a glossy coat of paint becomes a custom headboard with a contemporary feel. A large vintage sign will add down-home country charm to a space. Use it as the focal point in your bedroom, and choose wall colors and accessories to match.

Bring the outdoors indoors with window shutters. Paint them a cool aqua color for a beach decor or antique white for a country feel. Once they're painted, you have two options. Either hang each shutter across the wall behind your bed. Or, to hold the shutters in place, consider attaching a strip of wood across the top and bottom.

If you need a headboard with storage, pull out your drawers — your dresser drawers. Or pick up an old dresser at a garage sale. Measure your headboard space and then fiddle with drawers on the floor. Use plywood scraps to fill empty spots between drawers. Before you do anything else, decide if you want to keep or replace the old pulls. Use screws to turn the drawers and plywood into one large piece. Then paint your new headboard. For a finishing touch, place wallpaper or staple fabric to the insides of each drawer. You now have an attractive and unique piece with shelves for books, photos, and small lamps.

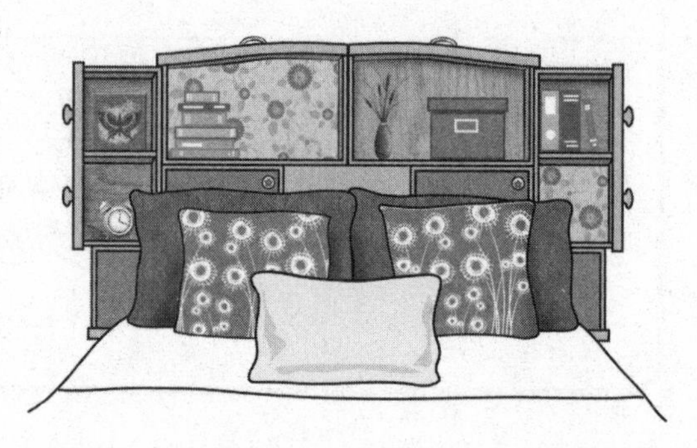

To hang any of these headboards, you'll need a heavy-duty mount like a French cleat.

Transform a bathroom for a bargain. You can add a lot of style to your bathroom with little effort and expense.

- Switch out an old medicine cabinet for a new mirror. Or frame your existing mirror with glass tiles or fluted door casings.

- Install matching towel bars, hooks, cabinet hardware, outlet covers, and toilet paper holder.

- Add sconces on either side of a mirror or window. Place battery-powered candles on them for a soft glow without the risk of a real flame.

- Brighten grout lines with a grout cleaner that removes ground-in dirt.

- Paint soothing colors on your walls and cabinets doors. Go with neutral colors or two harmonious hues. Add splashes of color with towels and accessories.

- Go with white sinks, toilet, and bathtub. They cost less and offer squeaky clean appeal.

- Coordinate light fixtures with the rest of the bathroom's hardware. For instance, install polished nickel light fixtures to match polished nickel towel bars and cabinet pulls.

- Toss out an old window treatment, and hang a Roman shade or install louvered shutters.

- Replace a standard shower head with a multipurpose one. Or pick out a handheld sprayer to ease rinsing off, hair washing, and tub cleaning.

Creative, low-cost ways to hang curtains. PVC pipes aren't just for plumbing. A paint job and decorative end caps will turn these pipes into window dressing for a fraction of the cost of curtain rods. Look for spray paint that's formulated for plastics. Or use a latex primer and latex or acrylic paint. Either way, you'll want to rough up your PVC pipes with sandpaper to help the paint adhere better. Allow the paint to air dry and cure completely. Gently run your curtains through your pipes and hang. Use hot glue to attach finials to the ends for a finishing touch. If you want to add a sheer panel to your window treatment, use a bungee cord. Simply string the cord through your curtains. Then strap the cord on to the wall brackets behind your curtains.

Suck up oil spills. Spring into action by spreading a thick layer of Kitty Litter on a fresh driveway or garage oil spill. Let sit for 12 hours, then sweep away. Next, sprinkle on a layer of dry cement and let sit for a day or two before sweeping off. The cement powder will suck up what's left of the oil and even bleach the driveway back to its original color. For old oil spots, spread on a little paint thinner before covering it in kitty litter.

Keep tiny tools from getting lost. Put Styrofoam scraps to use holding small tools like drill bits and mini-screwdrivers. Lay the foam flat and push the tool headfirst deep into the foam. Label each resulting hole with a magic marker so you know which tool or bit fits into which hole, and return them to the same spot when you finish using them.

How to deal with asbestos

Many older homes contain asbestos, a mineral fiber once used in roofing and siding shingles, insulation, joint compound, vinyl floor tiles, pipe insulation, and other building materials. Unfortunately, inhaling these fibers can lead to lung disease, including cancer.

Household materials made with asbestos are most likely safe as long as they're in good condition and not crumbling. If they are damaged, however, don't try to remove them yourself. Call a certified asbestos professional to repair or remove them.

Jog your memory in style. Making a magnetic memory board is easier and cheaper than you think. Try one of these simple ideas.

Open up your kitchen drawers, and look for an old metal burner cover or pizza pan. If you don't have either of these, you can pick up one at a dollar store. On the lip, drill two small holes several inches apart. Trace your pizza pan on to a piece of scrapbook or contact paper, and cut it out. Then spray paint the edge of your pie plate. When it dries, brush Mod Podge on the inside of your plate and press your paper into it.

Wait until it's completely dry then brush another layer of Mod Podge on top of the paper. Seal it with a clear, acrylic spray. Tie ribbon or yarn into the two holes and hang.

You can try the same idea with a cookie sheet. Instead of covering it with fabric, spray paint the entire sheet with a fun color. Sand or prime a nonstick pan before you begin. If you have a pan with greasy buildup, let it soak in 2 tablespoons of baking soda, a squirt of dishwashing detergent, and hot water for 15 minutes. Then scrub with a scouring pad. Drill holes in your cookie sheet and run ribbon through them for hanging.

For lovers of rustic decor, here's one more magnetic idea — use a salvaged piece of metal like an old tailgate as a memory board. Post messages and hang photos using souvenir magnets.

Safety and security solutions

Age-proof your home. Your body ages, but your house stays the same — the same steep stairs, hard-to-reach cabinets, and slippery bathtubs. Or does it?

Rebecca Stahr, a 50+ Housing Specialist and founder of aging-in-place consultants LifeSpring Environs, believes otherwise. "There are literally hundreds of ways safety concerns can be reduced and alleviated" around the home. "Choices do exist. Doing nothing, that's the wrong choice." Check out these simple changes she suggests you can do yourself.

- install grab bars in the shower, by the toilet, and in other wet areas
- lay rubber strips in bath tubs and showers to prevent slipping
- replace stationary shower heads with hand-held, flexible ones
- put a telephone in the bathroom, one you can reach from the floor
- install roll-out drawers in cabinets for easier access to pots, pans, and other kitchenware

- pull up rugs, hide electrical cords, and get rid of low-seated furniture
- use more and higher-wattage light bulbs
- paint surfaces in contrasting colors so you can see them better

Schedule extra check-ins when traveling solo

You might be tempted to shed your responsibilities and skip your daily safety check-ins when you travel. But if you travel alone, you should protect yourself by checking in even more often than usual. For example, when Laura goes to Florida on vacation every year, she uses her iPad to send her daughter-in-law regular updates about her plans and locations throughout the day. You may prefer to call or text instead, but be sure to include all the information your contact would need to help you or find you if trouble were to happen. You may also want to include your route and roughly when you expect to reach your destination or provide your next update. Remember, the more often you check in, the safer you'll be.

Smart routine if you live by yourself. Schedule a daily check-in with another friend or relative who lives alone. That's what Jane Sullivan did. She asked her friend, Margaret, to be her safety partner. Every day at 10 a.m. Jane would call Margaret.

If she wasn't able to reach her after a few minutes, Jane would go to Margaret's house to check on her. If Margaret didn't hear from Jane by 10:30, she would go to Jane's house to make sure she was all right.

You can set up a similar arrangement if you live alone, but you're not limited to your phone. Some people text each other with their cellphones or use instant messaging on their computers. Others may use Skype to video chat with a webcam and computer. You might even use social media, but only if you can set limits to make sure no one but your friends and family can see and respond to your posts.

For added protection, choose more than one safety partner. You might want to check in with one partner in the morning and another right after dinner. This is a cheap, effective way to make sure help is never more than a few hours away.

3 crime prevention tips for people who live alone. Keep strangers from realizing you live alone, and you may protect yourself from home invasions and other dangers. Use tricks like these to help.

- Call out a good-bye to your dog or cat or just yell "Bye, honey" every time you leave the house. Shout "I'll get it" whenever the doorbell rings unexpectedly.
- When you leave home, leave the television on, or turn on the radio and tune it to an all-talk or all-news station.
- Invite a friend or two over whenever you're expecting a repairman, salesperson, or other stranger to visit your house.

Boost your home's security with smart landscaping. You can't surround your home with a water-filled moat like the castles of the Middle Ages, but you can still make your yard hostile to burglars. Roughly 70 percent of burglars are amateurs who take advantage of easy targets. That means they prefer yards with more places to hide and fewer barriers to a speedy, silent break-in. If your house doesn't fit that description, they may seek easier pickings elsewhere.

Flowers beneath a window are a welcome sight for a thief because he can easily get to the window to break in. But if you plant a hedge of prickly pyracantha beneath that window, climbing over that won't be easy or quick. The thorny hedge may force him to spend more time in plain view of the neighbors while struggling to break in, a problem that may make your home too risky to rob.

So consider growing prickly plants or hedges under your windows, along fences, and around plants or yard features burglars could use for hiding. Good plant choices include spiky hollies, rosa rugosa and other thorny roses, fence climbers like bougainvillea or smilax, palms, cactus, berberis, and pyracantha.

Ask local landscapers about other defensive plants that grow well in your area. Just make sure you plant these yard defenders well away from walking paths and places where they might harm children or pets. Also, be sure to keep them trimmed to 3 feet or less so they make lousy hiding places.

Burglars also like grass and mulches they can cross silently. Surround the prickly plants beneath your windows with an attractive gravel mulch, and you'll hear crunchy, intruder-scaring noises when anyone walks through it.

Turn ceiling lights into motion detectors

Make that dark garage, basement, or attic a safer place. Just unscrew the light bulb in your ceiling fixture, and screw in a motion-sensing light socket. When you're done, screw the light bulb back in. Make sure the wall switch is flipped to its ON position before you leave the room. The next time you enter, the light will switch on automatically and stay on for at least several minutes.

Product reviewers say the motion detection works best when it's at least 2 feet away from the nearest wall and is not blocked by a shade. You can find this type of sensor online or at home improvement stores like Home Depot.

Know what to do when a stranger knocks. Experts warn that some door-to-door salespeople may be burglars. For example, someone may pose as a home security system salesperson so he can enter your house and "case the joint" for a later burglary. To help prevent robberies and other crimes, don't open the door when a stranger knocks or rings your doorbell. Instead, ask who it is and what they want. Or, if you have a peephole, check to see who's there. If the person claims to be:

- a delivery worker — ask who she is delivering to. If she can't tell you, look up her employer's phone number and call to be sure she works for them.

- a repair worker, meter reader, or employee of a business, utility company, or government agency — ask the person to stand by. Look up his employer's phone number, and verify that he works for them. Don't use a phone number the person gives you unless it matches the number you look up. Only open the door if the person is legitimate and can show you a photo ID, preferably a company ID card.

- a security alarm salesperson or any other door-to-door salesperson — call his employer to verify that he works for them. If he does, ask him to leave his office contact details and company information outside the door, so you can research the business and decide whether to schedule a sales appointment.

If the person wants to call 911, a roadside assistance service, or a family member, offer to make the call. Con artists and criminals may quickly vanish after you make this offer, but people with a legitimate problem are likely to stay.

Schedule a free home security check-up. "Many homeowners suffer from a victim mentality, believing that there is little they can do to deter a determined burglar. This isn't the case," says Michael Fraser, former host of BBC's *Beat the Burglar*. "Most burglaries are committed because an opportunity has arisen." To make sure your home won't present opportunities for burglars, call on the experts — the police. Ask your local police department if it offers a free home security audit. Many police departments do. This means you can make an appointment for a police expert to walk through your home, point out the weak spots that put you at risk, and explain how to fix them. It's that simple, and it could make all the difference.

Warning — you may be inviting a robbery. You wouldn't tell a thief when you're going on vacation — or that you just got a new diamond pendant or big screen television he can steal. But you may be sharing this information with thieves or other troublemakers even if you don't mean to. It's so easy to share sensitive information in a public place without realizing it. For example, you could be overheard while:

- walking down the street with a friend as you chat about when your new work schedule will keep you away from home.
- talking over the sound of a blow dryer at a hair salon as you describe the expensive new birthday present you just received.
- speaking loudly into your cellphone in a public place because the other person is having trouble hearing you. If you're making an appointment by phone, you may even give out your phone number and other personal information.

Sometimes you don't even have to speak. You can tempt a home invader just by posting vacation photos on social media while you're away from home.

So be careful about what you say or type when you're in any place that may not be private. Don't mention your schedule, travel plans, expensive or rare possessions, account numbers, or personal information unless you're sure no one can overhear you or read your lips. Also, watch out for places that may seem private when they really aren't, such as public restrooms, your yard, a street, parking lot, restaurant booth, city bus, or subway. If you absolutely must speak about sensitive information in public, lower your voice and cover your mouth.

Give your home an extra layer of protection while you're away

Call the police before you go on vacation, and ask if they offer a vacation home check program. These programs arrange for police officers or volunteers to either drive by participating homes or perform a walking check of the house while a homeowner is away. And many towns offer the program for free.

Simply tell the police when you will leave and return from vacation and what you would like them to do. Some people prefer not to have the police check their house as it may tip off potential thieves that they're away. Once you've signed up for a vacation home check, you'll probably enjoy your vacation even more thanks to this extra layer of protection.

Critical tips for surviving a break-in. Keep your cool, and follow this expert advice to increase your odds of surviving unharmed.

- If someone breaks into your home while you are there, cooperate with them. They may relax and be less likely to hurt you.
- If you think you hear someone breaking in at night, leave — if possible — without alerting them. Then call the police from a neighbor's house or your cell phone.
- If you awake to someone in your bedroom, pretend you are still asleep. Wait until the coast is clear, then call the police.

- Don't look an intruder in the eye. Intruders are more likely to hurt you if they think you can identify them to police.

- Give a code word or phrase to a friend who calls you often. If they happen to call during a home invasion, you can tell the intruder your friend will be suspicious if you don't answer. Then you can alert your friend to dial 911 by saying the code word.

Trip up thieves while on vacation. Secure your automatic garage door when you leave on vacation by unplugging the auto-opener and bolting the door panels shut from the inside. Then leave the house through your front door.

Best way to deter burglars. Burglars decide how to break in based on which door looks easiest to open. Encourage burglars to look elsewhere by following this advice.

- Choose exterior doors made of metal or solid hardwood at least 1-3/4 inches thick, with door frames made of equally tough material. Doors should hinge on the inside with hidden or nonremovable pins and close securely in their frames.

- Install extra-tough doors and locks leading from the garage into your home. Burglars love entering through garages because they have plenty of cover from prying eyes.

- Buy deadbolt locks with a bolt that extends at least 1 inch and hardened steel inserts to keep burglars from sawing through it.

- Make sure your deadbolt has a reinforced strike plate anchored in the door with extra-long screws for added security.

- Consider a double-cylinder deadbolt on doors that have glass within 40 inches of the lock. You need a key to unlock these from inside, too.

Defend against car burglaries. Thieves who break into cars love readily visible goodies, so keep your car from offering a showcase of loot. Always hide your new purchases, purse, electronics, and other valuables so a potential burglar can't see them. Yet be aware that some thieves spy on parking lots to catch people putting purchases or valuables into a hiding place. Here's how you can frustrate them.

Any time you leave your car, lock your trunk and all your doors, and close all your windows. When you can't avoid keeping valuables or new purchases in your car, either pull over and hide them in your trunk before you reach your destination, or plan your shopping so you don't need to hide things before you're ready to leave.

If you must offload purchases to your car and do more shopping, move the car to another section of the lot, preferably a well-lit, busy area far from your original parking spot. If your car has no trunk for hiding things, stash your items under the seat, or cover them completely.

Of course, your best bet is to avoid keeping valuables and purchases in your car for any longer than necessary. Always unload them at home as soon as possible.

Smart strategies for dealing with a lost purse or wallet. First of all, don't cancel your credit cards. Instead, call your credit card companies and ask them to issue you cards with new numbers. Canceling your cards could harm your credit score. Here are four other surprising things you must do.

- File a police report and hang on to the paperwork. You may need it in the future to prove your wallet was lost or stolen.
- Call the credit bureaus — Equifax, Experian, and TransUnion — and place fraud alerts on your accounts. Or ask them to place credit freezes once you've ordered new cards. A credit freeze will keep scammers from being able to open new accounts using your name.
- Inform the Department of Motor Vehicles that your license has been stolen. They can flag your file to prevent a thief from using your number.
- Visit your bank to cancel your checking account and any accounts linked to it. Open new accounts, and request a new debit card.

Clever ways to frustrate pickpockets. The purse you choose or the place you keep your wallet could make the difference between becoming a pickpocket's victim or leaving the crook frustrated. Pickpockets love a purse that is easy to reach into, so foil them by choosing a purse that's tougher to open. Purses with clasps, zippers, or snaps are good choices.

Look for one that also has a strap you can hang diagonally across your body so you can keep your purse in front of you. Men who put their wallets in a back pocket are tempting pickpockets to strike. So experts suggest both women and men should carry money, identification cards, and credit cards in a front pocket or a pocket that buttons or zips. Pickpockets avoid these.

Guard your loved ones against "ghosting." This form of identity theft brings the dead back to life. Con artists scan obituaries and steal death certificates to assume the identity of a deceased person. They use the information to open fake credit card accounts, apply for loans, and file for tax refunds. Since the deceased can't monitor their own credit reports, these rogues rack up thousands of dollars worth of charges and pocket thousands more in tax refunds. Here's what you can do to protect a loved one.

- When the official death certificate becomes available, request at least 12 copies. You will need these as proof that your loved one has died.
- Thieves scan obituaries looking for information they can use to create an identity. Don't give it to them. Keep your loved one's birth date and mother's maiden name out of the obituary.
- Cancel the deceased person's driver's license.
- Unless you notify the credit bureaus Equifax, Experian, and TransUnion, they will not be aware of the death. Send them copies of the death certificate, and ask them to place a deceased alert on the person's credit reports.
- A surviving spouse or executor of the state may request free copies of the deceased's credit report. Request one periodically and look for suspicious activity.

- Inform the Social Security Administration of your loved one's death. Be prepared to send the SSA a copy of the death certificate.
- Send copies of the death certificate to financial institutions, mortgage companies, insurance agencies, and the Veteran's Administration if the person served in the military.
- Always make copies of all of your correspondence.

Tricks to brighten your home in a blackout. Don't worry if you don't have enough flashlights when the power goes out. You may have other lights available, and some won't even need matches or batteries. For example, if you have solar landscape lights, bring them inside at sunset. Drop each one into its own tall mason jar or drinking glass, and place them wherever you need light. Put them back outside to recharge the next morning. If you don't have solar lights, leftover glow sticks from a recent kids' party are good substitutes — and they're cheap.

If you can't come up with other lighting, use this trick to get more light from your flashlight. Turn the flashlight's narrow beam into a wider glow by filling a milk jug with water. Rest the flashlight so the lighted end is pressed against the flat outside surface of the jug. The light shining into the jug will be reflected by the water so you get a pleasantly lighted area several feet wide.

Store water safely for emergencies. If you're on well water or untreated public water, add a small amount of household bleach before storing it as part of a disaster kit. Use only regular liquid bleach that contains 5.25 percent sodium hypochlorite, not scented or colorsafe bleach. Stir in 16 drops per gallon of water and let stand 30 minutes. Sniff the water carefully. You should smell a slight bleach odor. If not, stir in another 16 drops and let stand 15 minutes.

You don't need to add bleach to water before storing if the city treats your tap water with chlorine. Keep it in food-grade plastic bottles, such as 2-liter soda bottles, in a cool, dark place. Milk jugs don't seal tightly enough. Replace stored water every six months, whether it's self-treated or city treated.

Cut air pollution inside your home. Indoor pollutants are fairly commonplace in our homes, says a spokesman for GREENGUARD Environmental Institute. Furnishings, building materials, and cleaning products can all give off gases containing volatile organic compounds (VOCs). Controlling VOCs at the source is the best way to limit exposure and protect the air you breathe.

One VOC, formaldehyde, is especially widespread in homes. It's often a part of laminated furniture, shelving, and wall coverings. In many cases, the adhesives that bind wood together contain added urea formaldehyde. Start being choosy about the furniture you buy. Avoid wood furniture products that contain higher levels of adhesives, such as particle board, medium density fiberboard (MDF), or plywood. Solid wood is a better option.

Unhealthy products give off fewer and fewer VOCs over time, so you don't necessarily need to kick old pieces to the curb. Instead, take steps to maintain and protect them using low-emitting materials. For instance, formaldehyde also evaporates from paints, varnishes, and chemicals used for sealing and finishing walls. When refurbishing or re-staining furniture use sealants and stains that are certified for low chemical content and emissions. And make sure to perform staining outdoors and with proper protective equipment, such as gloves and a respirator.

Whether you're stripping furniture, painting walls, or cleaning the kitchen, you can avoid dangerous chemicals by selecting products that are certified for their levels of chemical emissions and content. One option is to look for labels like GREENGUARD and Green Seal on products you buy.

Burn cleaner, healthier candles

Paraffin candles made from petroleum products can give off harmful compounds, including formaldehyde, while burning. Soy candles, made from hydrogenated soybean oil, burned cleaner than paraffin and about as clean as beeswax in lab studies. So think about trading in your petroleum-based candles for natural soy or beeswax.

Useful oddities to add to your emergency kit. Outdated and frivolous items can become surprisingly useful during a disaster. Consider adding these to your emergency kit.

- An old phone. If you keep an old cellphone charged, you can still use it to call 911 during an emergency, even without a contract. That could come in handy if your current cellphone dies and you have no power for your cordless home phone. An old-fashioned corded phone is also helpful during a blackout. Unlike cordless phones, your corded phone will still work if the electricity is out.

- Paper maps. GPS units, smartphones, and computers may be useless after a disaster when power may be out and you can't connect to the internet, but paper maps never need electricity. Include paper maps of your local area and your state in your emergency kit so you can use them if you have to evacuate or travel locally after a disaster. You'll know why you need them after the third time a detour sign, downed tree, or other problem forces you to turn around and hunt for a new route.

- Glow bracelets. Use these to mark door knobs, stair rails, tripping hazards, your phone, vital supplies, and other important things during the pitch-black nights that come with power outages.

Keep your room number secret

When the hotel clerk tells you your room number, he is broadcasting it to everyone within earshot, even if he doesn't mean to. Take steps to prevent that security lapse. When you check in, tell the clerk you'd like to keep your room number confidential. Ask him to write the number down so no one can overhear it. If strangers are nearby, you can even ask him to fold the paper before handing it to you, so no one can see the number.

4 ways to charge your cellphone during a blackout. Your cellphone may be vital for getting help or emergency information when the power goes out. For those who have given up landline service to save money, it may be even more important. Fortunately, you have several options for phone charging during a lengthy power outage, especially if you plan ahead.

- Laptop. If your laptop is almost fully charged, you can probably plug your phone charger or a USB cable into one of the laptop's USB ports. This transfers power from your laptop battery to your phone.

- Car charger. Newer cars may offer an AC outlet port you can use with your regular phone charger. But if your car doesn't have that, a car charger can plug into your car's cigarette lighter or charging port and use power from your car's battery. If you didn't get a car charger with your cellphone, you can buy one. Or, if you're really stuck, ask a neighbor if they have one that fits your phone. Just remember, if you turn on your car's engine to charge, pull your car out of the garage to avoid carbon monoxide poisoning.

- Cranking charger. Some emergency radios include a hand crank to generate power and a USB connector port for charging your phone. You can also buy a hand-crank phone charger without the radio. These may not be as cheap as a car charger, but you can probably buy one for under $50.

- Battery-powered charger. You can pick up a charger that runs on AA batteries or a rechargeable power bank for less than $20. Be sure you always keep plenty of AA batteries on hand or keep the rechargeable battery fully charged. You may also need a charging cable that has the proper connectors for both your phone and the charger.

Disaster help for people with disabilities

Handicapped people need special help reaching safety during natural catastrophes. If you're one of them, register with your local fire or police department or your local emergency management agency. Also, register with your electric company if you use critical medical equipment that relies on electricity.

Take steps before disaster strikes. Plan two escape routes from every room, and let everyone in your home know where they are. Keep the routes easily accessible at all times and free of obstacles. Make sure you can find them by touch or feel, since you may not be able to see in the dark.

Keep one credit card in protective custody. Take two credit cards with you on vacation, but only carry one with you while sightseeing. Lock the other one in the hotel safe as soon as you check in — for its own protection. If someone picks your pocket, you won't be stuck without a credit card. You can simply retrieve the second credit card from its "protective custody" in the hotel safe. Just be sure you contact your other credit card company right away to report and cancel the stolen card.

Uncover roadside assistance options you didn't know you had. If you're shopping around for the right roadside assistance program or would like to find a better one, don't forget to check the options hiding in policies you already own.

- Credit card agreement. Look for a roadside assistance package in the terms. Most credit card packages charge you only when you use their services, and the price for basic services and towing will probably be cheaper than paying out-of-pocket. Other packages may pay a portion of the cost for each use until you pass the annual limit on service calls.

- Car warranty. Review the terms of your car's warranty or extended warranty to see if it includes roadside assistance. Many do, but they only cover one car. Also, make sure your warranty hasn't expired.

- Cellphone plan. You may discover a roadside assistance fee buried in your cellphone bill. If not, find out if a roadside assistance option is available as an add-on to your plan.

When reviewing roadside assistance plans like these, be sure to check:

- whether you must pay extra to add other family members.
- the average response time to service calls.
- whether limits are placed on the number of service calls or which repair shops your car can be towed to.
- the percentage of costs covered and whether you must pay upfront and be reimbursed later.
- whether towing after an accident is covered.

What to do if you're stranded in a winter storm. Thousands of Georgia drivers were stranded on interstates for up to 22 hours during a 2014 winter storm. Two weeks later, the same thing happened to thousands of drivers in Raleigh, N.C. Here are five things you can do if this happens to you.

- Stay with your car. Only leave to go for help if that help is available within 100 yards.
- Make sure everyone else can see your vehicle. Tie brightly colored cloths on your antenna and side mirrors, and turn on the dome light at night.
- Check that nothing is blocking your tailpipe. To save gas and prevent carbon monoxide poisoning, only run the engine and the heater for 10 minutes out of every hour. Also, roll down the windows facing away from the wind just a little to keep carbon monoxide from building up.
- Move your arms and legs vigorously from time to time, but don't leave the car.
- If you have a cellphone, call for help. Post an urgent message to your friends on social media if your cellphone can connect to the internet.

To avoid getting stranded in winter storms, always pay close attention to the weather and road conditions before going out on the road and while you're traveling.

Scam protection: don't get swindled

Beware of your own family. It may not be a slick, professional con artist who swindles you out of your money. For many seniors, financial swindles come from their own children, grandchildren, nieces, nephews, brothers, and sisters. Be suspicious if a relative you've trusted to handle your finances keeps you from checking your accounts.

Also, watch out if a relative seems eager to take you to a lawyer to sign a power-of-attorney or talks to you about changing a will, deed, or beneficiary designation on insurance policies. If you do set up a power-of-attorney, keep your relative honest by designating a lawyer, accountant, or another family member to receive regular account updates.

Shop safely online. You can't beat the convenience of shopping online from your own home. It's a great way to avoid the hassles of crowds, parking, and driving all over town. But you must be careful. Here are some easy tips for safe online shopping.

- Look for "https" and the closed padlock symbol in your browser's toolbar before giving your credit card number online. These are signs that you're on a secure site that encrypts, or scrambles, your private information.
- Pay with a credit card. It offers more protection than a debit card.

- Shop only with stores you trust. Beware of companies without a physical address or phone number to make it easy to handle disputes.

- Seek out seals, like the Better Business Bureau Reliability Program, VeriSign Secured, or TRUSTe. But even if a site displays these seals, it could be shady. Check out the seal issuers' websites to verify that the company is legit.

- Be especially careful with auction or classified-ad sites, like eBay or Craigslist. For eBay, if a seller has poor or little feedback, reconsider dealing with him. For Craigslist, only deal locally with people you can meet in person.

Protect your identity from thieves. Concerned about identity theft? You should be. In one year alone, about 10 million Americans were victims. And it's estimated that an identity was stolen every four seconds. In his book, *Stealing Your Life*, Frank W. Abagnale, author of the best-selling memoir *Catch Me If You Can*, explains this common crime.

The scary thing about identity theft is that it can happen to almost anyone. Possible victims include anyone who has a credit card, bank account, mortgage, car loan, debit card, driver's license, Social Security number, phone service, health insurance, or a job. Paying bills and using the internet also puts you at risk.

Once someone steals your identity, they can use it to wipe out your bank account, take out loans in your name, or adopt it as an alias while committing other crimes. You may be denied credit, charged for purchases you didn't make, harassed by collection agencies, or even arrested.

Learn how to prevent this costly crime with these tips from Abagnale's book.

- Check your credit report regularly.
- Don't give out your Social Security number.
- Protect your computer. If you use a wireless connection, make sure it's encrypted.
- Keep track of billing cycles. A missing bill may mean an identity thief changed your address.
- Examine financial statements carefully to make sure all the purchases are legit.
- Guard your mail from theft. Get a post office box and put outgoing letters in a drop box.
- Invest in a shredder.
- Practice safe shopping online.
- Avoid sketchy ATMs, like the portable kind in delis and hotel lobbies.
- Be suspicious of calls or e-mails from a business asking for personal information.
- Put strong passwords on your accounts.
- Keep your credit card close when shopping or eating out. Make sure salespeople and waiters don't have a chance to copy your card.
- Use safe checks, from your bank, and use them sparingly.

- Store your Social Security card, passport, and all financial and tax records in a safe spot in your home.
- Cancel credit cards you don't use.
- Opt out of marketing lists that get sold and resold.
- Read privacy policies for your bank and other businesses, and choose all the restrictions available to you.
- Place fraud alerts on your credit reports.

While nothing is foolproof, Abagnale points out, making things more difficult for thieves may prompt them to give up on you and target someone else.

Don't let swindlers steal your identity — and your home. You can protect yourself from a new form of fraud called "house stealing." Scammers steal your identity and create fake ID cards. Then they visit their local office supply store to buy forms that transfer property. Next, they file the paperwork with the proper government offices. This gives con artists license to sell the home or property and pocket the profits — all behind the real owner's back. These predators also prey on vacant houses and vacation rentals.

You can take a few steps to protect yourself, according to the FBI. Don't throw away any letters or payment books you get in the mail from a mortgage company. Read the documents carefully, and then call the company. Check your county deeds office regularly to see if any new paperwork has been filed on your home. If you suspect you've been scammed, call your local police immediately.

Shred your paper trail

Identity theft doesn't have to be high-tech. In fact, it's more likely to occur when you complete paper forms by mail or in person than over the internet. Protect yourself by tearing, cutting up, or burning documents that contain your personal information. Or buy a document shredder to safely dispose of things like bills, bank statements, pre-approved credit card applications, ATM receipts, pay stubs, medical or dental records, and tax forms when you no longer need them.

Safeguard your Social Security number. For identity thieves, Social Security numbers are like the numbers on a winning lottery ticket. Make sure no one hits the jackpot with yours. Know the law. Many may ask, but only these three must know your Social Security number.

- your employer
- your bank or any financial institution that's involved with taxes or income
- credit bureau, when you're requesting a copy of your credit report. Also, if you're opening a credit account, the company might want to check your credit record and will need your Social Security number.

If your state puts Social Security numbers on driver's licenses, ask if you can use a different number. Other companies might ask for your Social Security number, but you're not legally compelled to give it to them. Keep in mind they can refuse to do business with you if you decline.

Let relatives rest in peace

Identity thieves want you — dead or alive. When a relative dies, stop crooks from using his identity by contacting the credit bureaus and having a "deceased" alert put on his reports. You can also report the death directly to Social Security. Include a copy of the death certificate. The Direct Marking Association also has a "Deceased Do Not Contact" list, which will eliminate telemarketing calls or direct mailings to your deceased relative.

First aid for medical ID theft. A robber may demand "your money or your life" — but crooks who practice medical identity theft could cost you both. Thieves use your health insurance identification or Social Security number to get medical care or make phony insurance claims for reimbursement. Often, they pay employees at hospitals or doctor's offices for this information.

Like all identity theft, this crime takes a financial toll, but it can also mess up your medical history and health care records. If someone else's information finds its way into your records, it could appear as if you've been treated for conditions you never had. You could even be given the wrong blood type during a transfusion. Here are some ways to protect yourself from medical ID theft.

- Guard your health insurance card. Don't loan it or show it to anyone except trusted health care professionals.
- Be suspicious of clinics that advertise aggressively, promise to waive co-payments, or provide transportation.
- Ask to view your medical records.
- Shred any health care or insurance documents you don't keep.
- Read your insurance company's explanation of benefits letters carefully, and question any claims for services or drugs you don't understand.
- Request a yearly list of benefits paid by your insurer, so you can spot fraudulent claims, even if the thief changed your billing address.
- Access your insurance billing statements online rather than receive paper mailings. Keep track of your account.

Drive away with your identity intact

Be careful at car dealerships. Instead of getting a new car, you may lose your identity. When you take a car out for a test drive, the salesman will ask to make a photocopy of your driver's license. That's so they have proof you're licensed in case of an accident. Make sure to get that photocopy back when you leave. Otherwise, a shady salesman could pass the information along to identity thieves.

Beware of eavesdroppers. You can walk away from a crowd, use hushed tones, or lock yourself in a restroom stall. No matter — if you're talking on your cellphone in public, anyone can overhear you. To protect yourself from wandering ears, keep the conversation short and never give out personal information such as a Social Security number or credit card number. If you must, cover your mouth and speak quickly. Always assume that someone is listening. And remember, public restrooms are just that — public, not private.

Freeze credit report to foil fraudsters. If you're hot under the collar about the possibility of identity theft, try this cool option. Freeze your credit report. This makes it impossible for thieves to open new lines of credit in your name. In fact, it keeps all new creditors from accessing your credit report.

To put a freeze on your credit report, write a letter to each of the three major credit bureaus. It could cost as much as $10 per request. But if you can prove you've been a victim of identity theft, it's free. If you plan to apply for new credit, you'll need to "thaw" your report a few days ahead of time — and this also comes with a fee. Then you'll need to pay again to put the freeze back on. Credit freezes work best for people unlikely to need new credit.

Another option is a fraud alert. Anyone can request this free service, and you just need to contact one of the credit bureaus, which will then alert the other two. In theory, lenders and merchants call you or take extra steps to verify an applicant's identity before opening a new account. But not everyone abides by the alert, which expires after 90 days.

Beware of fake police and other impostors. Your phone rings and your caller ID displays your local police department's number. The caller claims to have a warrant for your arrest. But he promises you can avoid criminal charges if you pay the fine by immediately wiring money or paying with a pre-loaded debit card.

Don't rush to obey. Scammers can falsify the caller ID information you see, and they can find personal information about you that may make the call seem genuine. The Better Business Bureau named this Arrest Warrant scam as one of its top 10 scams of 2013. And it's not the only impostor scam you may face. You could also get threatening calls, text messages, visits, or emails from fake officials who claim to be from the IRS, Medicare, Social Security, the FBI, your utility company, or the courts. The emails, calls, and credentials may seem official, and visitors may even sport uniforms or badges.

If anyone demands money or personal information, don't give it — especially if the person asks you to wire money or pressures you to act immediately. No government agency will ever call or email to ask you to wire money or provide a Social Security number, credit card number or other personal information. So look up the phone number of the organization the "official" works for, and call to confirm the person's identity and whether their demands are legitimate.

Bank safely from your smartphone. But first, secure your phone. Start with a complex pass code, and enable the autolock feature. Make sure the passwords you use for mobile banking are not automatically saved on your phone. Most banks don't keep passwords on phones, but it's best to ask.

You can also set up your phone with remote tracking. If your phone is lost or stolen, this feature will purge your personal data.

When banking from your phone, use your bank's app and not the website. Download it from an official app store. Don't save your username on your phone, and don't use the same password you use for other apps. If you lose your phone, call your bank immediately, and ask if it's possible to have your app shut down. Thankfully, if your phone and bank app are hacked, your liability limit is only $50. And most banks waive this charge.

End credit card offers for good

Identity thieves love to go through mailboxes looking for preapproved credit cards. Don't let them. Here's a quick and easy way to put an end to credit card offers that come through the mail — and the risk of identity theft that comes with each one.

Opt Out Prescreen is the official consumer credit reporting industry website. Visit *www.optoutprescreen.com* or call 888-5-OPT-OUT (888-567-8688) to cancel offers for five years. Or to stop receiving them permanently, log on to the website and print out the Permanent Opt-Out Election form. Fill it out, and mail it back with your signature.

Whether you call or go online, you'll need to provide personal information, including your birth date and Social Security number. Your information will be kept confidential and will only be used to process your request.

Outsmart a cyberthief with powerful passwords. It's easier than you think. You can create strong, hard-to-crack passwords for all your accounts by following these seven steps.

- Never use words or phrases you can find in a dictionary.
- Never use your hometown's name.
- Use the first letter of each word in a sentence, then insert a number or special character. For instance, the famous musical line "The rain in Spain stays mainly on the plain" can become "tr1Ssm0tp."
- Never use the title of a song, book, movie, or television show.
- Use personal information in an unusual way. For example, just using your anniversary date is a no-no. But something like "0n11/27/82weWed" would challenge even the savviest cyberthief.
- Never use the names of cartoon or fictional characters such as Batman or Cinderella.
- Make it long. The longer your password, the more time it will take a cybercriminal to figure it out. Try a sentence with a number or special character thrown in.

Remember to create solid usernames, too. Use the same guidelines as passwords. The main difference between usernames and passwords are the special characters. You may only use a dot, dash, or underscore in a username. With passwords, you can use math symbols like plus and equal signs.

Action plan for ATMs. Use caution when using an automated teller machine, or ATM. Thieves may be lying in wait — or using technology to steal your card number and PIN. Here's how to protect yourself.

- Examine the ATM for any suspicious attachments or extra cameras. Devices called skimmers capture information, while crooks set up cameras to spy your PIN.
- Do not use an ATM when people are lurking nearby, and never accept a stranger's help to retrieve a stuck card.
- Memorize your PIN. Do not write it down anywhere, especially on your ATM card.
- Shield the keypad with your body when entering your PIN.
- Do not linger. Have your card out as you approach the machine. Take your receipts with you, and put away your money right away. If you're making a deposit, sign the check ahead of time.
- Avoid using an ATM at night. If you must, park close to a well-lit ATM and bring a friend with you.
- Stick with bank ATMs. Other machines may be rigged to gather customer information.

Shield yourself from check washing scams. The red flag on your mailbox doesn't just alert your mailman that you have outgoing mail — it also tips off thieves. If you pay your bills by check, it can leave you vulnerable to a scam called "check washing." This is how it works.

Criminals may drive through your neighborhood early in the morning, spot the red flag, and steal the envelope containing your check to the phone company. They can take the check home, put a piece of Scotch tape over your signature, and use an everyday household chemical to wash off all the information on the check other than your signature. Then they can make the check out to themselves, fill in any amount, and cash it. Protect yourself by mailing your checks at the post office, but avoid mailboxes that are too stuffed, which allows thieves easy access. You should also use pens with permanent ink.

Fend off Medicare crooks

Beware of scammers posing as approved Medicare Prescription Drug Plan providers. They may call you and request your checking account number for an automatic withdrawal of the $299 enrollment fee. Do not provide it — or any other personal information. Do not let any door-to-door salesmen peddling drug plans into your home, either. For more information on legitimate plans, call 1-800-MEDICARE or go to *www.medicare.gov*.

Identify insurance fraud. Insurance gives you security and peace of mind — but only if it's legitimate. Fraudulent companies take your premiums, but don't pay your claims. Here's how to spot insurance fraud. Watch out for companies that accept everyone or whose policies cost far less than what other companies are charging.

Avoid agents who pressure you to act quickly, discourage you from getting advice from a lawyer, demand cash payments, or ask for personal information that has nothing to do with insurance — like your bank PIN or password. Make sure the company and agent are properly licensed in your state before doing business with them.

Why you should check out charities before giving. It's better to give than to receive — unless you're giving to a scam artist rather than a legitimate charity. Follow these suggestions to make sure your money goes to a worthy cause.

- Question cute kids who go door-to-door. You may feel tempted to buy magazines or other products to support youth programs, but these young salespeople may work for a for-profit company. Ask for verification of the organization's name, address, and purpose.

- Support firemen and policemen, but don't fall for phone or direct mail appeals. Usually, these come from outside solicitors who get 70 cents or more of every dollar they raise. Your donation might not even go to firemen or policemen at all, and it may not be tax deductible.

- Never give money by phone, and don't let callers pressure you into making a donation. Request literature to find out more about the organization. Send a check directly to the charity instead.

- Play the percentages. Find out what percentage of funds go to the services the charity provides and how much goes for fundraising and other costs. Sometimes, you'd be surprised how little money reaches the people in need.

- Learn more about specific charities at websites like *www.charitywatch.org*, *www.guidestar.org*, *www.give.org*, or *www.charitynavigator.org*. You can also check with the IRS at *www.irs.gov*.

Shopping savvy

Never ever pay full price for anything. Find the lowest price on thousands of products. Here's the scoop.

- If you're savvy about computers and their prices and you know exactly what you want, browse the computer manufacturer's website. You may find specials that offer a lower price than retail stores.

- Get expensive jewelry for up to 50 percent off at a pawn shop. Bring an appraiser with you if you're worried about the value of an item.

- Buy children's clothes at consignment and resale stores. You may even find clothes for yourself.

- Shop at flea markets and thrift malls for collectibles, nostalgic goods, antiques, and much more.

And don't forget the web. You can find deals on all sorts of items at *www.overstock.com*. Or try *www.shopping.com* and *www.shopzilla.com*. These price comparison sites not only give you plenty of options but also display the TRUSTe seal next to reputable merchants.

3 costly "bargains" to be wary of. These often-touted bargains may not be bargains after all. Here's what you need to know.

- Online shopping. You can find fabulous discounts online, but sales tax and high shipping costs can wipe out your savings. Check shipping rates before you shop. If you're lucky, you may find information about sales tax on the same page. If not, check the "store locator" or "find a store" link to see if the seller has a location in your state. Expect to pay sales tax if they do. Sometimes you won't find this information because the site simply doesn't charge sales tax. But if you're surprised by a sales tax charge near the end of your purchase process, just shut down your browser before clicking the button that finalizes your order. Another vendor may sell the same product at a lower total cost.

- Television-shopping networks. Shipping can also wipe out the savings of "bargains" bought from television-shopping networks, especially if the product is big or heavy. Besides, if you're not careful, the ease of buying from these networks may tempt you to spend more than you planned.

- Outlet stores. These stores are supposedly filled with overstocks at discounted prices. But many retailers just send their lesser-quality clothing to the outlet stores. Instead of quality goods at bargain prices, you're just getting cheaper goods. Seek better bargains elsewhere.

Secret path to free shipping. You can't find what you're looking for in the store, but you don't want to pay the shipping fees from ordering online. No problem. Many retail stores offer in-store delivery if you buy from their website. That means your website order will be delivered to a location near you at no charge. Sears and Walmart are just two of the retailers who offer this convenient service. Check your favorite store's website to see if they offer this, too.

Simple guide to the best discounts

Just because something is on sale does not mean it's a good deal. Retailers know how much people love markdowns. They set the price of goods like clothing artificially high, so they can then offer big discounts and still make plenty of money.

When is a sale truly a good deal? According to the website Shop It To Me, clothes that are at least 42 percent off are actually good deals in November and December. Expect even bigger discounts after the holidays, in mid- to late-January. You'll get around 46 percent off.

Stop getting burned by restocking fees. Watch out. The next time you return an item to a store, you may not get all your money back unless the item is defective. That's because some retailers now charge a "restocking fee" for up to 50 percent of the original price. Take these steps to avoid such fees.

- Restocking fees may be more likely for items like appliances, computers, and electronics. Before you buy these products, look for a copy of the store's restocking fee policy. The store is required to display it where you can easily see it.
- Check for restocking fee notices at online vendor sites. Online vendors may be even more likely to charge these fees than regular stores.
- Notice which online and local shops don't charge restocking fees. Shop at these stores for happier returns.

- Always be ready to provide your receipt when returning an item.

- If you buy from a store that charges restocking fees, be careful when opening the item. Avoid damaging the packaging and don't throw anything away. Marred packaging or missing items can trigger a restocking fee.

Don't let hidden charges trip you up. Everyone hates those irritating fees merchants tack on toward the end of a transaction, a practice known as drip pricing. Many unsuspecting customers don't even know they've been added until it's too late. But a wise consumer needs to stay alert. To protect yourself, take a few simple steps.

First, ask. Ignorance is not bliss when it comes to drip pricing. Read the fine print, and ask a salesperson to reveal fees up front. This will help you comparison shop before completing a sale. Next, steer clear of companies that play the hidden fees game. And let them know why you won't do business with them. Lastly, if you've been the victim of drip pricing, challenge the charges. Show a manager proof that you were quoted a lower price such as a reservation confirmation or an ad without mention of additional fees. If you charged your purchase, you could request a chargeback or ask your credit card company to dispute the fees.

Don't hesitate to report a company to the Federal Trade Commission for drip pricing. And tell the company you're going to file a complaint. Your actions may change their mind.

Stop telemarketers once and for all. You can end most unwanted telephone sales calls by registering your phone number with the National Do Not Call List. Just dial 888-382-1222 from the phone number you want to register, or go online to *www.donotcall.gov*. Registration used to expire after five years, but now the Federal Trade Commission (FTC) says it may make registration permanent, so stay tuned.

Political organizations, charities, telephone surveyors, and businesses you already deal with are allowed to continue calling you. Let them know separately if you want them to stop. Telemarketers, however, have 31 days to take you off their call lists. If they keep calling anyway, there are six ways to make them wish they'd never dialed your number. Complain to:

- the FTC at 888-382-1222 or *www.donotcall.gov*. Give them the company's name or phone number and the date of the call.
- the Better Business Bureau in the company's home state.
- the Federal Communications Commission at 888-CALL-FCC or 888-225-5322.
- your state attorney general.
- your state public utility or public service commissions.
- small claims court. If you ask the company to take you off their calling list, but they call again within 12 months, you can file a claim against them in court.

Sharpen your bargaining skills. You negotiate every day — you just don't realize it. From deciding what's for dinner with your spouse to choosing a movie with your grandkids, bartering is a way of life. But how do you haggle with corporate America, be it an online retailer or a financial institution? Here are a few tips to guide you through a negotiation — and help you get what you want.

- Find out what you can about a product or an issue. The more you know about it, the easier it will be for you to make a reasonable offer.
- Be collaborative, not confrontational. Once you allow emotions to get in the way, you've lost. Maintain a calm, friendly tone, and look for win-win outcomes.
- Listen to and acknowledge the other side. This increases your ability to persuade.
- Find common ground. If you and the other person share an interest and spend time discussing it, he will be less likely to argue with you.
- Ask for 15 to 20 percent off a listed price for a used item. For example, if a sofa is selling on Craigslist for $200, offer between $160 and $170. Chances are, the seller will accept your offer. Most tend to price their items at 15 to 20 percent higher than what they really want.
- Never pay full price in a situation where negotiating is the norm. Car salesmen, for example, expect to be offered a lower price.

- Ask for a little something extra. If a company offers you a free shipping voucher to compensate for an error, ask for an additional 20 percent off your next purchase.

Get the best secondhand clothes

You'd like to buy some snazzy secondhand clothes, but you've been sorely disappointed by the selection in the stores. Try shopping in early spring or early fall. Many people clean out their closets around that time, so that's when secondhand shops often have their widest array of styles, colors, and sizes.

Get your favorite items on store shelves. Have you ever fallen in love with a product in one store and wished another store would carry it? With a little patience and perseverance, you can make it happen. Approach the store manager first. "A store manager can look through his computer system and see if he can order the item," says Frank Garcia, a supermarket manager in Miami. If the manager says he will get back to you and he doesn't, email the store's corporate office. Most corporate offices will forward a request to a local store fairly quickly.

"If a customer sends corporate a message, and corporate then sends it to me, I am required to respond to both the customer and corporate within 24 hours," says Frank. "A good manager will do whatever it takes to carry the item and make the customer happy."

The savvy shopper's calendar of steals and deals. Everyone knows about annual closeouts for cars and Christmas decorations, but that's just the tip of the iceberg. You may be surprised at other pre-season bargains, end-of-season sales, semi-annual closeouts, and scheduled deals at the same times every year. Use this calendar to help you catch the fabulous sales you've been missing.

Month	Sales
January	appliances, clothing, household linens, furniture, toys, luggage, and sleepwear
February	computers, air conditioners, exercise equipment, mattresses, lamps, furniture, and jewelry
March	winter coats, air conditioners, clothes washers and dryers, gardening and landscaping equipment and supplies, and winter sports equipment
April	paint, outdoor furniture, and gardening and landscaping equipment and supplies
May	televisions, jewelry, handbags, luggage, and outdoor furniture
June	summer sporting goods, sportswear, men's and boys' clothes, and sleepwear
July	swimsuits, electronics, major appliances, summer clothes, and air conditioners
August	summer clothes, coats, furniture, and shoes
September	children's clothing, air conditioners, paint, camping goods, fans, patio and pool items, and tires.
October	children's clothes, coats, fall and winter clothes, major appliances, school supplies, bicycles, fishing gear, and women's coats
November	boys clothes, blankets, water heaters, ranges, household linens, used cars, and jewelry
December	microwave ovens, jewelry, and Christmas merchandise

Retailers' secret you need to know. You can haggle with department stores, big box discounters, electronics sellers, and more. The trick is to know when to haggle, how to do it, and who to haggle with.

- People who sell big ticket goods often have a monthly sales quota to meet. Try haggling late in the month when they're more interested in making a deal.

- Haggle when the store isn't busy. Store employees are more likely to negotiate when they're not swamped with lots of customers.

- Do research on prices before you haggle, so you'll know how deep a discount you can reasonably hope for. You can even bring in the store's newspaper ad, a competitor's ad, or a web printout to help support your request.

- Be patient, considerate, and as nice as possible — even if you have to wait for approval or jump through a few hoops to get your deal. The savings will be worth it.

- Pick the right person to negotiate with. Only approach experienced and knowledgeable employees. The store may not allow newer hires to negotiate.

Once you get the hang of retail haggling, you may also find success at jewelry stores, banks, and hotels. You can even try to wring better rates out of your cable company, phone company, credit card company, and internet provider. Just call, tell them you're thinking about switching, and ask if you can get a better rate. You may be surprised at your own success.

Score huge savings by shopping online. The internet can be a bargain shopper's dream. It's bursting with coupons and special deals that could save you hundreds of dollars on all sorts of gifts. You just have to know how to find them.

Start by signing up for Facebook (*www.facebook.com*) or Twitter (*www.twitter.com*). Besides staying in touch with friends and family, these websites can be a gateway to crazy coupons and secret deals. Visit the Facebook page of a brand or retailer and "like" it to receive coupons or alerts about special sales and offers. Open a Twitter account and "follow" the same brand or retailer to qualify for super discounts.

Or let websites like *www.bradsdeals.com*, *www.retailmenot.com*, *www.fatwallet.com*, and *www.mybargainbuddy.com* do the legwork for you. These scan the internet all day, every day for deals on everything from clothing and coffee to computers and jewelry. Another website, *www.restaurant.com*, specializes in discounted gift certificates to local restaurants. Simply type in your location to see all the available offers.

As the holidays approach, specialty websites pop up to help you track sales. Try *www.bfads.net* to see Black Friday store ads weeks before they are published on Thanksgiving Day. You can also search ads for the best deal on a given item and organize your Black Friday shopping list.

You can even find free shipping from almost any store, any day of the year, at *www.freeshipping.org*. This website lists current code words you can type into a retailer's website during checkout to score free shipping on your purchase. Or simply put off buying your Christmas gifts until Free Shipping Day.

One day a year, hundreds of retailers offer free shipping on online purchases. To learn this year's date, visit *www.freeshippingday.com*.

Best time to return merchandise

Avoid weekend afternoons. Instead, show up during the first hour after the store opens. This is a great way to skip the long lines and endless waits. What's more, experienced employees usually prefer to work the day shift, so there's less chance you'll be the victim of a trainee's mistake.

Credit card perk saves you money. Some people prefer shopping with a credit card for convenience or safety. If you're one of them, make sure you take advantage of a valuable but often overlooked credit card perk — price protection, or price rewind. Many credit cards promise that if you use them to buy an item now and you find it cheaper at a later date, they will refund the difference. This may be especially helpful if you do your holiday shopping in advance. No more worrying that your gifts will go on sale later on.

You may have to jump through some hoops to claim your refund, such as documenting the lower price and submitting it to the card company along with proof of your original purchase. And some items aren't covered, like jewelry, closeout specials, or online purchases. But spending a few minutes untangling the red tape could earn you a fat refund. Check your card's benefits for details.

Know when buying more saves less. Don't let a warehouse club leach money from your wallet. Get the savings your membership pays for with these clever ideas.

- Dare to compare. Some warehouse club items are true bargains while others cost you extra. To tell the winners from the losers, compare the per-unit price to what you'll pay at other stores. Limit your warehouse store shopping list to items that are cheaper there than anywhere else.

- Do the math. Your bargains should save you more than your membership fee costs. Use your per-unit price comparisons to determine how much you're saving and then estimate how much that savings will add up in a year. If it's less than your membership fee, don't renew your membership. But if your savings outweighs that fee, you're a savvy shopper who should keep your membership. Just remember to compare prices every year to make sure you're still saving money.

Save more than before at warehouse clubs. You'd love to take advantage of deals on perishables at your warehouse club, but you'll never finish that triple, extra-large package before the food spoils. So take a divide-and-conquer approach. Talk to friends about splitting the cost — and contents — of large packages of perishables.

You may even wish to shop as a group for the most convenience. Bring pencils, paper, and a small calculator to help divide costs accurately and keep track of how the items should be divided up. If you comparison shop on price, this clever method may boost your club savings well above the cost of your membership.

Win big with flea market do's and don'ts. You can get terrific deals on plenty at flea markets if you just know how to shop. Remember these tips.

- Don't buy used items at a flea market if they'll quickly become outdated. For example, a year-old HD DVD player may be cheap, but finding DVDs to play in it may be tough. Be wary of buying used electronics, computers, and other items that may have short life spans.
- Arrive when the flea market opens to catch the best finds. Snatch up anything you really want because it may not be available in an hour.
- If you plan to shop for a specific product, check its retail price before shopping the flea market.
- Check back late in the day for the biggest bargains. Sellers are more likely to make a deal on items they don't want to tote home.
- Flea markets don't take returns so carefully check items for flaws before you buy.
- Flea market vendors almost never deliver. Don't buy anything large unless you can transport it home yourself.

- Be ready to pay in cash. Flea market vendors rarely take checks and credit cards.

- Bring a backpack, rolling backpack, or tote bag to hold your purchases.

Trade unwanted gift cards for cash. Your nephew gave you a generous gift card for your birthday. Trouble is, you don't shop at that store. Here's how you can turn unwanted gift cards into cash.

Online dealers will buy your gift card, then resell it to someone looking for a card from that store. You won't get the full value of credit on the card, since the dealer needs to make a profit. You'll probably get between 60 percent and 90 percent of the card's face value — certainly better than losing it entirely. It's best to compare offers from different websites to find the best deal for your particular card. Some dealers give you the choice of cash, credit at certain online stores, or a different gift card.

Typically, your gift card must have a balance between $25 and $200 to be traded. Pay attention to a card's expiration date, since dealers place limits on what they will accept. Happily, new laws mean gift cards will have looser restrictions and a longer shelf life before expiration.

Check out offers for your gift cards at *www.PlasticJungle.com*, *www.GiftCards.com*, or *www.raise.com/sell-gift-cards*.

Never forget another birthday gift. Designate a drawer, bin, or shelf in your closet to store gifts you buy throughout the year. Then, when you see a great item on clearance or score a super deal with a coupon, snatch it up and put it in your presents pile. For really good finds, consider buying two or three of the same item and setting them aside when you need a gift to give on short notice. The same goes for cards. Grocery and drug stores occasionally offer coupons on cards for special occasions. When that happens, stock up. The next time you forget a friend's upcoming birthday, you'll be ready.

Slash shopping time with themed gifts. Want to make holiday shopping a breeze this year? Pick a theme for the gifts you'll be giving. Decide in advance that everyone will get something sweet from the candy store, or something new for their kitchen. Then you can do all of your shopping in one store and avoid the madness of multiple trips to the mall to find the right size or perfect color.

Take themed gift-giving to the next level by personalizing it. For instance, grab a few picture frames the next time they go on sale at the arts-and-crafts store. Raid your photo albums, and insert special images into the discount frames. Give your daughter a photo of your mother as a little girl, or a friend a picture of the two of you on vacation. They'll appreciate the gifts, and you'll finish your shopping in record time.

Technology tricks for every device

Watch TV for free. Tired of watching your cable bill go up? With a digital antenna, you can stop paying for cable and start watching television for free. Simply plug in the antenna to the input on your TV. You may pick up anywhere from a few channels to more than 40, depending on the make and model, your home's distance from TV towers, and where you position the antenna inside your home. You will need a digital tuner, a standard on televisions since 2007. Older models may need a digital converter box.

Prices range from $10 to over $100. Buy from a store with a hassle-free return policy, and test a few models to see which antenna works best for you. And don't worry that your TV will sport outdated rabbit ears. Digital antennas come in sleek and attractive designs.

Swap cable for streaming to save big. When you think of a stream, you may envision a gentle babbling brook. But in the world of technology, the word stream refers to the way in which movies, music, and TV shows are delivered to a tablet or television via the internet. Programs flow continuously in real time versus being downloaded for viewing at a later time.

"Streaming" allows you to drop your high-priced cable and still enjoy your favorite programs. Simply select a service like

Hulu, Netflix, VUDU, YouTube, Apple iTunes, or Amazon Prime. Check each service's website to see if it offers your favorite shows. The cost of each channel varies. Some are free with ads while others require a monthly subscription. Others charge by the show or for one- to two-day movie rentals.

In addition to picking a service, you will need a set-top box — a device that streams internet video to your TV. Popular manufacturers include Roku, Apple TV, Amazon Fire, and Google Chromecast. Prices range from $35 to $100.

To decide if streaming is right for you, consider your viewing habits. Are you a fan of daytime television, live sports, and 24-hour cable news? Then probably not. But if you love watching hours of reruns and hate paying your cable bill, then yes — you're ready to dive into the world of streaming.

6 strategies for saving money on electronics. According to *Consumer Reports*, the key to getting the best deal on electronics lies in these six tips.

- Avoid buying expensive extended warranties.
- Be skeptical about low, low prices. The item may be refurbished, not new.
- Haggle for a better deal. Bargaining can work just as well for electronics as it does for other items.
- Check for online coupons to major electronics stores at coupon clearinghouses like *www.couponcabin.com*.
- Use shopping bots, also known as web robots, such as BizRate, DealTime, MySimon, Shopping.com, and Yahoo to compare prices when buying online.

- Buy it with your credit card. You'll get more protection if something goes wrong with the product. Some, like American Express, even extend the manufacturer's warranty for free.

Tap into the best phone apps for seniors. Can an app a day keep the doctor away? Possibly, if it's a health app, a mind game app, or one of the thousands of other beneficial apps on the market. But what exactly is an app and why would a cellphone user want one? Here's the lowdown. The word "app" is short for application, and it's simply a piece of software that you can load on to your smartphone. Some apps provide entertainment like the popular Angry Birds game. Others provide services from digital coupons to heart rate monitoring. Many are free, and others cost a few dollars.

Whether you own a smartphone or are thinking about getting one, consider making apps part of your mobile experience. Here's a sampling of apps that will make your life easier and just plain better.

Health — WebMD provides information about diseases and symptoms. My Medical is a digital file cabinet for your medical records. Instant Heart Rate can take your pulse from your fingertip through the lens of your phone's camera.

News and weather — Read, watch, or listen to your favorite news programs with apps from NPR, CNN, or Fox News. Check current conditions and forecasts on The Weather Channel.

Social — Share family pictures with friends and relatives on Facebook. Twitter gives seniors a chance to follow up-to-date posts from their favorite resources be it a retail store or a beloved grandchild.

Music — Stream free music with Pandora or Spotify.

Games — Lumosity for iPhone or Mind Games for Android will keep your mind sharp.

GPS — Google Maps and StreetPilot by Garmin will get you where you need to go.

Inspirational — The Bible and popular devotional books like "Jesus Calling" and "Streams in the Desert" are available as apps.

Shopping — Retail Me Not delivers coupons directly to your phone. Or you can scan and save coupons to your phone, and then redeem them in stores with SnipSnap.

Everyday living — EyeReader and Magnifying Glass with Light will magnify your reading material and shine extra light on it. If you have trouble remembering where you park your car, try the Find My Car app.

Cancel your cellphone contract without penalty. It's easy enough to sign up with a cellphone carrier and take your new phone home right away. Trouble comes if you want to switch to a new carrier before your contract time is up.

One survey found nearly half of all cellphone customers would consider switching carriers if they didn't have to pay an early-termination fee. These fees can run to $350 depending on how much time is left in your contract term.

But there are ways to get out of your cellphone contract early, without paying huge fees — although your mobile provider probably won't tell you how.

- Have a really good reason. If you're moving out of the country or to a place the carrier doesn't cover, or if you are a soldier being deployed, you may be able to end your contract with no fees.

- Ask nicely, and keep asking. When you make your case to your wireless provider, you'll probably talk to a customer service representative over the phone. Don't accept the "no" you'll get from the first call. Instead, call back, ask for an executive in charge, and escalate the issue — whatever it takes to get the attention you need. You can even use social media — Twitter and Facebook, for example — to voice your concerns and try to resolve the issue.

- Try for a trade. As much as you dislike your carrier, there's someone else out there eager to join up. You can sell the remainder of your contract to one of those folks through websites like *www.celltradeusa.com* and *www.trademycellular.com*. You'll probably pay a fee of around $20 to $25, but that's much less than an early-termination fee.

- Switch to a smaller company. Small carriers and those categorized as mobile virtual network operators (MVNO) may be so eager to get your business, they'll buy out your contract if you sign up for a new plan. MVNOs, like Boost Mobile and Virgin Mobile, are good services to try.

If you can't get out of your contract, lower your bill by cutting text messaging, switching to the smallest data allowance, and reducing your number of minutes.

Save money with phone alerts. Avoid overage charges by paying attention to your mobile's alerts. According to the Federal Communications Commission, cellphone companies must tell consumers when they get close to, reach, and surpass their plan's limits on voice, data, texting, and international roaming. You can set up alerts to arrive via text message or email. Once you receive a notice, limit or stop your usage until the start of a new billing cycle.

3 more ways to cancel your contract

You found "the one," signed on the dotted line, and began your two-year commitment. Now you want out of your contract. Here are some other steps you can take to try and drop your plan.

- Read the fine print. You may have a way out and not realize it.
- Stay up to date with changes made to your agreement. By law, if a carrier changes its terms, consumers must be notified and given 30 days to break their contract.
- Tweet or post. Airing a grievance on social media is like running a commercial during Super Bowl. It's fast, effective, and can reach thousands within seconds. No company wants to look like the bad guy in front of its customers. Use Twitter, Facebook, or any other social media outlet to broadcast your desire to bail, and see if you get a response.

Score the best price for your old phone. When it comes to selling your old cellphone, you've got plenty of options — from online sites to brick-and-mortar stores, and the "go to" staples of eBay, Craigslist, and Amazon.

For good payouts and quick turnarounds, check out Gazelle *(www.gazelle.com)*, You Renew *(www.yourenew.com)*, and Exchange My Phone *(www.exchangemyphone.com)*. All three sites offer quotes online, free shipping, and payment options such as a check, PayPal, or an Amazon gift card.

Best Buy and Radio Shack all run trade-in programs for phones. So does Target in partnership with NextWorth, an online service. The process generally starts online. You then drop off the old phone at the store or mail it in using a prepaid label. Payment is in gift cards.

Charities will also take your old phones off your hands, and put them to good use. Verizon's HopeLine program provides used cellphones to victims of domestic abuse. Cellphones for Soldiers supports troops stationed overseas. And the National Cristina Foundation uses them to help people with disabilities and at-risk students.

3 ways to wipe your phone's data. You're ready to sell or donate your old phone. Before you do, take the following steps. They're easy to follow, and will keep your personal data from landing in the hands of a stranger.

- A Subscriber Identity Module, better known as a SIM card, is a memory chip that holds an account holder's name, phone number, contact list, text messages, and other data. Pop the card out with a pin or paperclip. You may be able to use it in your new phone.

- Your phone may come with an extra slot for an SD or micro SD card. An SD card allows you to store music, photos, videos, and digital books. If you inserted an SD card into your phone, make sure you remove it.
- Returning your phone to factory conditions eliminates any trace that the device was ever yours. You can do this by opening up your "Settings" tab and looking for the reset or erase option.

Cut a deal when your contract is up

Most service providers will do whatever it takes to keep you as a customer. Take advantage and ask for the terms that work best for you the next time your contract expires. If they're not willing to work with you, take your business elsewhere.

Charge your device faster than ever before. You take out your tablet to dig into your favorite novel and the battery is about to die. What gives? You just charged it. While charging your tablet or phone is as simple as plugging it in, you can get that battery icon to 100 percent much faster by following a few simple guidelines.

To start, turn off your device. If it's on and you use it while charging, more juice may be going out than coming in. If your device stays on while charging, you can reduce the amount of power being used by putting it in Sleep mode or Airplane mode.

Sleep mode puts your tablet on standby, while Airplane mode keeps a phone or tablet from sucking up power to connect to Wi-Fi, cell service, or Bluetooth.

To get the fastest charge, use the cable that came with your tablet or phone, and plug it into the wall using the AC adapter. While you can charge a device using a USB port on your computer, it will go much slower.

Easy ways to boost your battery. It's inevitable—every time you need to make a call, your phone's battery is in the red. If it's any consolation, you're not alone. But there are a few simple tricks you can perform to make your cellphone's battery charge last much longer. And there's no reason not to do them.

- Turn on airplane mode via your phone's settings menu. This will turn off Wi-Fi applications that drain your battery, and charge your phone in half the time.

- Change the brightness setting from auto to manual, and keep it as dim as you can without straining your vision.

- Set your device to lock or time out after a minute of not using it.

- Never place your phone in a desk drawer. Your phone will work harder to find a signal, zapping its power in the process.

- Keep your phone from getting too hot or too cold. A temperature between 32 and 95 degrees will best conserve your battery.

Best battery charger is in your garage. When your power goes out and you need to recharge your cellphone, turn to your car for help. Your vehicle's battery packs enough power to charge up your phone during an outage. It can juice up tablets, too.

Tablets a threat to your heart?

Sitting hunched over your tablet all day may give you more than a stiff neck. A recent British study found that use of mobile devices could lead to heart problems later in life.

The hunched-over position constricts breathing and blood flow, forcing the heart to work harder. Essentially, it's more difficult for you to take full breaths when you drop your head and round your shoulders to look at your device. Plus, your ribs struggle to move, which keeps your heart and lungs from performing properly.

But don't feel like you have to pack away your tablet for good. Just spend less time using it, and hold it at eye level when you do. Your heart may thank you.

High-tech solution for the hearing impaired. Have you heard? Bluetooth technology will help you hear your cellphone conversations crystal clear. A Bluetooth device can turn a pair of hearing aids into a wireless headset with no audio interference. The results are an enjoyable cellphone experience for hearing impaired individuals. The technology also allows people who wear hearing aids to listen to MP3 players, hear the television, conduct video chats with ease, and tune into GPS apps with driving instructions. Check with your audiologist for more information or search online for an accessory that will work with your hearing aids.

Dim your phone to catch some Zzz's. If your body's natural sleep rhythm is disrupted night after night, your cellphone may be the culprit. According to a Mayo Clinic study, checking your phone in bed exposes you to bright light. That light can interfere with your production of melatonin, the hormone that regulates your sleep-wake cycle. Essentially, the light from your phone may trick your body into thinking it's daytime. Researchers suggest a simple way to get around this. Turn down the brightness setting on your device, and hold your phone at least 14 inches from your face. You may find your sleep problems put to rest.

5 simple tips to speed up a slow computer. Is your computer as slow as molasses these days? Don't drop hundreds of dollars on a new machine. The one you have may be almost full and just in need of a quick tuneup.

Computers are like cars. They run smoothly 99 percent of the time, but occasionally they need new tires and an oil change. Consider the Disk Cleanup program your mechanic. It frees up space by emptying unnecessary files from your computer's memory banks, making it peppier and more nimble. Type "disk" in the Search box on your Taskbar, and click **Disk Cleanup**. Windows will run a quick check to see how many files you can safely delete, and how much space this will free up on your hard drive. Then, you'll see a window like this.

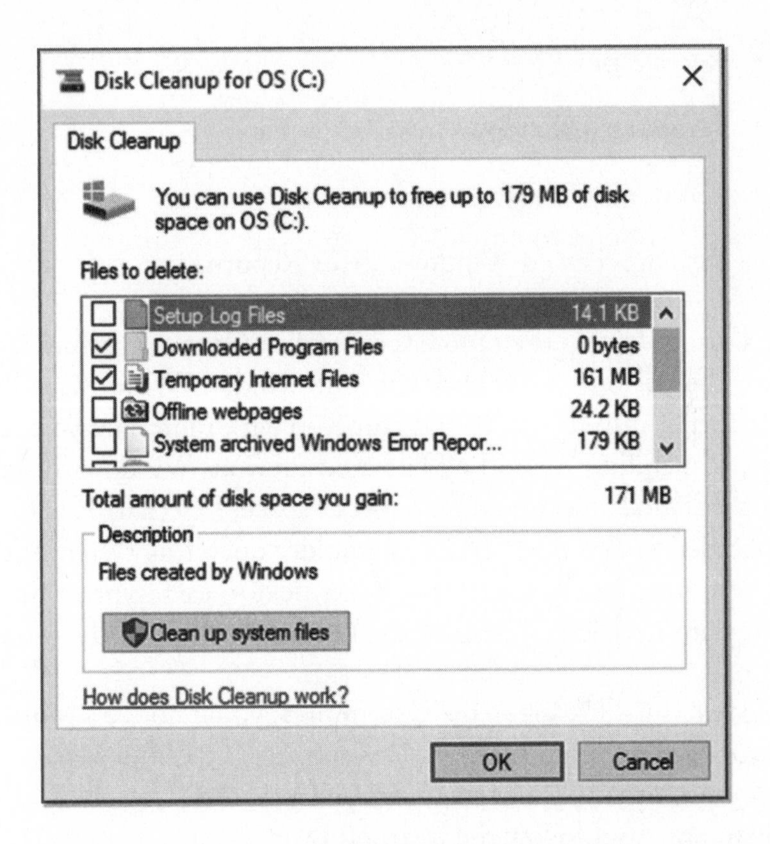

Now comes the fun part — dumping stuff. It's like cleaning out your attic, without having to haul bags of trash to the curb.

1. The idea of throwing out computer files can be a little nerve-wracking, especially if you don't know what they do. Click on any category in the list to see a summary about them in the space under **Description**. In general, you can safely delete these types.

- Downloaded Program Files
- Temporary Internet Files
- Recycle Bin
- Temporary Windows Installation Files
- Temporary Files
- System archived Windows Error Reports

2. Want to free up even more space? Click **Clean up system files** near the bottom of the Disk Cleanup window. Windows will dig deeper into its "attic" and come up with more files you can delete, including Setup Log Files and Previous Windows Installations. The latter can take up lots of space, especially if you upgraded to Windows 10 from an older operating system such as Windows 7 or 8. Check the boxes next to each type of file you want to delete, then click the **OK** button to clear them out.

3. After you click **Clean up system files**, you'll notice a **More Options** tab next to the **Disk Cleanup** tab at the top. **More Options** lets you delete programs you never use. Just click **Clean up...** and follow the instructions.

4. The same **More Options** tab also lets you delete old restore points from your hard drive. Your computer occasionally takes a snapshot of all its settings and saves those "pictures" to the hard drive. That way, if new software or devices start causing problems, Windows can rewind itself back to the last time it worked smoothly, before the trouble started. That's great, but restore points can start to stack up. Clicking **Clean up...** under **System Restore and Shadow Copies** deletes all but the last restore point.

5. Disk Cleanup only deletes files created by Windows, the operating system. It doesn't touch leftover files created by other programs, like Firefox or Google Chrome. For that, you can download a free program such as CCleaner made by Piriform. It will clear out junk files left by non-Microsoft programs. You can get a basic version for free at *www.piriform.com/ccleaner*.

Buy refurbished for rock-bottom bargains

When you're in the market for a new electronic, don't pass up the incredible value of a refurbished product. Refurbished items are generally restored to their original condition, often with newer replacement parts. Plus, they undergo thorough inspections before heading back to store shelves to be sold at a discount.

Other products that retailers may label as refurbished include items returned in opened packages, devices with cosmetic flaws, products that arrive in damaged boxes, recalled items, and floor models. All of them carry discounted price tags.

One word of caution — make sure you ask about return policies and warranties. Only do business with a retailer that will take back a refurbished piece of merchandise in case you change your mind or discover it doesn't work.

Smart way to save on ink. The price of ink stinks. So don't make this common mistake that wastes up to 40 percent of the ink in that expensive printer cartridge. Here's what to do instead. When the warning light comes on telling you the cartridge is low, don't replace it right away. Alerts often kick in long before the cartridge is close to being empty. Hold out until the print quality of your documents diminishes, or you need to print a big job. You may get more copies out of your cartridge than you think.

Make great home movies. Making your own home movies sounds like fun, but get your first video camera and you may feel in over your head. Enter expert Joyce Bertolami, professional videographer with more than 30 years' experience and co-owner of the Joy of Video in Woburn, Mass. She offers these tips for capturing your best home-movie memories.

- Know what your camera can and can't do. According to Bertolami, understanding your equipment is an "overriding factor in producing a video worth watching." Learn how to use features like the manual controls to get consistently good shots in every situation.

- Invest in a camera stabilizer. "I have seen many videos shot freehand that were painful to watch because of the erratic camera movement," she says. "Despite the fact that today's video cameras possess excellent image stabilization systems, the tripod remains a valuable tool."

  Unfortunately, tripods are not very mobile. If you want to move around more but still get stable shots, invest in a monopod. "In our business of wedding and event video production, monopods allow us to be very creative while providing excellent camera stability."

- Learn to work with light. "Proper lighting is essential in producing a good video." For most home movies, the available light is enough. Bertolami's advice — "practice with your camera in different lighting conditions" to learn what works best and how to adjust your camera settings.

That said, leave heirloom events to the pros. "Creating a home movie can be an enjoyable hobby, but for the most important special events in your life — like weddings, anniversaries, and graduations — you should hire a videographer to create a professional production."

Get a grip on gadget grime. Germs — they're everywhere, thriving and multiplying on your tablet, keyboard, and computer mouse. They land on your gadgets by the thousands thanks to sweaty hands, sticky fingers, coughing, sneezing, and food spills.

You don't need to spend much money to get your tech gear squeaky clean. Just make sure you turn off, unplug, and remove batteries from any device before scrubbing.

- To clean your keyboard, turn it upside down and shake it gently. Spray compressed air between the keys. Finish cleaning with antibacterial wipes. Or mix a little alcohol with water, and spray it on a microfiber cloth.

- A computer mouse is a hotbed for viruses. Spray compressed air around the track ball, and use a disinfecting wipe over your mouse and on your mouse pad.

- Gently dig out crud from ports with a toothbrush, cotton swab, or a cleaning brush made especially for electronics.

- As with cellphones, you never want to spray glass cleaner directly onto a tablet screen. Opt for a special screen cleaner like iKlear or AM Get Clean. Spray on a microfiber cloth.

- Remote controls are petri dishes for cold viruses. Blast between buttons to blow out dust and dirt, and sanitize with fast-drying wipes like Wireless Wipes.

Protect your hard drive from a fatal crash. It's as inevitable as death and taxes — one day, your computer's hard drive will stop working, and it will take every photo, letter, song, and file down with it. That wouldn't be so catastrophic if you knew when your hard drive would bite the dust, but you don't. It could happen today, or it could happen five years from now.

The best insurance policy is to create copies of all your files and save them to an external hard drive, a little box that plugs into your computer.

In Windows 10. The good news is, you don't have to copy every file and folder by hand. Windows 10 will do it for you, automatically, every day so that you never even have to think about it.

Start by plugging an external hard drive into your computer with a USB cable. Type "file history" into the Search box on your Taskbar and click **File History (Control panel)**. This opens the window where you set up and schedule your backups. Your computer should find the external drive you have plugged in, and show it here.

You'll have to turn on File History the first time you create a backup. To do that, click **Turn On**. Windows 10 will immediately begin to back up your files. You don't have to do a thing. When it finishes, you will see the phrase **Files last copied on** followed by the current date and time. Now if your hard drive crashes or if you permanently delete an important document, you'll have a copy tucked away safely.

Windows 10 will automatically back up your files to the external hard drive once an hour, if your computer is turned on. You can change that frequency, if you like. Click **Advanced Settings** on the left side of the File History window. Here you can change the backup schedule and choose how long the computer keeps old backups.

For Macs. Once you have a neat feature called Time Machine set up, you'll always have a backup copy of your hard drive on an external drive. As soon as you plug it in, your Mac will probably ask you if you want to use it for Time Machine. Click **Use as Backup Disk**. If it doesn't take you to the Time Machine settings, click on the Apple icon, then System Preferences > Time Machine, and click to turn it on.

Got a laptop? You can still use Time Machine. It will take "local snapshots" that are stored on the laptop when you're away from the external hard drive, then merge them with the existing backups when you plug in again.

On the cloud. Cloud-based services can also back up your files, folders, and photos. Instead of residing on an external hard drive, they live on servers owned by the company you choose. OneDrive, Dropbox, and iCloud are a few examples.

Plug in to protect against power surges. A good surge protector will sacrifice itself during power surges and lightning strikes, saving your computer, television, printer, and other expensive electronics. However, not all surge protectors pass muster. Look for one with these features.

- meets UL 1449 testing standards
- protects all three electrical lines entering the outlet — Line to Ground (L-G), Line to Neutral (L-N), and Neutral to Ground (N-G)
- has a clamping voltage rating no higher than 330V on all three lines
- contains telephone and coax cable jacks, since power surges can travel up these lines, too
- will turn off the power to plugged-in gadgets once it can no longer buffer against electrical surges
- features a light that tells you whether the outlet it's plugged into is properly grounded
- comes with a warranty that promises to replace any plugged-in devices if they are damaged by a power surge

Wise way to protect valuables against theft. Ask your local police department about borrowing their engraving pen, and use it to engrave your state and driver's license number on your valuable electronics, including televisions, cameras, computers, and cell phones. This will help authorities find you if the item gets stolen and later found. You can also include the words, "in case of loss" along with your phone number or e-mail address. Don't engrave your Social Security number or anything an identity thief could use.

Travel tips for a great getaway

Where to look for special deals. Senior travel discounts haven't disappeared. You just have to know where to look.

- Airlines. Since September 11, 2001, airlines have dramatically cut back on their senior discounts, but you can still find them if you ask. Southwest offers Senior Fares, where people over age 65 qualify for discounted, fully refundable airline tickets. Other carriers, including United and American Airlines, also offer senior discounts, but you must ask for them when booking your ticket.

- Hotels. Get a 15-percent discount or more at Marriott hotels around the world if you're age 62 or older just by asking for the senior hotel discount when you book. Hyatt hotels promises discounts up to 50 percent off the going rate of rooms in the continental United States and Canada. Other hotels also offer senior rates, so ask for them when booking.

- Senior groups. There's power — and savings — in numbers. AARP members reap discounts of 10 percent or more on certain hotels, flights, rental cars, vacation packages, tours, cruises, and entertainment. Book these deals through *www.expedia-aarp.com/flights*.

Surf your way to low airfare. If you want to find good travel deals on airfare, the internet is the place to go. According to Damon Darlin, an editor for *The New York Times*, and Jay Cooke, a former editor for *Lonely Planet* travel guides, these websites can help you plan your trip and save money — to boot.

- Farecast at *www.farecast.com* predicts the cost of airfare on particular routes. A new feature even tells you whether a particular fare is a real deal or not. Type in a departure city, and a list of deals will pop up with designations such as "record low" or "$105 less than the average low."

- Airfarewatchdog.com at *www.airfarewatchdog.com* digs deep for deals, according to Cooke, and includes listings for low-cost carriers Southwest and JetBlue. Most other travel sites do not.

- SmarterTravel at *www.smartertravel.com* offers consistent, steady deals, says Cooke.

- Southwest Airlines at *www.southwest.com* is well worth checking, if Southwest flies where you're going. They will likely offer a good bargain fare.

Don't forget to check other major travel websites such as Orbitz *(www.orbitz.com)*, Travelocity *(www.travelocity.com)*, Expedia *(www.expedia.com)*, and more specialized sites including Kayak *(www.kayak.com)* and CheapTickets *(www.cheaptickets.com)*.

Newfangled way to protect your possessions. Before you leave for the airport, take a picture of the items in your suitcase and create a detailed list. Upon arrival at your destination, go through your luggage and make sure nothing is missing. If you can't find an item, you can easily search for it in your photo and on your list. If it's missing, file a claim with the airline and your insurance company immediately. You will have picture proof.

Fly your valuables past the gate agent

Don't pack essential items in your carry-on and expect to board your plane without incident. Due to space limitations, a gate agent may ask you to check your bags as you board the plane. You risk never seeing your valuables again if you hand them over. Instead, pack the things you can't live without — jewelry, prescriptions, even souvenirs — into a separate, smaller bag. Then place the smaller bag in your carry-on. If you are asked to check your hand luggage, you can easily remove the smaller bag. Enjoy your flight knowing your valuables are safe and sound.

Turn your cooler into a carry-on. If you need a cooler on your next vacation, use one as your carry-on bag. Pick a soft-sided cooler with straps for easy handling. Fill it with your travel-size toiletries and valuables. When you reach your destination, empty it and use it to pack drinks and snacks each day. You won't have to buy a disposable foam cooler while on your trip.

Stroll through security with ease. No need to worry about airport security if you have a medical condition or disability.

The TSA now offers a card that can be downloaded and printed from its website. Use the card to jot down notes about your condition, disability, or medical device. You can show the card to a TSA officer, and trust him to discuss your condition discreetly. You won't escape being screened or patted down. But you will be able to protect your privacy by not having to explain your medical condition in front of other passengers.

Visit *www.tsa.gov* and click on "Disabilities and Medical Conditions." Then look for the link "TSA Notification Card." Make sure you call TSA Cares' toll-free number at 855-787-2227 three days before your flight to discuss any questions or concerns.

Up, up, and away: booking tips nab sky-high savings. Frequent fliers know the key to grabbing a great deal on airfare is to book your flight on the right date, at the right time. Book it too soon? You pay too much. Book it too late? You still pay too much. It's no wonder today's travelers have reservations about flying the friendly skies. Clear up the plane nonsense — and land the fairest fares — with proven tips from travel pros.

- Book on a Sunday and pocket the savings. Bet you thought you'd get a better price on Tuesday or Wednesday, right? The experts at Airlines Reporting Corporation (ARC), a tech firm that provides the U.S. travel industry with statistics on airline ticket transactions, say no. The average price of a domestic flight, according to ARC, is $495. But buy your ticket on a Sunday, and you'll typically save anywhere from $50 to $110. The average cost for booking a flight on Tuesday through Friday tops off at almost $500.

- What's the cheapest day to fly? That one's sort of up in the air. Most travel experts agree that Tuesday and Wednesday are the least expensive days to fly. Some travel gurus also include Thursday, and a few even recommend Saturday.

- Flexible fliers can save more. Try sites like *onetravel.com* and *cheapair.com* to explore low-cost options if your travel dates are flexible. You'll find the lowest-priced flights for the dates you enter, but you'll also see some alternative dates that could save you money. Closest may not be cheapest when it comes to choosing an airport. Name your departure city — not your nearby airport — when booking online. Most sites will show you prices for flights in and out of several nearby airports. You may be surprised to find the best deal is just a short commute away.

- Book in the zone. The experts at CheapAir.com say you'll get the best deal if you buy your ticket during these time periods.

  Front Runner: You'll get your pick of flight times and seats, but your ticket will cost an average of $50 more if you book your flight between 335 and 197 days before you plan to travel.

  Early Bird: This zone covers days 196 to 113 before you fly. Some flight options will still be available during this period, but your ticket's price tag jumps up around $20.

  Prime-time Buyer: This is the experienced traveler's sweet spot. Book your flight between 112 and 21 days before you travel, and you'll get the best overall prices.

  Long Shot: Fares change daily in this zone, from 20 to 14 days before your trip. You may be able to find a super deal depending on how full the flights are. But you may end up paying a whole lot more than you expected if you're planning to travel during peak seasons.

Down-to-the-wire Flier: You plan to book at the very last minute, hoping to grab a great rate. And you might. But you may spend an average of $75 more if you wait to book 13 to 7 days out. Even worse? Your cost could soar by over $200 if you purchase your ticket less than a week before you travel.

Snap your way back to your hotel. You don't want to waste time getting lost on your vacation. But you don't want to keep up with little bits of paper either. Instead, use your cellphone's camera to snap a shot of your hotel room door. If you forget your room number, you can check your phone. You can do this with your cabin number on a cruise, too. And before hailing a cab, take a photo of your hotel's street address. Then pull out your phone when you're ready to head back. This idea also works for airport parking. Take a picture of the location signs near your parking spot, and never get lost in an airport lot again.

Cruise your way to a bargain holiday. Ocean cruises used to be just for the wealthy. Not anymore. If you know your way around the cruise market, you can enjoy a budget vacation on the high seas.

- Get help from the professionals. Consult a travel agent to plan your first cruise. An agent who specializes in cruises can find a low price on a trip that matches your needs and lifestyle. You might also get freebies, like cabin upgrades and credit for on-board extras. Look for an agent affiliated with an organization like the American Society of Travel Agents or the Cruise Lines International Association. But once you have a few cruises under your belt, you can find great deals through websites like *www.cruisecritic.com* or *www.cruisemates.com*.

- Search for last-minute deals. Cruise lines depend on a strong Wave Season — the period between January and March when lots of cruises are booked for the year. That's a good time to check prices.

- Don't sink your savings. No matter how low the price of the cruise, costly extras can blow your discount. Cruise lines encourage you to spend, spend, spend on excursions, souvenirs, professional photos, on-board gambling, and drinking. Don't do it.

- Benefit from a down economy. When neighbors are tightening their belts and staying home, you can snap up good deals. Some experienced cruisers say they won't book unless the cruise is $100 a day or less per person. If you notice a price of $80 — or even $40 — a day, it's time to pounce. A down year may help you net a deal like saving $1,000 off the price of a cruise to Europe, or free airfare when you book the cruise.

- Book early without fear. If you book a trip and the price goes down before you sail, many cruise lines will refund the difference in price — if you ask. Find out the cruise line's policy before you book.

Recycle magnets to remember dates

On your next cruise, spend less time sorting through piles of paperwork. Pack several magnets — like the ones you peel off your Yellow Pages. They will stick to your cabin walls with ease. Use them to post daily activity schedules and invitations to special events, like the Captain's Welcome Aboard party.

"Pinning up papers with magnets helps me stay organized onboard," says Charlotte, an avid cruiser. "I want to make sure I don't miss out on a fun activity or a special offer. Instead of going through stacks of invitations, I just put them on my walls. They're so much easier to find this way."

Dodge a dispute with a snapshot. Rental cars and condos come with their fair share of risks. Rental companies rake in cash from unsuspecting consumers by blaming them for preexisting damage. Even if you jot down the details of any damage on your paperwork, a rental company can still come after you. To protect yourself, photograph or video record the exterior of your rental car. Look for nicks, dings, and scratches. Also check the wheel rims and windows. And don't forget the vehicle's interior. Look for stains and tears on seats and floor mats. Use your camera with a date stamp or your cellphone's video recorder.

This tip works for vacation rentals, too, from beach condos to mountain cabins. Look for stains on carpeting, cracked mirrors, and broken door handles. If the owner slaps you with a claim, you can easily prove the damage was already there.

Take a bus for a buck. You want to travel from one city to another, but don't want to deal with airports. And the cost of filling up a rental car just isn't in your budget. Check into Boltbus and MegaBus — both companies offer cheap bus fares to more than 100 cities across North America. BoltBus primarily serves the Northeast and West Coast. Each route sells at least one $1 seat. The trick to snatching up that seat is timing — the sooner you book, the greater your chances of grabbing a fare for a buck. Call 877-265-8287 or visit *www.boltbus.com* for more information. MegaBus serves cities across North America with free Wi-Fi and power outlets at each seat. The bus line also sells $1 fares. Booking way in advance will help you find the lowest ticket prices. Call 877-462-6342 or log on to *www.megabus.com*.

Call ahead of time or get declined. You don't need to worry about your credit cards getting declined on your travels. Simply contact your bank and credit card company in advance to give them a heads up. Otherwise, your credit cards may get turned down when they pop up for purchases away from home. Companies refuse transactions to protect your account. Still, being declined can be inconvenient and embarrassing.

Call or email ahead of time, and have your itinerary handy with dates, locations, and accommodation details. This will give them a chance to place travel alerts on your cards. And remember to take your debit card with you — you can use it to withdraw cash as needed. Plus, jot down your credit card numbers, expiration dates, and toll-free numbers. Then leave this information with a friend. If your cards are lost or stolen while you're on vacation, you will be able to access all the numbers you need quickly and easily.

Don't pass up sightseeing perks. Buy multi-day passes to attractions. You'll save money and time by not waiting in long ticket lines. Say you want to explore Colonial Williamsburg. A single-day ticket runs around $42 and gets you into all of the Revolutionary City's sites. The ticket includes 35 exhibits, trade shops, museums, and complimentary shuttle bus service for one day. For a few dollars more, you can purchase a multi-day pass for the same attractions, including three days worth of shuttle service.

You can also check into buying a CityPASS in 12 cities or regions across North America including Atlanta, Boston, Chicago, Dallas, Houston, New York City, Philadelphia, San Francisco, Seattle, Southern California, Tampa Bay, and

Toronto. A pass bundles prepaid admission to each city's top attractions.

For example, San Francisco's CityPASS includes unlimited transportation on all trolleys, buses, and historic cable cars for nine days, plus a bay cruise and admission to an art museum, an aquarium, and the California Academy of Sciences — all for around $90. Purchase individual tickets and fares, and the cost would range from $130 to $160 for seniors over age 65. Visit *www.citypass.com* for details.

Never lose frequent-flier miles again

Don't let frequent-flier miles and other loyalty-program points go to waste. Three simple computer programs will keep track of them for you so you can use points before they expire. Both Points Loyalty Wallet at *www.points.com* and MileTracker at *www.miletracker.com* are free. MileageManager at *www.mileagemanager.com* charges $14.95 a year but offers a few more bells and whistles.

See America for only $10. Enjoying the natural beauty of your nation is a perfect way to spend your golden years. Now you can do it for just $10 with an America the Beautiful Senior Pass from the National Park Service. This lifetime pass entitles people over the age of 62 and three other adults — or a car full of people in a per vehicle fee area — free entrance to national parks and reduced fees for camping, swimming, boat launches, and other amenities. Disabled people of any age can get a lifetime park pass free. You can only get these passes on park grounds, so hop in your RV and start seeing America.

Pack backward before you move forward. Before driving off on a road trip, think about how you'll pack your car. Start by cleaning it out. Throw away trash, and put away anything you won't need on your trip. Next, check your spare tire and make sure it's in good condition with the correct tire pressure. Then, pack first what you'll need last. For example, if you plan on taking your golf clubs, pack them first. You won't need these while you're driving. Finish by packing anything you'll need easy access to.

5 ways to lighten your load. Packing light is not only smart, but it can save you money. Airlines that once allowed two checked bags per person now charge extra for more than one, not to mention the chances that checked luggage will get lost and cost a small fortune to replace. Lighten your load the next time you travel with these tips.

- Pack a pair of long underwear if you chill easily or are traveling in winter. They double as sleepwear, so you won't need pajamas.

- Roll up socks and stockings and place inside women's shoes. Then, place the shoes in a plastic bag, and tuck them inside the men's shoes to make the best use of suitcase space.

- Wear your just-in-case sweater, jacket, and heaviest pants the day you travel instead of bulking up your suitcase. Airplanes tend to get cold anyway.

- Save perfume samples from magazines and take these on trips instead of fragile perfume bottles. Do the same with shampoo and other samples. They take up less room, and you'll avoid the mess of squeezed bottles inside your suitcase.
- Take old shoes you no longer want, and throw them away at the end of your trip. Do the same with worn out undergarments and socks. Toss them after wearing.

Don't plan an escape without duct tape

It can fix just about anything — at least temporarily — from the hem of your favorite pair of pants to the broken handle on a suitcase. Even astronauts take it on space missions. So why not take a roll with you on your next vacation? Measuring 2 inches by 100 inches, travel-size duct tape is small enough to toss into a suitcase or carry-on. You can pick up a two-pack for around $4 online or at your local hardware store. Or you can make your own travel roll from duct tape you already have. Just wrap the tape around an old credit card or piece of cardboard. You'll end up with a flat roll that's easy to pack.

Sort and pack with repurposed zippered bags. You know those clear, plastic bags your sheets, curtains, and pillowcases come in? Don't throw them out. They come in handy when it's time to pack your suitcase. You can pack shorts and T-shirts in larger bags — and undergarments, hairbrushes, and accessories in smaller ones. The clear plastic allows you to find what you need easily and quickly when you open your suitcase. Plus, you can use one to "zip up" odors from dirty laundry, and keep the rest of your clothes smelling fresh. If you don't have any stashed away, ask a friend or check with your local thrift stores.

Spray foam keeps valuables safe. Foam spray may be, first and foremost, a sealant for air leaks around window jambs. But did you know you could use it to pack valuables, too? Just follow these simple steps. First, make sure to wear safety goggles and rubber gloves. Then, spray the foam into a plastic bag and seal the opening. Next, press the fragile item on top of the bag, and allow the foam to expand and surround it. It will form a protective mold around your treasure. Lastly, pack it in your suitcase. You can pick up a can of foam spray at any home improvement store for less than $5. Just remember to always follow the safety instructions.

Pack a week's worth of jewelry with ease. Your pill organizer isn't just for pills. You can use one to organize your jewelry for a week's vacation. Each compartment will keep jewelry tangle-free. Also, a pill box can be tossed into a suitcase without taking up space. Need more than a week's worth of jewelry? Try a pill organizer with morning and evening compartments. Need less? Try a contact lens case instead.

Veil your valuables in a vest. No need to lug a handbag or a backpack on your next vacation. Try a photo vest instead. With about 20 pockets, you can easily stash away small items from passports to prescriptions. Plus, you can tuck away money and credit cards in hidden pockets. And you don't have to worry about a thief running off with your purse. Just remember to reserve one pocket for one of your most prized possessions — your camera.

Pack your polish perfectly. Eyeglass cases make the perfect manicure kits. Just toss a nail file, clippers, and a small bottle of polish into a hinged case, and you're good to go. You could even throw in a couple of cotton balls, cotton swabs, and a tiny bottle of nail polisher remover. An eyeglass case will protect your clothes from spills. Plus, you can fit one into any little nook in your suitcase. If you don't wear glasses, ask a friend who does for an extra case.

Blow away wrinkles with hair care tools. You need to get the wrinkles out of your shirt or dress, but you don't have an iron handy. Time to plug in your hair dryer. First, sprinkle your garment with a little water. Then hold the dryer 1 to 2 inches away and keep it on low. Or, for small wrinkles, heat up your flat iron. Straighten out wrinkles like you would straighten your hair. Just make sure you clean your flat iron first with a damp cloth before you plug it in. And keep it on a low setting to prevent scorching your clothes.

Utilities: cash-saving energy tactics

12 ways to slash utility costs. You can save more money on your power and water bill than you think. To put the most money back in your pocket, don't forget these practical tips.

- Shower instead of taking a bath. Baths can use up to 70 gallons of water a day or more than 2,000 gallons every month.
- Switch from using your clothes dryer to using a clothes line or rack. This can really make a difference because the clothes dryer uses more energy than almost any other appliance in your home.
- Turn down the thermostat, and dress more warmly in winter. You can add two to three degrees of warmth just by putting on a sweater.
- Install a low-flow shower head in your bathroom.
- Only run your dishwasher or clothes washer when you have a full load.
- Turn off the water while washing your hair, and turn it on again to rinse. You'll save over 100 gallons of water every month.

- Wrap your old water heater with an insulation blanket to conserve heat, and save up to $20 a year. Many new water heaters don't need extra insulation. In fact, adding insulation can void the warranty. Check the tank and your manual for information or warnings about whether extra insulation can be added. Follow the manufacturer's instructions.

- Install aerators in your kitchen and bathroom faucets.

- Replace a broken lamp with a three-way lamp that lets you choose dimmer light when brighter light isn't needed.

- Insulate your attic yourself if it doesn't have enough insulation. You can do it for as little as $200.

- Humid air feels warmer than dry air, so use energy efficient humidifiers to help warm rooms in winter.

- Caulk and add weather stripping around all exterior doors and windows to reduce your heating and air conditioning use by up to 20 percent.

2 steps to saving more water. Spend five bucks at the hardware store and cut your water use by thousands of gallons a year, just by installing an inexpensive faucet aerator. First, check to see if your faucet already has an aerator. Look for tiny numbers printed on the mouth of the faucet. These tell you the flow rate. The lower the numbers, the better. If they are higher than 2.75 gpm (gallons per minute), install a new aerator. If you don't see any numbers, you don't have one. Stick your finger inside the faucet mouth and feel around. If you can feel "threads," then your faucet can accept an aerator.

Also, consider replacing old, leaky shower heads with low-flow models. These water misers use only 2.5 gallons of water per minute. You can easily tell if you have a water-wasting shower head by placing a 2-quart sauce pan on your bathtub floor. Turn the shower on full blast and situate the pan in the middle of the spray. If it fills up in less than 12 seconds, you need a low-flow shower head.

Wash your way to an extra $70

You can make your clothes last longer and save $70 or more in yearly energy costs if you use cold water for most laundry loads. If you'd like, you can add special cold-water detergent. Reserve warm water for unusually dirty clothes, and only use hot water for severe stains. This strategy can do more than just save money. Hot water sets protein-based stains like dairy foods, mud, clay, blood, human waste, and baby food, so you can't get them out. If you rarely wash in hot water, you're less likely to set stains like these and more likely to enjoy laundry savings.

12 ways to save money on outdoor watering. The average household uses as much water outdoors as indoors, so you can make a big dent in your water bill by limiting the water used in your yard. Start with these tricks and tips.

- Mulch trees, shrubs, and beds so they'll lose less moisture to evaporation and won't require as much watering.

- A lawn measuring just 32 feet by 32 feet can require more than 600 gallons to water 1 inch. Reduce the size of your lawn, especially in areas where grass struggles to grow. Replace the grass with native and drought-tolerant plants that need less water.

- Water your lawn once a week, instead of daily. Place an open tuna can nearby, and give the grass a good, slow soaking. When an inch of water has collected in the tuna can, turn off the water.

- Use drip irrigation around trees and shrubs.

- Fertilize your lawn less, and use slow-release fertilizers.

- Attach a pistol-style sprayer to your hose so the water won't run continuously.

- Collect water from your gutters with a rain barrel, and use it to water your flowers and grass.

- Adjust your mowing height to 2 inches, and leave clippings on the grass instead of bagging them. Your grass will retain more moisture and need less water.

- Sweep your patio and driveway with a broom instead of hosing them down to clean them.

- Water during the early morning when winds and temperature are lower and the water is less likely to evaporate before your plants can drink it.

- If you wash your car at home, don't turn on the hose until you are ready to rinse.

- Avoid planting grass on steep inclines that are hard to water.

Help your water heater last years longer. Discover the simple, inexpensive part in your water heater you should be replacing every three or four years. It's not the heating element, and you don't have to drain the tank. It's the anode rod. Replacing it regularly could help you delay buying your next water heater for years to come.

The anode rod is a metal rod that hangs inside your water heater's tank. It attracts compounds in your water that would otherwise corrode the tank walls. That's why the rod corrodes while the tank stays untouched.

Eventually, the rod becomes too corroded to protect the tank. If the rod isn't replaced, the tank corrodes until the entire water heater must be replaced. If you replace the rod in time, your water heater will not only last longer, but could double its life span. The trick is to replace the rod before your water heater corrodes.

To do that, you need to know this valuable secret — check the rod every year, even if you rarely need to change it. The life span of an anode rod varies depending on your water's characteristics, the amount of use the tank gets, the water temperature, how well the tank is made, and whether you have a water softener. Some lucky people will discover they can change the anode rod every five to seven years, while others must change the rod more often. Under the very worst conditions possible, some anode rods may last less than a year. Read on to learn how you can inspect the rod and change it yourself.

3 biggest energy mistakes

Correcting these can give you instant savings.

- Buying a second freezer or refrigerator for extra storage. If you need more storage, consider buying a bigger kitchen refrigerator. In general, it's cheaper to run one large model than two small ones.
- Insulating only your attic. Even though heat rises, floors over crawl spaces and unheated basements benefit from insulation, too, as do exterior walls and windows.
- Buying the wrong size heating and cooling unit. Don't listen to high-pressure salespeople. Buy the right size heating and cooling system for maximum efficiency.

How to replace an anode rod. You may be able to check and change the anode rod yourself if you are an experienced do-it-yourselfer. Here are the basic steps for doing the job.

- Collect a garden hose, socket wrench with 1 1/16-inch socket, breaker bar, and pipe thread sealant.
- Turn off the water supply and electricity or gas supply to the heater. Close the cold water shutoff valve.
- Using a bucket or garden hose, drain several gallons of hot water from the tank.

- Locate the anode rod, and loosen it with your socket wrench. If it won't budge, ask someone to hold the tank in place while you push harder to free the rod.

- Lift the rod out. Replace it if it's covered in mineral deposits or if the diameter is less than that of a AA battery. Replacements are available at home improvement stores.

- Smear the new rod's threads with thread sealant, insert the rod in the tank, and tighten the rod in place. Restore power and water to the water heater.

Your water heater may require different instructions than what you see here, so consult your water heater manual before you try checking or changing your anode rod. If you can't find your manual, download a copy from *www.manualsonline.com* or your water heater manufacturer's website.

If you don't have much do-it-yourself experience, call your plumber to check and change the anode rod. Even with the extra expense, you'll still save money by helping your water heater last years longer.

Earn cash from your electric company. Let the electric company pay you — for a change. When you sign up for their Power Credit program, Georgia Power will credit your electric bill $20. Other utilities may offer similar deals.

"Air conditioners cycle, meaning that they run for a certain amount of time (on), and then shut down (off)," explains Dean Harless, a retired Georgia Power energy efficiency manager. When you sign up for the program, the utility company installs a radio receiver on your AC. Then, when energy use in your community starts to overwhelm the power company, they send a signal to your receiver, telling it to shut off the AC.

"For example, if your air conditioner normally runs 15 minutes, the switch will allow it to operate for five minutes." The temperature in your home may rise a few degrees, but the AC makes up for it later, once the switch turns off again. This, in turn, saves the company money. "Since running the air conditioner is shifted to later in the day, it takes some demand off the system during the peak hours of energy demand. This helps Georgia Power avoid having to build more combustion turbines to handle a few peak hours each summer."

Harless says the utility company typically only flips this switch a few times each summer, so you probably won't even notice it. But each time they flip the "off" switch, Georgia Power gives you a $2 credit on your electric bill. Signing up for the program and having the receiver installed is free.

Tips and tricks for choosing the best bulb. Now that you've said so long to incandescent light bulbs, here's how to choose which new halogen, LED, or fluorescent bulb will work best in each room of your home.

Some CFL, LED, and halogen bulbs shine with the same cozy tint as standard incandescents, while others produce a noticeably whiter light. To tell which light a bulb provides, find "Lighting Appearance" on the bulb's label. Lighting tint is measured in Kelvin (K). Here's how to read the number you find.

- 2,700K - 3,000K (Soft White or Warm White) — yellow-tinted light like standard incandescent bulbs. This is ideal for overhead lighting in bedrooms and living rooms.

- 3,500K - 4,100K (Bright White or Cool White) — whiter or more blue-tinted light that appears brighter than soft white. Try this in kitchens and garages.

- 5,000K - 6,500K (Daylight) — the whitest or most blue-tinted light, similar to noon sunlight. This may be too harsh for some indoor locations, but perfect where you want higher-contrast lighting to help distinguish details. You may prefer this light for reading lamps, task lighting focused on a particular area, and overhead lighting in dark basements.

But that's not all because the tint of light isn't the only thing that matters. Consider these questions to make sure you choose the best bulb every time.

- Is the light fixture hard to reach? Choose LEDs for fixtures in hallways, staircases, cathedral or tray ceilings, ledges, and other places where changing a light bulb is difficult.

- Do you need light that shows colors accurately? Some lights don't show the true color of an item as well as halogen bulbs do. That's why they're recommended for lighting bathroom vanities. Just remember, halogen bulbs get hot enough to burn skin or set fire to objects that are too close.

- Does the bulb work with a dimmer? All halogen bulbs are dimmable, but check the labels of LEDs and CFLs. Most LEDs are dimmable if you have an LED-compatible dimmer, but some CFLs are not. Many LEDs also work with timers or motion sensors, but most CFLs don't.

- Will the switch be flipped often? If a light is turned on and off multiple times each day — as often happens in bathrooms — think twice about using CFLs. Frequent "cycling" like this shortens a CFL's life.

- Is the light a nonstandard incandescent? Some nonstandard incandescents, including three-way bulbs, candelabra bulbs, and decorative bulbs like globe lights, are still available in stores.

Watch TV for less

You might be surprised to discover that one television screen at its brightest can cost $10 or more in electricity every year. Your television and computer screens combined may cost up to $80 annually. To fix this, check the lighting around your televisions and computers to make sure it isn't making the screens appear dimmer. After adjusting the lighting, check the brightness setting for each screen. If it's set to maximum, reduce it to a comfortable level. This simple setting adjustment can shave $1.25 off your electric bill every month — and those savings add up more quickly than you might expect.

Stop paying for "phantom" electricity. Up to 75 percent of the power use for many home electronics happens after you turn them off. That's why they call it "phantom power." Discover how to save big bucks with one simple solution — simply unplug items when you won't be using them for several hours and when you leave the house. This could be enough to cut your electric bill up to 10 percent every month. To save time, consider using a power strip or surge protector that fully cuts power to several devices when you flip a switch.

Of course, some items must be reset or adjusted when you plug them in again, and you may need to leave your DVR plugged in so it can record programs while turned off. In fact, whenever you have a cluster of electronics that work together, such as those around a television set or computer, some can usually be unplugged while others must stay plugged in.

This is where smart strips can come in handy. A smart strip is a surge protector that cuts power to items that are shut down or on standby, but the strip includes a few outlets for devices that should always stay on, such as your cable box. Smart strip makers claim you'll save up to $150 a year by using their products — more than enough to cover the purchase price.

3 easy, energy-efficient cooking tips. Believe it or not, you can trim your energy bill while cooking, too. Try these energy-saving tips.

- If you have three dishes that need to bake at different temperatures, don't bake them all separately. Pick the average temperature and pop them all in at once. Don't bother preheating your oven for a dish that needs to cook more than one hour.

- Broil food when possible, since broiling doesn't require preheating.

- During warm months, run your kitchen exhaust fan while you cook, if your exhaust fan vents to the outside. It will suck out the hot air, cooling your kitchen more effectively.

Proven way to trap allergens

Cleaning or replacing your heating and cooling system's air filter not only helps it run more efficiently — it also reduces the allergens floating around your home. According to experts with the American Lung Association, air filters are one of the most effective ways to cleanse the air of allergens, but they only work if you change or clean them regularly. High-efficiency particulate air (HEPA) filters are the gold standard, since they catch almost all particles. Filters with accordion-like ridges have a larger surface area that may help them trap more allergens than flat ones.

2 ways to boost your HVAC's efficiency. Two simple steps can boost the efficiency of your heating and cooling system, lengthen its life, and save you money.

- Check the air filter every month and clean or change as necessary. A dirty filter blocks airflow through the whole system, forcing it to work harder, use more energy, and break sooner.

- Hire an expert to tune up your air conditioner in the spring and your furnace in the fall. A properly tuned system runs more efficiently.

Help your fireplace save heat. Everyone loves the warm, cozy glow of a wood-burning fireplace, but don't mistake it for an energy saver. It won't shrink your heating bill and may even increase it. Whether a fire is burning or not, the same system that pulls smoke out of the fireplace also pulls air out of the house through the chimney. That's air you've paid to heat, so you actually may be paying more to warm your home. When you use the fireplace, close all doors to the room and turn down the thermostat. Installing glass doors and a heat exchanger can help reduce your losses even more.

Close the damper when you're not using the fireplace, but keep in mind that it may still leak some air. During long periods of nonuse, a chimney pillow may help. This inflatable device blocks air from leaving your chimney. It's simple to install and can easily be removed when you want to start using your fireplace again. Manufacturers claim this remedy could save you $200 or more each year.

LEDs put more Christmas cash in your pocket. Toss your old Christmas lights and plug into LEDs — light-emitting diodes. LEDs look like the familiar strings of holiday lights, but they are cool to touch, less likely to start a fire, and can cut energy costs 85 percent compared to incandescent Christmas lights. Look for LEDs marked with the Underwriters Laboratories (UL) seal.

Get more heat from your firewood

The amount of heat firewood produces depends on its weight. Heavier wood, like seasoned hardwood, weighs about twice as much as softwood and gives off about twice as much heat when burned. White ash, beech, yellow birch, sugar maple, red oak, and white oak produce the most heat. If you have several different species in your woodpile, burn the softwoods in the warmer winter months and save the hardwoods for the coldest months.

Best way to repair leaky ducts. Heating and air ducts can be a major source of wasted energy in your home. Leaky ducts that travel through unheated spaces, like an attic or unfinished basement, can lose 60 percent of the hot air they carry before it reaches the register. It's easy to seal leaks yourself.

- Check for air leaks. Look for holes in the ductwork and joints that have separated.
- If you find a leak, don't bother with duct tape. It fixes almost everything except leaky ducts. Use mastic, a goo you apply with a paintbrush. Butyl or foil tapes work well, too. Buy tape marked with the Underwriters Laboratories (UL) logo.

Ceiling fans reap cool savings. Research by the Florida Solar Energy Center shows turning on a ceiling fan can lower your energy bill in summer, but only if you also raise your thermostat. Fans allow you to bump up the thermostat a whopping 6 degrees and still feel just as cool. That equals big savings. Turning up your thermostat just 2 degrees in summer can shave 14 percent off your cooling bill. The higher you raise it, the more you save. On the other hand, leaving the air conditioner set low while running fans will actually increase your bill.

Insulate with special paint

A new paint does more than pretty-up a room. It helps insulate your home and lower your utility bills. Insuladd is a special ceramic powder you add to regular paint then brush onto walls or your home's exterior. Insuladd contains tiny, hollow ceramic spheres. As the paint coating dries on the wall, it forms a thin film that manufacturer's claim keeps heat from escaping in winter and entering in summer. For more information or to order the product, visit *www.insuladd.com* or call 888-748-5233.

Easy fix to a chilly problem. That mystery draft that chills your legs on a gusty winter day could be coming from an electrical outlet. This may be the one place in the house almost nobody thinks to insulate, but insulating electrical outlets and switch plates may save up to 20 percent on your heating and cooling bills for years to come. Even better, it's easy to do.

For each outlet and switch plate, you can buy a foam gasket perfectly shaped to insulate that spot. Check online sellers as well as local stores to make sure you get the best price.

To install the gaskets, cut power to the room from the circuit breaker, and make sure the electricity is off. For each foam gasket, remove the cover plate with a screwdriver. Push the gasket in the outlet or switch slot so it fits securely, and put the cover plate and its screws back in place. When you have insulated all the switch plates and outlets in a room, restore power.

For added savings, install child safety plugs in the electric sockets you're not using, and close all your closet doors so you won't pay to heat or cool those spaces.

Quick fix for a "leaky" refrigerator. A one dollar bill can help you save money and electricity. You don't even have to spend it. Close your refrigerator door on a dollar bill, then try to pull it out. If it slides out easily, your refrigerator is leaking cold air — and precious money. Adjust the door latch so it closes more tightly, or replace the seal around the edges.

Seal vents during dusty remodel. Hanging plastic over doorways can keep dust from drifting when you are sanding walls or undergoing a major remodel. But don't forget your central heating and air system. Cover return vents with plastic and seal the edges with tape, so dust doesn't get sucked in. You run the risk of clogging the filter and shaving years off the life of your HVAC. Turn it off completely, if possible, to keep it from circulating any dust it does pull in throughout the house.

Slash your power bill. These six easy steps can save you more than $700 a year on utilities — and you're conserving energy, too.

Action plan	Potential yearly savings
Update old appliances and heating and cooling equipment with Energy Star qualified products.	$450
Wash your clothes in cold water using detergents formulated for cold water.	$63
Install an Energy Star programmable thermostat. It automatically adjusts the temperature at night and while you're away.	$100
Sign up with your utility company for load management and off-peak rate programs.	$100
Cool your home with a whole-house fan instead of AC.	$330
Replace your five most-used incandescent light bulbs with Energy Star compact fluorescent bulbs.	$60

Wardrobe wisdom

Secret to saving on clothing costs. Make a beeline for the back of a store to grab the best bargains. It's the single best way to save money on clothing. Retailers generally hang their clearance merchandise in the back, forcing customers to walk past their regularly priced items. Don't be tempted to look. Head straight back, then browse the racks along the walls for more deals. Leave full-priced clothes hanging.

You've heard the phrase "three strikes and you're out." Apply this baseball rule when you shop for clothes. No matter how badly you want that top, if it doesn't go with three items in your wardrobe, it's out. Don't waste your money on something that goes with nothing — you'll never wear it.

Of course, nothing beats the value of simply taking care of what you already own. If you have a skirt in need of a new zipper, fix it. A repair may cost you a little money, but it will save you lots of money in the long run.

Curb the urge to splurge online. Blowing your hard-earned bucks is easy on the internet. Shoppers must break out their credit cards to buy online — and therein lies the problem. Studies show that consumers spend more when they shop with a credit card than when they shop with cash. Websites will also lure you with free shipping offers and time limits. These never-ending deals get you every time. But they don't have to. Follow these five easy tips to end overspending online.

- Prevent one-click shopping by never keeping a credit card on file with an online retailer. Taking a few extra minutes to enter your information gives you time to ask yourself, "Do I really want this?"

- Forward your finds to a few friends. Ask them if they think the item is worth buying.

- Limit your budget and time online. Know how much you can spend before you log on. Then set a time limit. You can browse hundreds of fashion items and accessories in a short amount of time online. Don't get sucked in.

- Walk away. If you see something you can't live without, log off and get busy doing something else. Give yourself a few minutes or longer to think about it. If you still can't live without it, log back on and buy it.

- Clean out your computer's cookies. Web browsers track your buying habits online, and then show you ads for items you may also like. Go to your browser's preferences to delete your history and change your tracking preferences.

3 ways to dress for less. Follow these simple tips to save big on clothing.

- Time it right. Never shop for clothes when they first hit the rack. A little patience can lead to big savings. Most retailers mark down merchandise after nine weeks on the shelves. Some have even shorter shelf-lives and cut prices every four weeks. Just by waiting, you may save as much as 70 percent. Seasonal shopping also nets savings. For instance, near the end of July you can usually find bargains on warm-weather clothing, including bathing suits, as stores try to clear their shelves for "Back to School" season.

- Deal with cards. If you have a favorite store, it may be worth signing up for the store credit card, which can yield 10 to 20 percent discounts. Be sure to pay it off every month, though, because they often have higher interest rates.
- Dig department stores. You'll usually find better bargains in department stores than boutiques. They also feature more lenient return policies.

Never iron again

No time for wrinkles? No problem. Use these tips to find crease-resistant fabrics, and you may never plug in your iron again.

- Stick to knits like nylon, polyester, wool and wool blends, and cotton and cotton blends. Stretchy clothes, like those made of Lycra, keep their shape and smoothness, as does heavier denim.
- Tencel, an eco-friendly fabric made of wood fibers, resists wrinkling, dries quickly, and is completely biodegradable. Popular retailers such as Chico's and L.L. Bean carry apparel made of Tencel.
- Steer clear of most linen and rayon garments or you may find yourself slumped over an ironing board.

Get the best price on anything. Don't go running all over town trying to find the cheapest prices. Do some homework first to see if your favorite store will match competitors' prices and offer price adjustments. It pays to shop at stores that do. Walmart, Target, and Kohl's, for example, will match a price if you find the item cheaper somewhere else. Just bring in the competitor's ad that shows the lower price. Home Depot, Lowe's, and Sears go even further and offer to beat competitors' prices by 10 percent. If the item you bought goes on sale, many stores will refund the difference, usually within a certain amount of time. Just make sure you read the fine print so you're aware of loopholes in store policies.

Super shoe-shopping tips. You may get your kicks shopping for shoes, but make sure you follow these sensible suggestions to find the best footwear.

- Shop for shoes at the end of the day, when your feet are the largest. Your feet tend to swell during the day.
- Shoes should be comfortable immediately. You shouldn't need to break them in.
- Always try on shoes. A size 7 for one brand or style may not be the same for another.
- Walk around the store for five or 10 minutes to make sure the shoes fit comfortably.

If you have arthritis, the right footwear becomes even more important. Poorly fitting or poorly made shoes can make you alter your way of walking to compensate, leading to other problems. They can also aggravate bunions or bone spurs, frequent byproducts of arthritis. You also need to pay special attention to your footwear if you have diabetes. Avoid high heels, slip-on loafers, and sandals with straps between the toes.

Smart storage solutions. No one wants to take a favorite wool sweater out of storage — or any other article of clothing — only to find it's covered in mold or ruined by moths. Try these storage tips to keep varmints off your garments. Your favorite sweater will look fabulous from season to season.

Fabric	How to store properly
Cashmere and wool	Best stored in a cedar chest, or in a drawer or closet with cedar chips or cedar balls.
Cotton	Layer garments in a storage container with acid-free tissue between items of different colors. Drill a few holes in the container's lid to allow the fabric to "breathe."
Leather	Stuff arms, shoes, boots, and bags with acid-free tissue paper. Cover with cloth and leave in a cool location.
Linen	Cover in cloth, not plastic. Don't store in cardboard boxes or cedar chests.
Polar fleece	Keep in a cotton sack with cedar balls.
Rayon	Best stored flat in a cool, dry place.
Silk	Use a padded hanger and store in a dark, cool closet with cedar balls, cedar blocks, or lavender.

Smart way to shop for shades

Sunglasses are more than just a fashion statement. They're an essential accessory that safeguards the health of your eyes. Without proper protection, your eyes are more vulnerable to cataracts, macular degeneration, even skin cancer on your eyelids.

To protect yourself from these debilitating conditions, shop for sunglasses that block 99 to 100 percent of UVA and UVB rays or with a UV 400 protection label. For added security, try on wraparound styles. They block the sun's harmful rays from all sides and angles. And don't sweat spending a lot of money on pricey, name-brand sunglasses. You can find a good pair of sunglasses at drugstores and optical centers — reasonably priced.

Fashion lifesavers at your fingertips. What do a paper clip, a button, and your favorite bottle of wine have in common? They can all serve as fashion lifesavers.

The next time you're trying to fasten your favorite bracelet — the one that's impossible to clasp by yourself — just grab a large paper clip. Open up the clip so it looks like an S, and slide one end into the bracelet link. Hold the other end of the clip in the same hand, and secure the clasp with your free hand.

If you're going on a trip, even if it's only to the gym, throw a button or two into your bag. They make great earring holders. Attach your earrings to the button, and you won't risk losing them. They're a great addition to your jewelry case as well. Keep pairs of stud earrings affixed to your buttons, and you won't have to search to find a match.

Rain boots, fashion boots, cowboy boots — they're all difficult to store without falling over or losing their shape. But if you're a wine lover, you have a remedy right at hand. Simply collect your empty wine bottles, and insert one into the shaft of each boot. Your boots will stay upright and in shape no matter where you store them.

Quick fixes for fashion emergencies. You never know when you're going to face a clothing crisis. Wardrobe woes strike suddenly, like in the middle of a wedding or when you're running out the door to an appointment. But with a little savvy, you can repair the mishap in no time. Here's a short guide on what to do if ...

- your hem falls out. Hold it in place with duct tape or masking tape.
- your zipper gets stuck. Rub a bar of soap or a wax candle along the teeth, and slide it free.
- you rip your blouse. Pull the threads through to the inside of your garment and tape the tear.
- your earring back falls out. Grab a pencil and snip off the eraser for a new back.
- your shiny shoes get scuffed up. Reach for a permanent marker of the same color and touch up the scuff marks.
- you break a heel. Super Glue to the rescue.
- you find a wad of chewing gum stuck to your clothes. Lift with duct tape or spritz with hairspray then scrap away.

- your button pops off your shirt, blouse, or pants. Reach for a twist tie, remove the paper and "sew" the button back on with the wire.

Set knotty necklaces free

When your necklaces tangle into frustrating little knots, use these tips to untangle them. Place your jewelry on a hard surface. Gently tug at the kinks with straight pins. If this doesn't work, sprinkle baby powder or apply a couple of drops of baby oil on to the knots. This will loosen the links and make them easier to untangle with pins.

Easy ways to tie a scarf. A scarf can transform a boring outfit into a fabulous fashion statement. For fresh ways to wear this versatile accessory, follow these easy steps.

The double wrap:

1. Drape a super long scarf around the back of your neck and over your shoulders.

2. Wrap the ends around the front of your neck and over the shoulders.

3. Wrap around the back of your neck and over the shoulders again.

4. Fluff around the neckline.

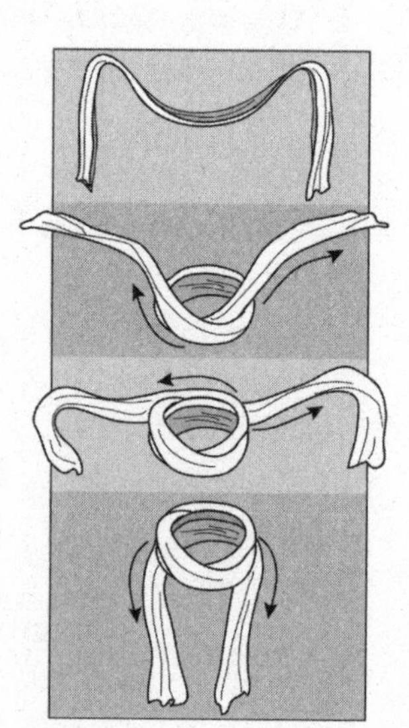

The slip knot:

1. Drape a long scarf around the back of your neck and over your shoulders. One end should hang longer than the other.

2. Tie a simple, loose knot about halfway up the longer end.

3. Slip the shorter end through the knot and tighten. Both ends should hang at about the same length. If they don't, try again.

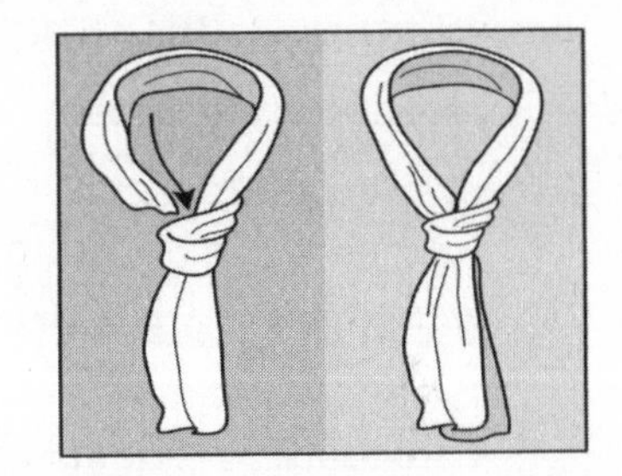

The hacking knot:

1. Fold a long scarf in half and drape around the back of your neck. The looped end should rest on one shoulder.

2. Pull both ends through the loop.

3. Adjust and fluff.

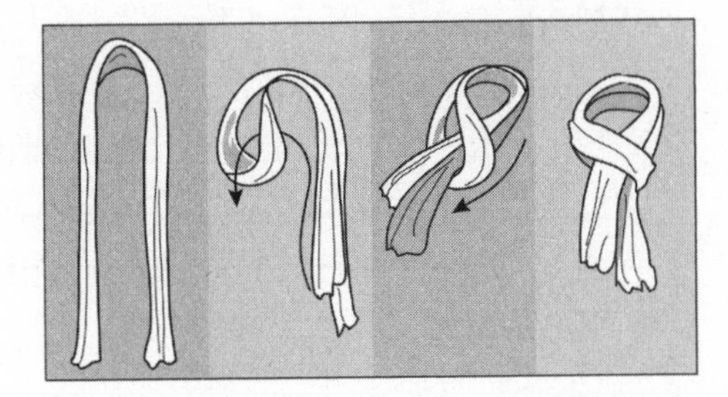

Tackle stains without pricey spot removers. Look around your house and chances are you've got everything you need to fight stains within reach. But first, check the garment's label. If it says "dry clean only," don't attempt to remove a stain. Take it to the cleaners and pay a professional to tackle it. Otherwise, squelch stains using the following guidelines, then follow the garment's laundry instructions.

- Butter or cooking grease — Dab on dishwashing liquid with a sponge. For stubborn spots, try rubbing alcohol.

- Coffee and tea — Pour hot water over the stain or reach for the dishwashing liquid.
- Ketchup and spaghetti sauce — Rub hydrogen peroxide on the stain or soak it in a mixture of 2 tablespoons white vinegar, 1 tablespoon dishwashing liquid, and cold water.
- Mustard — Blot to remove excess liquid, then try rubbing alcohol or glycerin.
- Red wine — Sprinkle with salt, then rinse with cold water. For a dried-in spot, rinse with club soda.
- Chocolate — Treat with a tablespoon of ammonia and 1/2 cup water — or try hydrogen peroxide. With chocolate, you want to blot the stain, not scrub it.
- Underarm — For whites, mix 1/4 cup each of baking soda, hydrogen peroxide, and water. Rub on the stain. For color garments that hide stains, but feel stiff from caked-on deodorant, fill your washing machine with cool water and add a cup of white vinegar. Soak for 30 minutes.
- Ink — Spray hairspray on the spot and blot. Place a rag or paper towel behind the stain to absorb the ink.
- Blood — Pour hydrogen peroxide or a solution of baking soda and water on the stain.
- Grass — Try a mixture of dishwashing liquid and hydrogen peroxide. If that doesn't work, a solution of hydrogen peroxide, baking soda, and hot water should do the trick.

Index

A

B

C

D

E

G

H

I

M

N

O

P

R

S

T

U

V

W

Z